*alic Fletcher* 1764 10/-

# The Saturday Book

*Seventh Year*

# Contents

Illustrations by *Philip Gough, Eric King, John Nash, Laurence Scarfe, Ronald Searle, Bernard Venables.*

*This book, published in November, 1947, was made and printed at the Mayflower Press (of Plymouth) at St. Albans, by William Brendon & Son, Ltd. The four-colour plates were engraved and printed by Grout Engraving Co. Ltd.*

*Edited by*
## LEONARD RUSSELL

*The*

# Saturday Book

*being the*

## Seventh Annual Issue

*of this*

## CELEBRATED CABINET OF CURIOSITIES

## &

## *Museum of Entertainment*

The *WHOLE COPIOUSLY ILLUSTRATED* and

*forming an*

## Indispensable Companion for Gentlemen & Ladies

*The Book Designed by Laurence Scarfe*

## HUTCHINSON

# Editor's Note

## The Saturday Book Office

47 Princes Gate, Kensington, S.W.7.

FAITHFUL readers of this book are aware that it is compiled annually to a simple formula: a formula so simple, indeed, that the editor almost feels guilty of unprofessional conduct in mentioning it at all.

There are, there must be, scientific editors who have scientific ways of discovering what their readers want, but this old slouch is not of their company. He hasn't an earthly what his readers want. He finds it impossible to form any impression of a representative SATURDAY BOOK reader. Many of them are kind enough to write to him about this and that, thereby pleasing him no end; but the dissimilarity of their tastes, their interests, their circumstances even, perplexes him. However, he decided long ago, in his customary unscientific way, that he had no gift for assessing the tastes of some imaginary being; instead, he would consult those of one person only: himself. And this, if you will forgive something that sounds like egotism but isn't, is what he has done again this year. He compiled this book to please and instruct himself.

Does it surprise him that, on former occasions, he has managed also to please and instruct quite a few other people? On the whole it does— but how pleasurably! At the same time he likes to flatter himself that more than a handful of people comprehend how devotedly he tends the things that go into this book. Not that he wants recognition of his own industry—certainly not that. But he does like to think that his selection and direction give a certain unity to the whole, that the book conveys, for all its diversity, some sense of his own enjoyment of the variousness of life.

This painful confession over, he must acknowledge particularly the assistance he has received from Laurence Scarfe, Edwin Smith, and Olive Cook, all three of them SATURDAY BOOK collaborators rather than contributors. Other things apart, the Art Album in this volume owes its execution to Miss Cook and Mr Smith; and here is the place for the editor to tender thanks, on their behalf and his own, to the National Gallery, the National Portrait Gallery, the Tate Gallery, the Victoria and Albert Museum, the Fitzwilliam Museum, Cambridge, the Birmingham City Art Gallery and Museum, Studio Briggs and others for permission to use photographs included in the Album.

# The Saturday Book

# ART ALBUM

## PART ONE

Rubens: A drunken pipe-player, detail from the
'Triumph of Silenus.'

Renoir.

Cézanne.

# THE ARTIST AT WORK

African sculptor (Cameroons)

European sculptor.

Lautrec, whose double photograph appears on the title-page, painting one of his favourite models, Berthe la Sourde.

Pictures on a gallery wall have apparently little connection with the workaday world; their air of remoteness and easy assurance hardly seems the product of toil. These glimpses of the artist at work show the error of such impressions. The gay spontaneous pictures of Renoir's old age are the result of an heroic struggle, for they were painted with a brush strapped to fingers crippled by rheumatism. Cézanne's art demanded constant study out of doors and he died from a chill caught whilst painting in bad weather. Even the sculptor who need not expose himself to the moods of nature must labour, if he wishes to produce an image larger than life, with the unwieldy pointing instrument.

The finished picture of Berthe la Sourde.

In the drawing by Rossetti, above, the artist submits to the searching gaze of his wife, Elizabeth Siddal, and becomes for once the model. A model, too, though this time pathetically, Géricault is seen below on his deathbed, painted by Ary-Scheffer.

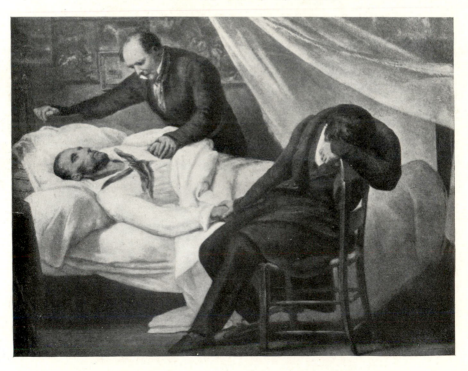

Crivelli : head of St. Catherine, from the Demidoff Altarpiece.

# WOMEN'S FACES

Ford Madox Brown : sketch for 'Farewell to England.' Right, Modigliani :
detail from portrait.

Piombo: from 'Daughter of Herodias.'

Gainsborough: detail from portrait.

Velazquez: from 'Christ in the House of Martha.'

Lotto: detail from 'Lucretia.'

Roman matron 1st cent., A.D.

Some of these faces, such as the Gainsborough, the Roman matron, the Baldovinetti and Lotto's Lucretia, record the features of individual women; others are idealized types. Yet each one was considered beautiful by the artist who chose to carve or paint her. The adenoidal smile and prim expression of Madox Brown's model cannot charm us, yet hers was the type of beauty the artist and his contemporaries most

Baldovinetti: from 'Portrait of a Lady.'

Vermeer: from 'Lady at the Virginals.'

Van Eyck: from 'Arnolfini and his wife.'

Douvermann: woodcarving, 'Virgin.'

admired. The female potency of Salome both attracts and repels, the egg-shaped face of Vermeer's subject enchants as a piece of painting but scarcely recommends the artist's taste in looks. Confronted with this display we must, it seems, reject all preconceived ideas of both women and beauty and conclude that types and standards vary with every age and individual.

Bellini: from 'The Circumcision.'

Engraving on a native bamboo-pole,
from New Caledonia.

# TO SEA

The painter, more than most, must strive to retain that freshness and simplicity of vision which is properly, not derisively, called childlike. The ship, therefore, that aggregation of delights which haunts the child's fancy, remains, often forever, a potent symbol in the painter's mind.

Claude: from 'Embarkation of the Queen of Sheba.'

Raphael: 'The Vision of the Knight,' painted when he was about 17.

# *JUVENILIA*

Turner: self-portrait at 17.

Lawrence: from 'Queen Charlotte,'
painted at the age of 19.

*Thursday. We went with Francis Moore to see Hilton's picture to day. The subject is from Spencer's Fairy Queen. where Serena is lying on the faggots just going to be*

*sacrificed by a party of wretches, and is rescued by Sir Calaphine who rushes upon them and kills every one. The figure of Serena is beautiful, the priests very spirited, the coloring rich and the figure of the knights himself. the only thing in it I dont like, There is something unpleasant in the look of the right arm. I dont know how it will look in the midst of the Titians of the National Gallery but as it appears now, I own I think the landscape is worthy of Rubens himself.*

**Friday.** 22ᵈ Mo Mayne went to Germany yesterday that is he set off, after having previously introduced to Papa one Col Shultze who is coming to breakfast tomorrow. I went to Finch lane this afternoon and procured a glorious quantity of my book.

Richard Doyle: page from his journal of 1840, when he was 15.

Gaudier-Brzeska: aged 15.

Géricault: aged 19.

Lautrec: painted at fifteen.

Picasso: painted at fourteen.

Cézanne: painted at eighteen.

Etruscan terra-cotta of Hermes, 500 B.C.

# SMILES

he smile, in art as in life, is provoking in its ambiuity. The origin of the range, unconscious smile n the faces of archaic reek and Etruscan statues obscure, though it is erhaps the result of the rtist's inability to make the ansition between cheek id lips. Mona Lisa's mile, the inspiration of a hole literature, is coniously suggestive and inntionally haunting. With als the smile almost bemes a robust laugh and e elusive, mysterious qualy is shattered.

Mexican mask.

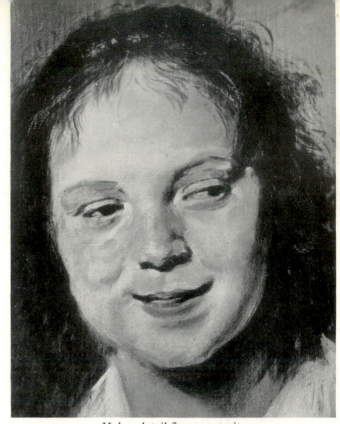

Hals: detail from portrait.

Leonardo: detail from 'Mona Lisa.'

George Cruikshank: 'The Cat Did It.'

# THE LITTLE DOGS AND ALL

Bewick: vignette, 'The Butcher's Dog.'

Gainsborough: detail from 'The Morning Walk.'

Umbrian School: from 'The Story of Griselda.'

Mieris: from 'Fish and Poultry Shop.'

Hogarth: detail from 'The Graham Family.'

Piero di Cosimo: animals from 'The Death of Procris.'

# CHILDREN

ivelli: from 'The Annunciation.'  Hogarth: from 'The Graham Family.'

Romanino: from 'The Nativity.'

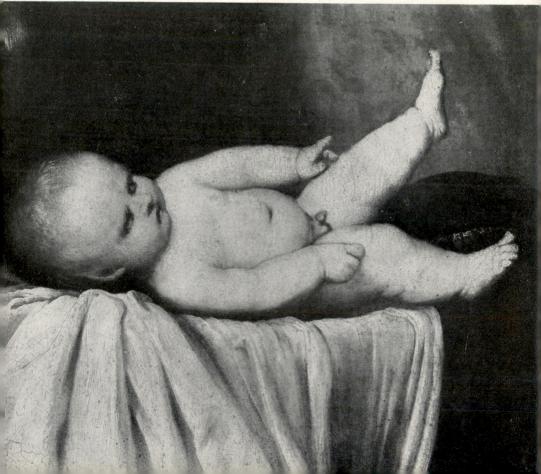

The child, as supreme symbol of his best patron, the Church, was among the painter's first subjects, and it is perhaps this illustrious precedent that connects, at least professionally, painter with baby. The ecclesiastical connection having declined, the painter shows now little interest in the smaller human fry. As part of the family portrait, represented here by Hogarth and Reynolds, the baby makes a bid for aesthetic survival, but the temptation to sentiment nowadays repels. Only the rare courage and rough simplicity of Van Gogh dares the napkinned subject, and we delightedly share his reward.

Van Gogh: le bébé de Roulin.

Reynolds: from 'Lady Cockburn of Eyemouth and her Children.'

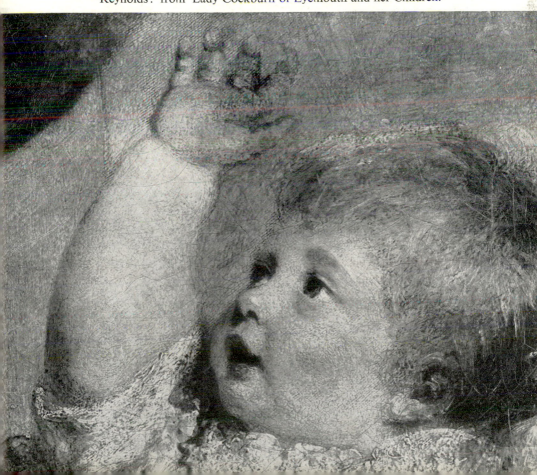

When motherhood was the subject of devout painting and the child an object of reverence, Rembrandt made this original drawing of one of those moments in child life which, though frequent, are usually shunned by all who are not forced to partake in them. In both conception and execution this free, vigorous drawing is the antithesis of Raphael's careful pen study of an idealized Holy Child. Millais' 'Mother and Child' is conventional in feeling, but the fine, nervous pencil line is surprisingly individual.

Rembrandt: pen and wash drawing.

Millais: pencil drawing.

Raphael: pen drawing.

Bordone: 'Daphnis and Chloe.'

Strang: 'Bank Holiday.'

Romanesque sculpture from Kilpeck Church.

The hopes and torments of love are the continual inspiration of literature, and passages from poetry or mythology often prompt the artist's treatment of the tender passion. The subject is otherwise less rewarding to him, and he inclines to deal with it summarily. The Romanesque sculptor strips desire of all its frills and almost of its humanity. Teniers paints the unlovely, ridiculous ardour of old age, Bordone gives a humorous twist to his oversentimental interpretation by introducing a cupid who disturbs rather than encourages the lovers. Only the Edwardian Strang handles his subject with sympathy, without disgust or irony.

Teniers: from 'The Surprise.'

# ATTITUDES

The impudent humanity of some abstract
forms is apparent to the least aesthetic, and we
acknowledge with a smile the aptness of the
bosomed urn (Etruscan, ca. 600 B.C.) whose
handles turn to arms, and the Staffordshire
stone-ware bell whose waisted form so well
recalls a woman.   A similar combination
of human and abstract endows the Indo-
Chinese sculptured frieze, below, with
super-human animation.

HANS HOLBEIN, (1497?–1543):      Mrs Pemberton, *V. and A. Museum*

# Miniatures

The tiny portraits which the Elizabethans called limnings, and often wore in enamelled lockets, derive the name by which we know them from the Latin 'miniate,' to colour red, and the term originally referred to the illumination of manuscripts. The word miniature therefore properly describes the technique rather than the small size of these paintings, and the meaning we give it is due to an etymological confusion. The Elizabethan limner worked with very fine brushes in opaque water colours upon small sheets of parchment stuck on card, but every variety of medium was used by later masters, oil, pastel and pencil, while in style the detailed precision of Hillyarde and Oliver yielded to a broader, sometimes, as in *Sarah Churchill*, almost impressionistic manner. Yet *Sarah Churchill* looks like a fragment from a full-sized picture rather than a complete work. Meticulous detail, crystal clarity are indeed essential to the miniature and, as in all minikin objects, are the source of our delight in these jewel-like circles and ovals.

OLIVE COOK.

PETER OLIVER (1594?–1647): Ann of Denmark.
*Fitzwilliam Mus.*

NICHOLAS HILLYARDE (ca. 1547–1619): Queen
Elizabeth. *Fitzwilliam Mus.*

HANS HOLBEIN: Self-portrait. *Wallace Coll.*

ISAAC OLIVER (d. 1617): Ann of Denmark.
*V. and A. Mus.*

NICHOLAS HILLYARDE: Man clasping hand
from a cloud. *V. and A. Mus.*

*NICHOLAS HILLYARDE:* Countess of Dorset and Pembroke. *Fitzwilliam Mus.*

*ISAAC OLIVER:* Henry Frederick, Prince of Wales.
    *Fitzwilliam Mus.*

*ISAAC OLIVER:* Sir Richard Leveson. *Wallace
    Coll.*

*LAURENCE HILLYARDE* (ca. 1582–after 1640): Unknown Man. *Fitzwilliam Mus.*

*UNKNOWN ARTIST:* Sarah Churchill. *V. and A. Mus.*

*UNKNOWN ARTIST:* King Charles II. *Fitzwilliam Mus.*

*SAMUEL COOPER (1609–1672):* Henrietta. Duchess of Orleans. *V. and A. Mus.*

*SAMUEL COOPER:* A soldier. *V. and A. Mus.*

*JOHN HOSKINS* (d. 1665): Queen Henrietta Maria. *Fitzwilliam Mus.*

*PIERRE ADOLPHE HALL* (1736?–1793): Portrait group.  *Wallace Coll.*

*FRANCOIS DUMONT* (1751–1831): The Dauphin.  *Wallace Coll.*

BERNHARD LENS (1682–1740): Lady Jane Codd.   V. and A. Mus.

PHILIP JEAN (1755–1802).  A child.  V. and A.
Mus.

JOHN SMART  (1741–1811):  Dorothy  Capper.
V. and A. Mus.

HORACE HONE (1756–1825): Col. Marston when a boy.  V. and A. Mus.

*GEORGE ENGLEHEART* (1752–1829): Portrait of girl.  *V. and A. Mus.*

*H. HONE:* Mary, Marchioness of Buckingham.          *A. ROBERTSON* (1777–1845): Portrait of lady.
*Fitzwilliam Mus.*                                                           *V. and A. Mus.*

*JAMES SCOULER* (18th cent.): Portrait of lady.  *V. and A. Mus.*

*SAMUEL SHELLEY* (ca. 1750–1808): Mrs Susannah Knott and daughters. *Fitzwilliam Mus.*

*BERNHARD LENS:* Unknown woman, **1710.** *Fitzwilliam Mus.*

# My Who's Who

### by FRED BASON

DURING twenty-five years, in my quest for autographs, I have met nearly eleven thousand famous people in all walks of life. For the most part the impressions of some of them which I give in this 'Who's Who' were written down immediately after I had met them. I believe a nobody like myself, born, bred and living in the slums,[1] to be a better judge of greatness and graciousness than most. These people did not need to pose to me, they had nothing to lose (or gain) by being civil to me. (AFTERTHOUGHT: *but lawyer must vet all entries . . . even though every word I've written is true. Don't want to spend a year of me jolly old life in clink!*)

### DR ALEXANDER ALEKHINE

I SAW HIM in 1937 when he was probably the greatest chess player in the whole wide world. I had been advised to ask for his autograph in French. (I can ask for autographs in ten languages, using the words 'Please will you sign my book?' I have to say 'Thank you' in English.) He asked in French if I was a player of chess. I was flummoxed, as I didn't understand what he was asking me, but a lady kindly interpreted his question. I said, 'Tell him no, but that I am hot stuff at *tiddley winks*!' She looked at me and I kept a straight face. Then she spoke to him and I caught the words 'tiddley winks.' He looked curious and interested. He signed my book, but as he still carried on a conversation in which the words 'tiddley winks' kept cropping up, I moved away, for I didn't want to be involved in a blooming international argument on the respective merits of chess and tiddley winks.

[1]Here is my own Who's Who: B. Aug., 1907, Walworth, London, lived there forty years. Educated L.C.C. school and hard school of life. Bought and sold books of every description 26 years. Author of six books and many articles. Broadcast twelve times, starred in three films, televised three times. Address: 152 Westmoreland Road, Walworth, S.E.17.

C

## SIR JAMES BARRIE

HE WAS A VERY canny Scot and there were no flies on him. He knew *all* the answers. I haunted the Adelphi many evenings before I happened to meet him. Out came my autograph album and off came my cap. Would he do me the honour? 'No, not in there!' 'But it's a perfectly clean page in a perfectly good autograph album!' 'I don't sign albums.' 'Would you sign in a book—a book by yourself?' 'I might.' And off he went. I bought a copy of *The Little Minister* and went to the Adelphi many nights after that (for about three weeks) with the book under my arm. At last I was lucky enough to see him just outside the Little Theatre. I opened the book and took off my cap and appealed for his autograph. 'I don't sign books for strangers. I don't give autographs. Go away.' 'But when I offered my album you refused and said you might sign one of your own books. So I bought a book by you, as you see, and now you again refuse.' He didn't answer and off he went towards the Savoy. I stood and watched him go. When he had gone about twelve yards he stopped and turned round. Then he beckoned to me. I ran towards him. He took the volume from me and in pencil at the very extreme top of the half-title he wrote 'J. M. Barrie,' then handed the book back without a word. 'Thank you ever so much, sir, I won't forget it. . . .' And although this happened about twenty-two years ago, you see I haven't forgotten!

## JOE BECKETT

IN HIS DAYS OF fame this boxer wasn't exactly a Sir Galahad. Pushed me and my book aside. I dropped my fountain-pen (that cost me fifteen hard-earned shillings) and his brother accidentally stepped on it. Was autograph hunting with a pencil for over five months, till I could afford a new pen. Ashamed to say that I was glad when Carpentier beat him in one round and said to myself, 'Well, you wouldn't sign my book *would you*!' I was very young at the time—about twelve. All my own fault. I was a little pest at twelve and never took 'No' for an answer.

## ARNOLD BENNETT

UNDER THE SURFACE I reckon him a kind-hearted man. Got a shy way, but when he thaws out is O.K., and will chat on this and that. (*Later.* Now had some twenty little chats with him after first nights and we've compared opinions. Has got funny ways but is a jolly good sort. Going to spend an evening all in my company to visit the Beggars' Theatre.)

I'm tempted to write and insert here a detailed account of our visit to this Lambeth theatre. Yes, it's worth it. Here goes.

Now, rather like my friend Somerset Maugham, Arnold Bennett was somewhat touchy. He chose his friends with great care, was very kind when you got to know him, and was interested in the unusual. Because I was a gallery first-nighter for an unbroken twelve years, he got used to seeing me (and my autograph book) at first nights, and we would often have a chat while he waited for his car and I looked out for celebrities to 'capture.'

Well, one night after a show at the Savoy Theatre, his car took a long time to arrive, and as he was getting het up I volunteered to go and look for it. I found it tucked away down by the Embankment Gardens, caught in a traffic jam. I told the driver to stay there and I'd bring Arnold Bennett to the car. I did this, and as we walked along I told him all about the Beggars' Theatre I'd visited the previous night.

On most occasions when we'd conversed I'd had a pretty sure feeling that he wasn't listening very closely, but this time he seemed really interested. He asked me if he could see the show. I told him that it was a very rough and ready place and that posh people were not admitted; but that if he liked to put on a shabby suit and look a bit seedy I reckoned we could pass muster as a couple of blokes rather on the rocks. I arranged to meet him at seven-thirty the very next night at the foot of Lambeth Bridge and take him to the place, but I said he must promise never to write about his visit or even put the incident into his Diaries. He promised.

Now, not even his best friend could ever have called Arnold Bennett distinguished-looking. He had a drooping, weeping apology of a moustache, a nose that seemed set on a crooked path, long teeth (and such a funny voice). Add to this a dilapidated black trilby with the brim at all angles, an old dark-brown raincoat, and trousers that didn't reach his boots, and you have Arnold Bennett as I saw him on our evening out.

'The Lambeth Walk' made Lambeth world famous, but it remains a borough of mean streets. Many parts of Lambeth were badly blitzed, and among the streets that have quite vanished is the little dingy turning that Arnold Bennett and I went down that night. I wouldn't be writing this now if the place was still standing, because I promised never to write about it while it was a theatre for beggars, as they didn't want curious strangers popping in and out. I knocked at the door of a drab-looking tumbledown two-story house.

'Who's you?' said the doorkeeper.

'Me?—I'm Freddie. A pal of Frankie, the pavement artist. I was here two nights ago and you said I could come again any time.'

'Oh, all right, but don't make a 'abit of it, mate . . . and who's this?' He pointed to Arnold Bennett.

'Oh, he's all right. He's a real pal of mine. Take it from me, he's all right. He's seen better days. He once wrote a book what got printed!'

The passage was narrow and not very high. We entered a room that was really two rooms in one because a partition had been knocked down. There were about seventeen people in the room, and it was rather crowded. You could barely see across the room for fog and smoke. The seating arrangements consisted of three very ancient sofas, several orange boxes, a tea chest, an old cabin trunk and some chairs in various stages of ruin. All these were placed around the walls, leaving the centre free for 'the acts'! A fat, beery old man who sat in front of the fire (and took most of its warmth) turned his head as we entered and beckoned us to go over to him. He was the theatre magnate, stage manager and casting director all in one. He held out his hand and I placed four pennies in it. (Tuppence a time—stay till you're warm or fed up!)

'Ta, mate,' he said, pocketing the money, and pointing to two seats in the corner.

'Silence, everybody!' said he in a powerful voice.

'Harris is going ter play to you, so pay attention. What you playing tonight?—oh, yes—I remember—it's "Parted." So silence all of you.'

Harris got his fiddle out of its case, walked into the centre of the room, and without any preliminary tuning up began to render (tear apart) 'Parted.' Everyone except Arnold Bennett applauded loudly.

'Did you expect Kreisler for tuppence, sir?' I asked him. He said he hadn't expected anything—much.

A fellow sitting next to me asked 'Who's 'im what you calls "sir"?' I was going to tell him to mind his own business, but instead, not wanting trouble, I said my friend had seen better days and that out of politeness and in memory of those days and to give credit where credit was due I still called him 'sir.' This satisfied my neighbour. (Giving credit where credit is due is always a safe line to play with working-class folk.)

'Now, Sarah, what about it?' said the old man. The room seemed to tremble. Many of the audience took up the cry, and after a few moments the door opened and a young woman came in. She paused at the door and acknowledged the applause.

'Do your stuff, girlie,' said the grimy old man next to me.

'Don't get anxious,' said Sarah, as she came to the centre of the room. She was dressed in a near-white blouse with wide red stripes. Her skirt was rather long and of some dark material. She had a many-coloured scarf round her neck and wore a big check cloth cap. She was 'in costume.' A chap with an accordion began to play a song called 'Frankie and Johnnie,' and she sang in a trying-to-be-Yankee style that wasn't displeasing because she had a sparkling personality. You had to look at her . . . and it wasn't because of her personality alone, for at the end of each verse she took off some of her clothes! The cap and scarf were thrown aside unnoticed. When the blouse went I sat up. When the skirt slipped down and revealed a rather nice pair of scanties and a lovely pair of legs I was most attentive. Her brassière came off in two stages and was upon the floor (and quickly picked up by a Negro) as she finished the final verse. And in nothing but scanties and a pair of shoes she paused at the door and acknowledged the applause with a smile and a wave of her hand. The coloured gentleman, with the brassière in his hand, made for the door also but the fellow who had played the accordion quickly took the thing from him and went after Sarah with it. (AFTER-THOUGHT: *she was certainly pinuptuous. But must make it clear that Sarah wasn't her real name, or all the Sarahs of Lambeth will be on us! All names except Bennett's are changed*.) Arnold Bennett said, 'Montmartre in Lambeth. She was certainly attractive . . . had a certain style.'

'The Pretty Lady,' I said, recalling one of his books. 'The Pretty Lady of Lambeth.'

'Yes, Fred, with bad teeth and a dirty mark half-way down her back!' That dried me up. (AFTERTHOUGHT: *Now I come to think of it, I don't suppose Sarah had had a real bath in a bath since she was a baby. They don't build bathrooms in mean streets!*) The Negro who had been keen to help Sarah was the next act and he recited Shakespeare by the yard.

'That man is very clever,' said Mr. Bennett, and he applauded louder than anyone else.

The fat old man then said, 'Now, ladies and gentlemen, for my final act tonight I have a special treat. My darling little granddaughter is going to sing "Swannee" to you. Kindly let us have no swearing or anything while she's doing her act, or you and me will 'ave words.' He waddled across the floor and opened the door. 'Sarah, bring Betty 'ere!'

Betty was an attractive little girl of about ten, and she did a nice little turn. Then I felt it was time to leave. The next stage of the evening would be a game of cards for those who wanted it and conversation for the rest. Conversation was very important here because they compared notes on pitches and police. There was also warmth and sleep for those it suited.

I tapped Mr Bennett on his arm. 'About time we went, A. B.,' I said.

'A.B.,' said a man to whom he had been talking in little bursts of speech, 'blimey, he ain't no Yid surely!'

'Of course not,' I replied, 'it's only initials.'

'What's his name then?' he asked. I felt sure Mr Bennett was going to tell him, and to shut him up I said, 'Any bottles! You know folk don't like giving names away!' He laughed, and looking at Arnold Bennett said, 'A.B. All Backside!'

Walking along the Embankment, I told Arnold Bennett a couple of Stock Exchange stories (he was something of a connoisseur) and by a miracle he'd heard neither before. The squeaky laughs he gave showed that he was in a good mood, and I ventured to ask him some literary questions, to which he gave carefully considered replies. We both agreed that Radclyffe Hall was the handsomest woman in London. (Did you ever see her? A lovely aquiline nose, keen steady eyes, a neat mouth, sleek close-cropped slightly grey hair with a little wave, wonderful smile, slight figure and the prettiest hands ever.) Mr. Bennett highly praised *The Well of Loneliness,* but said one must not forget that she wrote other great books, including *Adam's Breed.* He also praised Hugh Walpole and said *The Dark Forest* was a brilliant novel. I asked him to name the most promising playwright and he selected Patrick Hamilton. I scribbled notes about his remarks on the inside of a packet of cigarettes as I rode home on a 56 tram.

Arnold Bennett thanked me for the evening and called a cab. As he got into it he handed me a pound note. I refused it and said that what I would really like as a little present would be one of his own novels with his signature in it. Four days later he sent me *Accident,* suitably inscribed. But, alas, Hitler robbed me of it by blitzing my home.

I went to the memorial service of this great man at St Martin-in-the Fields and sat next to John Drinkwater. We had both lost a friend.

## MADELEINE CARROLL

MY IDEA OF THE sweetest angel this side of Heaven. Beautiful, gracious and kind. I was the first fan to get her autograph in the days when she was quite unknown. Loved her in secret since we were both in our teens. Watched her become a star. Still proud to have been one of her first admirers. She has no side and is friendly—in fact, she's my ideal. And if I had but one pound in the world and she needed it, then gladly would it be given to her.

## CHARLIE CHAPLIN

SAW HIM IN Bond Street alone, unprotected and unrecognized. Asked for his autograph. He looked carefully round this way and that. Many people about. He called a cab. I said, 'Blimey, sir, I ain't asking for a part in a film or a blooming cheque. Surely you can oblige! I live in Walworth. You knew my district when you were my age.' 'Just a moment, boy, *just a moment!*' Cab arrived. He got in. 'Come in here a moment, son.' I got in. 'Now, where's your book?' I handed over book and pen. He wrote a nice inscription and signed it. 'Thank you,' I said. 'Going Piccadilly way?' he asked. 'I'd go to Timbuctoo with *you,* sir! But why the taxi just to sign a book?' 'A precaution, boy. If I'd signed your book in the open there'd have been hundreds around in a minute and I'd have been late for my lunch!' We parted in Piccadilly.

## WINSTON CHURCHILL

MANY YEARS AGO I stood under the porch by the entrance to the House of Lords to get out of the rain. Next to me was an obvious copper in plain clothes, and next to him stood Winston Churchill. And although I had both book and pen I was *afraid* to ask in case the dick run me in or something. But I did find courage to say, 'Wish you could pass a Better British Weather Law, Mr Churchill.' He grinned and looked in a very amiable mood. For two pins I'd have chanced my arm (or my neck) and asked. I still so very much want his autograph.

## GEORGE FORMBY

HE CAN BE PUT DOWN as a good sort, but if you put him out of temper I reckon you'd have a very rough side of a real Lancashire hot-pot. As I was getting his signature someone in the crowd asked him for a song, and with a dead-pan glance he looked up from my book and said, 'Do you work for nothing?' in a manner that was very chilly and froze the speaker to vanishing point.

## HITLER

TWO YEARS BEFORE the war I wrote to Hitler asking if he would care to swop fag cards with me. I got no reply. A year before the war I wrote again. Hitler possessed the finest collection of cigarette cards in Europe, while I had probably the best selection in England. This time I did get a reply. It boiled down to the fact that the Führer was too busy to give attention to my request (I bet he was!). So I went to Berlin a month before the war started, without knowing German or anyone in Germany at all; I thought that on the spot I might be able to see him and arrange to exchange cards. What a blooming hope! I never saw him, but I did bring home 3,000 sets of German cards, arriving back with them the day before war broke out. (Reached London 1.30 Saturday afternoon and war began Sunday morning!) And the first ruddy incendiary bomb to fall in our street fell on my home and burnt the blarsted lot!

## JACK HOBBS

I'M NOT A CRICKET FAN but, of course, no collection of autographs is complete without representative sportsmen. I chose Hobbs because he was Surrey, and Surrey was my local team as it were. Bold as brass I hop off to the Oval armed with large album and long pencil. A commissionaire turns me away. Back I come. Again—a bit less gently— I'm thrust aside at the Players' Entrance. There's me and the blarsted cocky commissionaire and a couple of taxi-drivers. One of the taxi-drivers tells the commissionaire just what he thinks of him: says he ought to let me stay as I'm doing no harm. Words lead to words and it's almost a fight. Out of a taxi steps a kindly-looking man. He asks, 'What's up?' He's quickly told the situation by me and the other taxi-driver, who says, 'It's this way, *Mr Hobbs*.' 'Mr Jack Hobbs?' I say. The man nods. 'Then *do* please sign, sir. That's all I want, it's all I'm waiting for. When I've got it I promise never to ask another cricketer again.' I got it and I have kept my promise these twenty-four years. Hence in near eleven thousand autographs I have but one cricketer.

## LORD HEWART

A DEAD failure. Can't think what made me ask. It was outside the

Ivy Restaurant. I hadn't ever asked a judge. He was stout and looked kindly. I felt I'd take a gamble. Best manners and utmost politeness. Begged for the great honour. 'Most certainly NOT.' And in he walked to lunch. I immediately forgot Lord Hewart and captured Jack and Claude Hulbert.

## DEAN INGE

IN A BUNDLE of books I found a copy of *Assessments and Anticipations* by him which I had been unable to sell. Seeing that he was due to broadcast from Savoy Hill, I wrapped up the book and took it to the entrance and waited for him. Tall, thin, gloomy, he arrived. I raised my cap and put forward the book and pen. He looked at the book and then at me—up and down several times. (I was shabbily dressed and wore cap and choker.) He said, '*You* reading *my* book! I am *astounded!*' I didn't answer him till he'd autographed it. Then, as he handed it back to me, I said, 'No, sir—I haven't read it. I prefer Somerset Maugham. You see, sir, I sell books to make a living. It wouldn't sell unsigned, so perhaps it will sell signed.' He sighed such a sigh—and passed on, tall, thin and extra gloomy.

## W. W. JACOBS

EVERYONE KNEW HIS name, but very few people had ever met him. I looked up his address (it was Gloucester Gate) and haunted his front door armed with a tiny photograph for reference. I was lucky. After two hours he came out. I took off my cap and made my request. I was a real admirer and could easily have recalled to him whole paragraphs of his works. He signed my autograph book and suddenly said, 'Would you like a book by me signed by me?' I said I'd treasure it always. He went back into his house and within five minutes was back with a Tauchnitz edition of *The Skipper's Wooing* all nicely autographed. It escaped the blitz and is still a treasured possession of mine. That's the kind of man W. W. Jacobs was.

## ADMIRAL OF THE FLEET LORD JELLICOE

SAW HIM IN THE Strand. Hadn't got my book, but did so much want his autograph. What could I do? I said, 'Beg you to excuse me, my Lord. I would so much like your signature but have no book with me. If I wrote to you at the Admiralty would you honour me?' He said 'You seem anxious to capture me. Why?' 'You are a great man.'

'Well spoken, my boy. Look—I have a newspaper. I'll autograph that for you.' And he did. We saluted each other. He passed on and I went off with his newspaper. Carefully I put it on top of the piano underneath a few sheets of music to keep it flat, and went off happy to bed. Next morning I got downstairs early—but not early enough. My dad had lit the fire with my priceless Jellicoe newspaper!

## RUDYARD KIPLING

SNOBBISH AND stand-offish. One of my few failures. Saw him in South Kensington near a museum. Raised my hat. Begged the great honour. He pushed me aside with a 'No.' I repeated my request. 'I never sign and have no wish to be bothered. Will you go *away*.' He glared and sort of bristled. Even the policeman who had kindly pointed him out to me was amazed at this reception.

## SIR HARRY LAUDER

ONE OF THE FEW men I'd really raise my hat to. A noble man. Asked if I'd like a photograph of himself and his 'lassie.' I had a sort of idea that 'lassie' was a dog! But he sent a charming picture of himself and wife seated in front of their house. That was in 1926.

## RAMSAY MACDONALD

THE ONLY P.M. I ever captured. He was at the Palladium at a Sunday Charity concert, with his daughter. He was in an amiable mood, asking where I lived, what I did for a living and whether I was a Labour man. As I was only about fifteen I wasn't much interested in Labour. Seemed to me very human and quite pleased to sign my book. Shook hands with crowds of people.

## W. SOMERSET MAUGHAM

THE KINDEST CELEBRITY it has ever been my good fortune to meet. Put me on my feet financially when I hadn't thirty shillings in the world. *Not* by giving money, but by showing me how to write, autographing books for me to sell at a profit and ordering books from me which probably he didn't really need. But perhaps you've read my article about him in the fifth SATURDAY BOOK.

## CHARLES MORGAN

SAID TO BE RATHER aloof and not hail-fellow-well-met, but I can honestly say that on the only occasion I ever spoke to him he was very human and far from aloof. I saw him in St. Martin's Lane with his wife a week after *The Fountain* was published. I looked scruffy and wore old clothes and cap and had a sack of books on my back. I said 'Excuse me, sir. I ain't anyone. I just sell books for my living and I just want to say I think *The Fountain* is a magnificent novel—and jolly good luck to you.' His wife (I'm sure it was his wife, because Mr Morgan isn't the type to go around with chorus girls or other men's  wives) said, 'My dear, how very sweet! That's the nicest piece of praise I've ever heard.' And Charlie said that he would never forget that testimonial, and thanked me very heartily. Wasn't till they'd passed on that I remembered I had my album in my pocket—and I missed the occasion in my enthusiasm over a great novel.

## NONI

I PUT HIM IN because he is the finest clown I've seen. It took fifteen occasions to capture his autograph. No, he didn't refuse fourteen times, but he is so comically made-up on the stage that I could never visualize what he was like in real life, and I had to wait until he was appearing at two different music halls in one night and catch him in his make-up as he clambered into a taxi between acts. (*Later*) Doesn't look a bit funny without his make-up, and you'd pass him a hundred times without knowing he was Noni, successor to Grock and in my opinion his equal.

## BARONESS ORCZY

I WAS VERY YOUNG when I first read *The Scarlet Pimpernel*, and it took me fifteen years to meet the author of it. She didn't look a scrap like my idea of a Baroness. But she was a dear, sweet soul and made me feel quite at home, and I had a lovely afternoon in her company.

## PADEREWSKI

VERY, VERY FAMOUS and guarded like a king—but even guards are sometimes slack and I managed to slip through and ask for his autograph. He waved long slender hands in the air and said, 'My hands! My hands! I am very tired!' I must have looked as disappointed as I felt, for I had waited over two hours for that moment. A man in dress clothes rushed up and I was pulled away. Paderewski said to him, 'Take the child's name and address.' I thought it meant police and trouble. 'What right,' I cried, 'have you got to ask for my address? I was absolutely polite.' 'It's quite all right. Your request will be granted in due course if I have your address.' Six months later the autograph was sent me—but *it was not genuine*. Someone had obviously signed for him on a photograph.

## JAMES MASON

THEY SAID THIS film actor was a tiger and would snarl. They said he was temperamental and touchy. They said he was a law unto himself. They talked through their blooming hats, as they so often do, because they had never met Mr Mason. Mr Bason met Mr Mason and found him human, kindly and a very good sort. He doesn't suffer fools gladly. He detests cadgers and he hates fuss and bother, pomp and ceremony. Don't hero-worship James Mason. Treat him as he is— a man's man and a clever man at that.

## J. B. PRIESTLEY

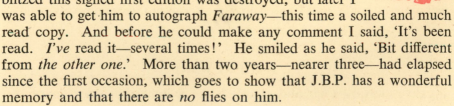

IT WAS AT THE Duchess Theatre that I first saw him, and I happened to be carrying in my attaché case a sparkling first edition of *The Good Companions*, which I had two hours previously gambled a pound on to buy as an investment. Would he autograph my copy of his book? He would. As he handed it back he said, 'It's really quite readable. You ought to read it some day!' And he hurried away before I had time to say that I don't pay a pound for a book I've not read: I had read *The Good Companions* three times. Unfortunately when we were blitzed this signed first edition was destroyed, but later I was able to get him to autograph *Faraway*—this time a soiled and much read copy. And before he could make any comment I said, 'It's been read. *I've* read it—several times!' He smiled as he said, 'Bit different from *the other one*.' More than two years—nearer three—had elapsed since the first occasion, which goes to show that J.B.P. has a wonderful memory and that there are *no* flies on him.

## SIR A. QUILLER-COUCH

JUST ONE OF THOSE lucky breaks we autograph hunters sometimes get. I'm on a railway station. Seated on the same bench is an elderly gentleman looking very dignified. Next to me is a younger man (might have been a nervous school teacher). He keeps saying rather loudly, 'Yes, Sir Arthur,' 'No, Sir Arthur,' 'Oh, no, Sir Arthur.' So I know that the old bloke is Sir Arthur! The nervous chap gets up with a 'Very well, Sir Arthur,' and off he goes. Out comes my autograph album. He's Sir Arthur someone. I'll take a chance—although I know it's *not* Conan Doyle. I raise my hat and most politely beg the honour of Sir Arthur's autograph. He seems amazed and pleased to be recognized, and he obliges with a signature which I eventually decipher as A. T. Quiller-Couch.

## BERNARD SHAW

SO MUCH HAS BEEN SAID about this superman that I won't add anything. I got his autograph when I was about fifteen. To me then he was just a funny old cove who, it was said, wouldn't sign his autograph unless you happened to be as famous as he was. I thought I'd be cheeky —I could only get a clip on the ear. It was in Kingsway after a debate at the Kingsway Hall. A crowd followed him the whole way down Kingsway but he  moved so fast that it had thinned to two by the time we reached the Strand. A middle-aged woman was begging him to help her son, who was in prison. He kept saying, 'I can do nothing. NOTHING.' And there was me almost running to keep up with him. I kept asking for his signature and he kept saying, 'No, no, NO!' Presently the woman gave up and lagged behind—I believe she was crying. That left me and Shaw. I was on the point of giving up. Then I had a brainwave. I said, 'Don't be so mean, Mr Shaw. You might be quite famous one day and then I won't bother you. I only want your autograph now for a souvenir *when you become well-known*!' He stopped and stared at me. Then he laughed, a merry laugh, took my book and pen, and signed with a flourish. And off he went again at a tremendous pace, leaving me panting but very pleased.

Thinking it over, I should positively hate to be as rich or as famous as Shaw. It must be a ruddy bother.

## PAUL ROBESON

I WAS A BIT OF a boy when he first appeared in London in *Emperor Jones*, but I had enough knowledge of art to recognize a great artist. I went to the stage-door and waited for him to come out after a show one foggy winter night. It was very dismal and dark and I had to wait quite three-quarters of an hour. As he came out I opened my book at random and asked him to sign. Then I saw that the page already had several names on it, so I turned over to a fresh, clean page. He said, 'Do you object to my signing on a page that has white men's signatures upon it?' 'Most certainly not, Mr Robeson,' I replied. 'I think you are such a great actor that you deserve a page to yourself. In fact, I wouldn't have the cheek to ask you to put your signature on the page with such people.' And he was so delighted that, unasked, he went back into the theatre and brought me out a nice photograph which I've kept over twenty years. And although five years passed before I next saw him, he remembered me and shook hands.

## A. GORDON SELFRIDGE

I WOULDN'T CALL HIM a celebrity, but as founder of Selfridge & Co. he is undoubtedly a famous name. He happened to be, like myself, a very keen first-nighter, and we got used to seeing each other at shows, till there came a time when he would nod and smile and recognize me and at times even have a few quick words as he waited for his daughter. So one night I asked if I could have his signature. He thought I was kidding and refused. 'But, Mr Selfridge, I really want it and I'll be *proud* to have it.' He signed then and said he couldn't remember anyone previously asking for it save on a cheque!

## DAME SYBIL THORNDIKE

A VERY DISTINGUISHED actress and a very noble lady. Always seems so *very* pleased to give her signature and *so* interested in what *you* have to say about her work, her plays or things in general! A dear kindly soul with a generous heart. Seems to lay stress on sentences like, 'How ARE you?', 'Did YOU really?' Never seems to dress fashionably yet is always just right.

## SIR RABINDRANATH TAGORE

ALAS, ONE OF my failures. I didn't get near enough even to ask. I feel pretty sure he'd have granted my polite request. But if he'd been King of All India he couldn't have been more closely guarded. It was in 1930 in London that I saw him, or, rather, the extreme top of his head. Looked a very distinguished old gentleman. I bet I'm one of the very few Cockneys to have read and enjoyed *Gitanjali*. He and I could have found much to talk about.

## TETRAZZINI

NOW ONLY A NAME, yet in her day the world's greatest soprano. Saw her in 1925. Untidy, fat and plain. Lots of temper. No charm or graciousness. 'And why ME!' she said. 'Because you are truly great, madame!' She purred like a pussy cat and out of a bag brought forth her photograph and signed it. I felt a proper hypocrite because I had never heard her sing. I had merely asked because she was a name to fill a page. (*Later*) I have heard a record she made when she was in her prime. She may not have been beautiful to look at, but, by golly, she had a truly wonderful voice. No one would have thought it to look at her. Still, she was as God made her, only He might have been a bit kinder with her. (AFTERTHOUGHT: *I do not know if she is still alive. If she is, I beg her to forgive this frank pen-picture. Perhaps with age she has matured into something like graciousness. I hope so, because I recall that the girl who asked for her signature almost immediately before I did got such a refusal that she warned me not to ask or I would probably get my face slapped!*)

## IRENE VANBRUGH

I KNOW A CHAP who saw *All The King's Horses*, a play of 1926 in which Irene Vanbrugh was the leading lady, forty-eight times. I thought he was crackers! No play could be that good outside Shakespeare. But he said it was once to see the play and forty-seven times to see Miss Vanbrugh. He said that each and every time she was just a little different, and it was the difference that compelled him to go so frequently. As he's a rich bloke (a timber merchant) I accepted his invitation to go twice (at his expense) to witness the differences, and blow me, he was right. *Never* twice alike and yet always *just right*. A born actress, a great actress. A nice lady as well. Did she make Pinero famous or did his plays make her famous? I once asked a theatre critic that question, and all he answered was, 'Miss Vanbrugh would have been famous in any age in any sphere.'

## EDGAR WALLACE

MOST HUMAN BLOKE I met till I met Willy Maugham. There was a first night of one of Wallace's plays at the Apollo at a time when all he touched seemed to turn to gold. But I considered it a very poor play (could easily have written something twice as good myself). I was friendly enough with Wallace to be able to go up to him and tell him I thought it a dull and uninteresting play which wouldn't run a week on merit. 'In fact,' I said, 'I bet you it doesn't run ten days on merit or anything else. Bet you 2s. 6d. against a signed book by you. Is that on?' He nodded and we shook hands on it. Play ran five days. He must have lost a packet on it. Fifteen days later, when I saw him at another first night, he came over to me and asked me to go to his car with him. I did so, and he got out of the car a signed copy of *The Flying Squad*, his latest book. It said, 'You win!' on the title page. Amidst all his work, all his troubles and worries, he remembered a bet made with a galleryite nobody!

## SIR HUGH WALPOLE

A VERY TOUCHY man of many moods. I never much liked his books save *The Dark Forest* and *The Secret City*. I was warned that if you made a fuss of him you got quite a nice autograph, but for heaven's sake don't forget you've immensely enjoyed his latest novel and lay the butter on thick. But I am no hypocrite, and when he asked me if I'd read *Harmer John* I said, 'Well, I'm busy enjoying *The Old Wives' Tale* for the third time.' It seems I said the *right* thing, for he spent five minutes praising it to the skies. But then I said the wrong thing. 'I think, sir, you've written only two books that matter, *The Dark Forest* and *The Secret City*. The rest, with the exception of *Mr Perrin and Mr Traill*, are so blooming wordy-wordy that you get lost in a jungle, and when you cut through there isn't any story!' Then, blow me, he got proper annoyed and asked who I thought I was to pass judgment on his work. And, would you believe it, he pulled back the autograph book that I held in my hand waiting for the ink to dry, and scribbled out his autograph with a pencil! 'In that case you don't need MY autograph!' I took off my cap and said, 'I am sorry, sir, I thought you were a great man—great enough to accept even my very humble but sincere opinion.' And then he suddenly changed. He smiled and apologized and signed all over again on a fresh page.

Bernard Venables

# James Agate's Table-Talk

THE DIALOGUE *which follows occurred at a dinner given to the late* JAMES AGATE *on February 7, 1947. Present as interlocutors were the editor of this book,* LEONARD RUSSELL, *and his wife,* DILYS POWELL, *with* ARTHUR J. LEE *as shorthand-writer. Mr Agate had been dogged by a severe illness for two months or more, but he would not on any account miss the opportunity of being what he called Boswellized, and on that evening he displayed all the old zest for life which was the wonderment of his friends and the delight of his readers. When he read the typescript of the dialogue, a fortnight before his death, he showed (to use a quotation of which he was particularly fond) one auspicious and one dropping eye. 'I like it,' he said. 'I Boswellize very well, don't you think? But'—and an expression of concern came over his Rowlandson face—'anybody who reads it will think I have no manners at all. There I am, at dinner in a private house, talking all the time. Can't you put in a note to say that I was specially invited to talk?' That is easily done. The intention was to preserve some impression of the table talk of a remarkable character of our time, and to that end social niceties were sacrificed.*

D

J.A.  Ah, we're to have fizz, I see!

L.R.  'Fizz'?  A bit Victorian, aren't you?

J.A.  I *am* Victorian.  I don't care if you call it 'bubbly' or even 'the widow.'  How many bottles?

L.R.  One.  Two if you insist.  Shall we start with the Bollinger?

J.A.  If you like.  Dilys, talking of Bollinger reminds me about a very old third cousin of my father's, a clergyman, who used to vary his grace according to the glasses he saw on the table.  When he saw champagne glasses he would say, 'Bountiful Jehovah!'  When there were only claret glasses he would say, 'O Lord, we are not worthy of the least of Thy mercies.'  Ha-ha-ha!

L.R.  You're not a red wine drinker, are you?

J.A.  No.

L.R.  Is that a life-long habit?

J.A.  No.  I know more about red wine than almost anybody living, not excepting some of those people who write books about it!  When the Manchester Midland Hotel first opened they had a wonderful cellar of all the best clarets—Lafite, Larose, Mouton Rothschild.  Three thousand a year was money in Manchester in 1904.  Fred Dehn, father of my godson Paul, and I set the fashion of drinking claret at dessert.  After champagne, of course.  Then whatever the disease that attacked the vines is called came along, and claret isn't the same.

D.P.  Look at poor Leonard getting desperate with that cork!  The only way to open Government-controlled champagne is to saw off the top of the cork and then use a corkscrew.  Or does that offend your sense of propriety, Jimmie?

J.A.  No.  It's the right thing to do.

L.R.  Is it, now?

J.A.  It's the right thing to do in the circumstances because the important thing is to get the champagne into the glasses.  Personally, I don't mind if Leonard takes a hammer to the neck of the thing.

L.R.  Here it comes.

J.A.  Now then, *mes enfants*, would you like to hear a sequel to the clergyman and the glasses?

D.P.  Yes, please.

J.A.  I went out to dinner one night, and out of mischief, seeing there were only claret glasses on the table, I told my hostess the story.  Three minutes later the parlourmaid was pushing round champagne glasses to everybody!  There's a silly woman for you!

D.P.  But I don't suppose you were *very* embarrassed, Jimmie.

J.A.  I like it.  Once I remember a man saying to his wife before dinner, 'Well, I'll go down and get a couple of bottles of champagne because I know Agate likes champagne.'  His wife said, 'Not two bottles.  You know I never touch it—and the doctor has warned you against drinking too much.'  And then when the champagne was opened she said, 'Well, thank you—perhaps just a sip!'  And I said, '*No, you don't!*  You told us you weren't going to have any and you aren't going to have any!'  But by that time her husband was well on his way to the cellar. . . . Leonard, can I tell you my best musical story?

L.R.  That's what we're hoping.

J.A.  It doesn't bore you, all this chatter?

L.R.  **Go on.**

J.A.  Some years ago I was lunching at the Waldorf, and I saw at the table behind me about ten or twelve unkempt, unwashed hangdog fellows, obviously instrumentalists from one of the big orchestras.  Suddenly I heard a purring voice saying, 'You may take it from me, gentlemen, that Brahms never composed anything that mattered.'  Without looking round I said in a loud voice, 'Rubbish —Sir Thomas!'  The voice went on, 'You may take it from me, gentlemen, that with the exception of four symphonies, four concertos, two hundred songs and a vast quantity of chamber music, Brahms never composed anything that mattered.'  Ha-ha-ha.

I remember, too, years and years ago, George Alexander coming to Manchester in some drawing-room play, striding up to a blackmailer and saying, 'Sir, your conduct is de*spi*cable!'  I pointed out in the *Manchester Guardian* next day that the accent was on the wrong syllable: that it should be on the first.  I happened for some reason to go to the theatre again during the week.  Again the scene in which Alexander confronted his blackmailer.  But this time he said, 'Sir, your conduct is—*dastardly*!'

L.R.  You've now finished with *Ego*?

J.A.  Yes.  I was playing with the idea of a *Postscript to Ego*, to be published posthumously.  But the work is too much and if I go on something will suffer.  After all, my *Sunday Times* theatre work comes first.  So I've finished.  I delivered *Ego 9* on the last day of the year.

D.P.  You'll miss it.

J.A.  Yes, greatly.  After all (*laughing*) you miss a hair shirt, you know !  And I've got such a grand close to it that, as an artist, I couldn't go on.  (*Intones*) 'As I write these last words I see my brother Edward rubbing his long nose and murmuring, "Isn't it extraordinary that a man who has written so much can have said so little!" And I hear old Leo saying in his rasping voice, "Tell me, James, will your *Ego 9* be choral?"'

D.P.   Charming!

J.A.   You can't go on after that. I'm not going to make the mistake of Berlioz, who ended the Symphonie Fantastique twice. The Symphony ends with the March to the Scaffold. The Ronde du Sabbat merely tries to finish something that is already finished.

D.P.   I see.

J.A.   He should have lengthened that last movement and turned it into a symphonic poem.

D.P.   I don't know the symphony well enough to judge.

J.A.   And I don't know enough about music to tell Berlioz what to do.!

L.R.   Your family was strongly musical, wasn't it? The glimpses you give of it remind me of a long-short story by Arnold Bennett— I forget the title. I seem to remember two brothers working in a pottery factory and coming home to play Scriabin all the evening, or to read books newly arrived from Paris. Is there a French strain in your family?

J.A.   No, although my grandmother, my mother and my aunt were all educated in Paris. My grandmother was engaged to Guizot, the French statesman, at one period, but chucked it because she thought she had hip disease. Actually, he chucked her. And then —well, my grandmother used to give piano lessons to the Greek colony in Manchester at a guinea a lesson at a time when people were charging *a guinea for twelve lessons*. And with this money she kept my mother and my aunt at two of the most expensive schools in Paris and in Heidelberg—knowing she was dying of cancer.

L.R.   Oh, dear.

J.A.   Somebody said to her, 'I think Mr. Agate is sweet on your elder daughter.' (That was my father.) And she replied, 'I should not permit the alliance. Mr Agate is in trade!' (*Laughter.*) I wonder if somebody would pass me the salt? My father's oldest friend, Gustave Garcia, was a nephew of Malibran, the great singer, and Pauline Viardot, also a singer and Turgenev's mistress. Their father was the great Manuel Garcia for whom Rossini wrote Almaviva, the Count, in the *Barber of Seville*. Now here's something a bit odd, even remarkable. Pauline Viardot made her début in the same week as Rachel, and I possess the notice in which Alfred de Musset combined the two events. Years afterwards I was to write my little study of Rachel, and old Mme Viardot was to give my sister May her first lesson in how to speak French verse.

L.R.   Where does the Garcia who died the other day come in?

J.A.   He was the son of my father's old friend. For thirty years old Gustave Garcia spent Christmas with my family, and he used to sing to us the Mozart arias with ornaments used by Malibran which have never been printed. He was a most extraordinary man. Often he spent his summer holiday with us. He would bring a rod and line—we had a little country house then—and start fishing in the pond, and I would say to him, 'There are no fish in the pond.' He said, 'I don't want feesh—I don't like feesh—I enjoy feeshing!' And (*laughing*) he went on fishing! When he wasn't fishing he cycled. I have cycled hundreds of miles with him.

D.P.   Jimmie, I can't imagine you bicycling—I don't seem to see you as a very sporting character.

L.R.   And there's his prowess at golf—he used to be a good player, you know.

J.A.   My dear children! My mother said to me one day, 'Jimmie, I want you to make me a promise. I want you to promise me you won't smoke or drink until you're 21.' I kept that promise. My father said, 'I'm going to ask you to make me a much more difficult promise—to have nothing to do with sex until you're 25.' And I kept that promise! Now, *how do you think I spent the time*? (*Laughter*.) I played cricket and lawn-tennis and football, and cycled and walked. I even had a go at lacrosse.

D.P.   And golf?

J.A.   I didn't take up golf until I was 33.

D.P.   You must have made a promise to someone!

J.A.   It happened like this. Playing for Chapel-en-le-Frith *versus* some other village I made 98 not out. I should have made a century, but alas I made the winning hit and the match was over. I went to the local golf course to meet my brother, who was just coming in from a round, and told him about my near-century. He said, 'Well, have a go at this!' And teed up a ball which I promptly hit smack-dab, 250 yards down the middle of the fairway.

I said, 'This is a daft game—too easy!'

He teed up another ball—and then twenty or thirty more. I never got a single one of them off the floor—they all went about a yard, to cover-point and square leg. After that I never touched a cricket bat again. I determined to be as good at golf as my brother was, and I got down to two in eleven months.

D.P.   But tennis, now, Jimmie: I can't somehow picture you in flannels on the tennis court—am I wrong or not?

J.A.   Yes, dear.

D.P.   I'm wrong again—unexpected activities!

J.A.    I wasn't very good at what, Dilys dear, you should call lawn-tennis. Lawn-tennis is no more tennis than the Dog Derby is the Derby. I have played both lawn-tennis and tennis. Tennis is a magnificent game.

L.R.    But to this day you keep up your interest in cricket—you're always at Lord's in the summer. Personally, I'm nearly demented by all this stuff in the evening papers about the Test Matches.

J.A.    I think they're overdoing it. But then my interest in professional cricket may be waning a little. *Tout passe, tout casse, tout lasse.* Things don't last a whole lifetime.

D.P.    Not even cricket?

J.A.    Well, nowadays, I'd almost rather see a village cricket match. . . . My dear children, do you realize that I bowled out W.G. Grace for a duck at the age of seven! It was on the sands at Blackpool. An enormous, black-bearded man came along and said—we had two walking sticks for the wicket—he would like to bowl to me. He did, and I hit him all over the place. And being a very well brought-up little boy I offered him my small bat and said, 'Perhaps you, sir, would like an innings?' I bowled to him, and the soft ball hit a pebble, and shot along the sand. He realized that with his size and tummy if he made any effort to get down to the ball with my tiny bat he might rupture himself. So he left it alone and saw it go between the walking sticks. And my father, who was supposed to be fielding at square leg, and was really reading the *Financial Times,* laughed like blazes and told me afterwards, 'That was W. G. Grace!' Now here's the most remarkable coincidence. At lunch the other day at the Savoy I happened to lunch at the next table to John Clements with Kay Hammond and her little son, who is wildly keen about cricket. I beckoned the kid over and told him my W.G. story. Clements said, 'This is the most amazing coincidence. I told young John here in the lounge before lunch how my father had heard W. G. say at a banquet that he had been bowled first ball by a little boy of seven whose name he never knew!'

L.R.  A very nice story.

J.A.  And this is very nice champagne.

L.R.  It isn't bad.

J.A.  What is it?

D.P.  It's Bollinger. It's not bad, is it?

J.A.  Very nice indeed. Well, just a drop.

L.R.  Don't be so modest, James. It isn't like you. . . .

J.A.  I was horrified to find in New York they gave you an enormous amount of cocktails before lunch and nothing to drink with lunch. They get sozzled first and then eat to get sober.

D.P.  You won't have salad?

J.A.  No thanks. Jock—Alan Dent, you know—came in to see me this morning. I was in bed—I haven't been very well. He looked through the window and said, 'That flag that you've had up since VE-Day is now tattered. It has the most horrible Ibsenite implications. I challenge you, Master Builder! Crawl along your window ledge and bring it in. This is Jock Wangel talking.' Ha-ha-ha! He's great fun, isn't he?

D.P.  I haven't seen him for ages—he's vanished. Where is he?

J.A.  He's off to Italy to make a film of *Hamlet* with Olivier.

D.P.  Is he now!

J A.  I said, 'Why are you doing it in Italy?' He said, 'Because we're going next to Elsinore to make a film of *Othello*!'

D.P.  I used to see him at the movies: he's completely gone now. Anyway, I never see him at the Press shows.

J.A.  You sit so near the screen that you can't see anybody! Did I tell you about the young friend I had with me one day? I saw nobody else downstairs except you sitting right up against the screen. I said, 'That's the famous Dilys Powell.' Then the figure turned sideways and the awed young man said, 'I didn't know Miss Powell smoked a pipe!'

D.P.  The only person who liked sitting as near to the screen as I do was your old secretary, Leo Pavia. He used to sit in the third row of the stalls—very happy. I miss him now that he's dead.

J.A.  (*Waving his hand as if to an invisible presence*). I think of him every day of my life.

D.P. Charming old boy! My memory of dear Pavia at the buffet after Press shows: a very large pair of elbows to keep off all-comers. Such an appetite! I adored him!

J.A. He could be absolutely unbearable. I kept a book on purpose to throw at him! Somebody's Life of John Barrymore. I got so good I could just miss him by inches. I once said to him, 'Leo, Lady Beetlewash has asked us to dinner tonight'—say any name you like—'Lady Freshwater has asked us to dinner tonight, and if you don't act daft you will be allowed to play the piano in the drawing-room afterwards.' Well, at dinner that night his face got redder and redder and finally purple with the things he suppressed. Presently Lady Hinton Bagpaize—that's in East Anglia, I think; you remember that Wilde named most of his characters after railway stations—said, 'Mr Agate, I think you must be wrong when you say Cora Pearl appeared on the French stage. You know how very keen the French are about preserving the inviolacy of their artistic society. Cora Pearl was a woman of infamous character!' Whereupon Leo said: 'Lady Kentish Town, I hold no brief for Mr Agate's critical opinions. They are his. But on matters of fact Mr Agate is invariably accurate. Cora Pearl *did* appear on the French stage. She appeared at the Bouffes Parisiens in June, 1867, in Offenbach's *Orphée Aux Enfers*. I know because my aunt, who was also a harlot in Paris, was in the chorus!' And then he got really excited. 'That is to say, my aunt was not a harlot—she was kept sometimes by one man, sometimes by two. In the end she married. . . . *But* Lady Swiss Cottage,' he shouted, thumping the table, 'I will not allow you to say that my aunt was a harlot!' And all the time blandly unaware that he was saying anything to give offence to anybody. Ha-ha-ha!

L.R. Let me put a little more—well, keep it by you.

J.A. I'll have another wee drop. (*Pours*) I'm like the Scotsman who was offered three gifts by the good fairy. First he said he would like enough whisky to go into Loch Lomond. Then he wished for enough time to sup it in. 'And the third?' the fairy said. 'And the third wish——?' He couldn't think of any more. 'Well,' she said, 'unless you say what your third wish is you can't have the other two.' And then the Scot said 'Weel, I'll hae a wee drap mair whisky!'

L.R. One thing about your Egos, Jimmie, looking back on them, is your persistent habit of mistaking spoken wit for written wit. The two things are so entirely different. You yourself are a remarkable raconteur, and you must meet at the Savage Club and elsewhere others who are nearly as good as you are. But when you transfer the raconteur's stories to paper without considering that he has been *acting* his stories—well, what was wit in the telling often becomes only facetiousness in the reading.

J.A.  Oh!

L.R.  You often say that so-and-so was in wonderful form at the Club last night, and boldly cite his witticisms. But they reach the reader on the morning after as it were—when they smell of stale cigar smoke.

J.A.  You mean, they don't quite——

L.R.  Well, isn't verbal wit—repartee, puns and so on—necessarily of the lower order of wit? You don't read—who shall I say—Voltaire for that. His is written wit, the other is acted wit. What I mean is if you're going to try to convey an impression in print of the man who sets the table on a roar you don't do it successfully by merely setting down his actual words.

J.A.  Oh!

D.P.  Jimmie has a story about a tram. It makes me laugh, but I should say it's only funny when he tells it.

L.R.  I don't think I know it.

J.A.  It's about old Professor Miall. He was having supper at the Savage Club and was eating first a layer of toast, a kipper, then another layer of toast, another kipper, and finally a top layer of toast, and was ploughing through all this. Suddenly Basil Macdonald Hastings leant over the table, put his eyeglass in his eye and said, 'My dear fellow, what are you eating—a *tram*!'

L.R.  That's a perfect example of acted wit.

J.A.  Doesn't that quite fit in?

D.P.  It's only funny as you tell it.

J.A.  It's awfully difficult to know. Take Lilian Braithwaite when she said about some young actress going out of the Ivy, 'There goes that clever girl—off to Hull!'

L.R.  That might come off in print.

J.A.  And about another actress she didn't like—if Lilian can dislike anybody. 'She's going to America—it must be a very small part.' I said, 'Why?' Lilian said, 'She's going in a very small boat.' (*Laughter*). You can't tell; it's very difficult. How about Mrs Pat? 'I adore your Egos—everything everybody writes in them is so good.'

D.P.  That's wit by any standard. . . .

J.A.  Garvin wasn't a good talker or a great conversationalist. He was a magnificent monologuist!

L.R.  Garvin?

J.A.   Yes. I used to meet him at the Ivy. I never succeeded in finishing a sentence!

D.P.   I can hardly believe that, Jimmie.

J.A.   He silenced me——

D.P.   My dear!

J.A.   Just as Mrs. Kendal silenced Shaw, who told me he never got a word out in her presence. I went once to get Mrs Kendal to do something for me on the B.B.C. and she talked for an hour and a quarter without stopping. Then somebody began to tune the piano in the next room, and I did the unpardonable thing. I got up and rang the bell! She said, 'Extraordinary behaviour, Mr Agate!' I didn't say a word. The parlourmaid came in and I said, 'Tell that man to come back and tune the piano tomorrow!' Old Madge K. said, 'Really!' I said, 'My dear Mrs Kendal—it was before she was a Dame—'do you suppose I'm going to allow a vulgar piano-tuner to prevent me from hearing the most beautiful voice in Europe?' She said, 'Tell me what you want me to do on the wireless' (*laughter*). She also said—later, 'Would you like to see my husband's collection of Sicilian pottery?' Well, I can't describe to you the monstrous impropriety of the various animals ! But as they were collected by Mr Kendal they were all perfectly proper. She went up to one particularly revolting animal, stroked it, and said, 'Wonderful glaze, don't you think?' In my opinion she was the third best actress I've ever seen.

D.P.   Bernhardt the first, Réjane the second, I suppose.

J.A.   And Mrs Kendal the third.

L.R.   Why has her fame been so eclipsed? Apart from you nobody ever mentions her.

J.A.   No, I know.

L.R.   She was a great actress in more than one mood?

J.A.   A great comédienne and a great tragic actress as well. I remember seeing her in a play called *The Likeness of the Night*, by Mrs W. K. Clifford. The great scene was when she called upon her husband's mistress. At the first rehearsal she said, 'Where are the doll and the hoop?' And the stage-manager said, 'They're not in the play.' She said, 'They are if I play it, because I shall see them there on the floor and I shall realize that the other woman can give my husband children and I can't, and my face will grow grey.' I saw that scene, and her face did grow grey! But she was a holy terror, an unchained fury. An actor told me about the first night of a play in which some twelve-year-old had to play the village child, and the little girl's mother had put a chaplet of flowers round her head. Mrs Kendal was in the wings two minutes before the child came on, and tore the flowers from her. 'Do you think you're going on my stage looking like the village harlot?' Two minutes later the child came on. 'Mrs Kendal's mothering of her was so pathetic,' said the actor, 'that I couldn't help crying. In fact I had to go and re-make up.' Wonderful woman!

L.R.  Is anything known of Mr Kendal?

J.A.  Yes, he was a stick, a bad actor—but a very good collector of pottery! You know that Mrs K. once said to her stage manager, 'Bring a kitchen chair and set it in the middle of the stage.' She then called for the company, and when the company was assembled knelt down and said, 'Oh Lord, we pray Thee out of Thy infinite mercy that Thou will cause some notion of the rudiments of acting to be vouchsafed to this company for Jesus Christ's sake, Amen.' She got up, dusted her knees and said, *Well, now we'll see what that will do !* ' And yet though she was also in my opinion a better actress than Ellen Terry, when she and Ellen Terry appeared together Ellen played her off the stage for charm.

And here's a story old Odell told me when he was nearly ninety—you've heard of old Odell, haven't you? I said, 'Mr Odell, when did you last appear?' He said, 'I was to have played in 1874. I was to have played with the Kendals. But that woman stopped me. She was a *bitch*! At the dress rehearsal I tore my part into two, then into four, then into eight, and then into sixteen pieces, and went up to her and said, 'Here, Mrs Kendal, is my part, and Mr Kendal can tell you what to do with it.'

L.R.  Ten years since I heard the name old Odell!

J.A.  I came across him in the cast of a play—1848!

L.R.  He wasn't a mere imaginary Thespian then?

J.A.  Oh, he'd played at Warrington or somewhere. But he could certainly tell a story. . . . The best raconteur, the wittiest man in England today, is still Seymour Hicks. One night Peter Page and I motored over from the Malvern Festival to Birmingham to see Seymour and give him supper. He kept us up—it was the Queen's Hotel—till two o'clock in the morning telling stories, and the waiters clustered round the doorway and wouldn't leave.

L.R.  It's like Foote and the young Negro waiter.

J.A.  We mentioned Réjane. When I was nineteen I saved up enough money to go to Paris in order to see Réjane, because Sarah came to Manchester frequently but Réjane never. It was in August, a heat wave. She just walked through her part. After the second act I sent her a note which said, 'This is impermissible. I am a young man who has come all the way from England to see the best actress in the world, and you are not acting.' The play was something called *La Montansier* and Coquelin was in the cast too. In the following act she gave a marvellous performance, and when the end came she gave me a little bow all to myself. I was alone in the front row—nobody else in the first five or six rows. That must have been round about 1895.

L.R.   You weren't practising dramatic criticism then?

J.A.   No, I wrote my first notice in 1907. In 1895 I was at my father's cotton mill, getting ready to sell calico in my father's office. Then in 1917, I think it was, one day at Arles during the war, I saw a carriage come round the square, past the statue of Mistral and stop in front of the hotel. And Réjane got out. She was playing *Madame Sans-Gêne* that night, and I asked her to sup with me. And you know, she was a complete frump off-stage! On the stage she had everything that the world has ever possessed of elegance and *chic*, but she was a complete dowd off! She said she thought she might permit herself to accept because she had a son in the French Army, and it would not be improper for her to sup with an English officer. We had supper, a very modest one, and—now let me get it right—I said, 'Madame, the note I sent you this afternoon was not the first time I have written to you. I wrote to you over twenty years ago.' She said, 'Are you the English boy who wrote to me one evening when I wasn't giving a performance?' I said, 'Yes.' Réjane said, 'You taught me a lesson that has lasted all my life. You made me realize that there may be somebody in any theatre at any time to whom you are opening a new door, a new gateway to beauty. You put it into my heart that no artist is ever entitled to give a bad performance.'

L.R.   In that third act, when she was herself, what sort of a hand did she get—did the French applaud?

J.A.   My impression is—I'm not certain about this—my impression is that the French applaud either not at all or very little. And they certainly don't applaud in America. There are no curtain-calls in America—the curtain comes down and that's the end. The one person I ever forgave for making a curtain speech was Irving. He always made the same speech; never varied it by a single syllable. He came forward—he was delighted to play again in this city, and to think that he was still the audience's humble, obliged, obedient servant. And that was all.

D.P.   Cheese?

J.A.   No cheese, dear. What's that—chocolate? Oh yes!

L.R.   What about Olivier's speech after the first night of *Oedipus*?

J.A.   I hated it! I wouldn't even stay to see *The Critic*. Dilys dear, may I—I must have some of that cream!

D.P.   Of course you shall have some, darling!

J.A.   Dilys, somebody said to me the other day, 'What's the wittiest impromptu, the wittiest sally, you've ever heard?' And I said something said by a man called Majdalany—you know whom I mean?

D.P.   Of course—the film critic.

J.A.   It was at the first night of *Mourning Becomes Electra* at the Westminster. We went into the pub next door after the first act, and there were two cats engaging in—shall we say—dalliance? The barman was squirting soda out of a syphon at them, and Majdalany said, 'Have a heart—why interfere with the fun?' The barman said, 'They're mother and son.' Majdalany said, 'An Oedi*puss* complex!' Now, is that verbal wit only, or is it something more?

L.R.   It's terribly quick—excellent. But not, I think . . .

J.A.   Not even if you spell it with two 's's'?

L.R.   Well, Jimmie, if you plead for it like that I'll say it was the finest thing I ever heard!

J.A.   Well, children, I drink your healths. What's the time? I must look at my watch—I enjoy looking at my gold watch. Recognize it? It's the one Lord Kemsley gave me at that lunch to commemorate my association with the *Sunday Times*. He's been so good to me in many ways.

    . . . Now let me tell you one last thing. I had written an article for a little magazine, and I tried to make it as witty as possible. Indeed, I took a great deal of trouble over it. Well, my article ended in the middle of a page. All right. But it was immediately followed by another article which began, 'The wittiest man in London, Mr Alan Melville, lives immediately over the flat occupied by Mr James Agate.' Ha-ha-ha!

## Two Poems by Walter de la Mare

# The Kiss

In the long drouth of life,
Its transient wilderness,
The mindless euthanasia
Of a kiss

Reveals that in
An instant's beat
Two souls in flesh confined
May yet in an immortal freedom
  meet.

From those strange windows
Called the eyes, there looks

A heart athirst
For heaven's waterbrooks.

The hands tell secrets.
And a lifted brow
Asks, 'O lost stranger,
Art thou with me now?'

All stumbling words are dumb;
And life stands still;
Pauses a timeless moment; then
  resumes
The inevitable

# The Dunce

Then Science said,
'Now, listen, child, to me.
Have I not taught you all
You touch, taste, hear, and see?

'Nought known as knowledge now
In print is pent
Which my sole method
Did not circumvent.

'Think you, the amoeba
In its primal slime
Wasted on dreams
Its destiny sublime?

'Yet, when I bid
Your eyes survey the board
Whereon life's How, Where, When
I now record,

'I find them fixed
In daydream, and you sigh.
Or, like a silly lamb,
You bleat me, "Why?"

' "Why is the grass so fresh and
      green?
The sky so blue?"

Get to your Chemistry,
You dullard, you!

' "Why must I sit and learn
Yet pine to play?"
Where's your Psychology,
You popinjay!

' "Why stay I here,
Not where my heart would be?"
Wait, dunce, and ask that
Of Philosophy!

'Reason is yours
Wherewith to con your task;
Not that unanswerable
Questions you should ask.

'Stretch out your hands, then—
Grubby, shallow bowl!
And be refreshed, child!
Mind, and (maybe) soul!

'Then, when you grow into
A man—like me—
You will as learn'd, and wise,
And—happy be.'

# CLOUDSCAPES

## and their

## meaning

### PHOTOGRAPHS AND COMMENTARY BY

### C. J. P. Cave

THE cloudscape shown in Figure 1, on the opposite page, exhibits two very different forms of cloud. The clouds that look like cotton-wool are known as cumulus; but these are of the small detached type such as one sees on a fine summer day. On such a day, after a clear morning, clouds begin to form, but in fine summer weather they never reach to great heights, nor do they cover the whole sky. In the late afternoon they begin to dissolve and by nightfall they die away altogether and leave a clear sky. This is the sequence in fine spring and summer weather. The cumulus clouds in this picture are probably only about two to three thousand feet up.

The other thread-like clouds, known as cirrus, are at a much greater height, probably 20,000 or even 30,000 feet. Such clouds may be seen in various types of weather, but when they are observed moving very fast from a southerly or westerly point they may very likely indicate bad weather coming in from the Atlantic. These cirrus clouds are composed of ice crystals, not of water drops, as are most other forms of cloud.

Low clouds and high clouds: the lower ones with the rounded tops typify fine sunny weather. The thread-like ones are very much higher, and often may be seen coming from a different direction to the lower clouds and the surface wind. Owing to their great height, they can be observed to be still in sunshine for a time after the sun has set on the surface.

Under certain conditions of temperature and moisture the cumulus clouds continue to grow, and may reach towering proportions. Such developments occur especially in late spring and summer. Here masses of cumulus cloud are seen billowing upward. The ascending currents of air, of which these clouds are the visible expression, are known to those who fly in sailplanes and are used by them to gain height; they are often arranged in long lines, and the sailplane pilot, by gliding along them, is able to fly long distances.

When a cumulus cloud has attained to a very great height the top spreads out into a soft edged white mass, as above; the top of the cloud has reached above the freezing level, and the extended top, instead of being composed of water drops, is composed of ice crystals like the cirrus clouds, and is known as hybrid cirrus. The whole cloud has now become a shower cloud and under it is heavy rain and perhaps a thunderstorm. This is a picture of a distant and intense thunderstorm and its top has reached a height of perhaps 30,000 feet.

This is another thunderstorm, a spring thunderstorm, moving away to the east, and the sky is covered with masses of cirrus, perhaps derived from the cumulus clouds which have passed by. It is not only by day that cumulus clouds develop into thunderstorms; in the latter half of the summer particularly they may form late in the day, causing one of the most striking phenomena of the weather, the night thunderstorm. Sheet or summer lightning is the reflection of a distant thunderstorm, perhaps so far off that the clouds are below the horizon and much too far off for the thunder to be heard.

Less spectacular but perhaps more beautiful, are the clouds of the middle layers of the atmosphere, which may be between 10,000 and 20,000 feet up. They are often beautifully rippled, and those with the finer ripple markings are often called mackerel skies. After a spell of bad weather they sometimes prelude the coming on of better, and after a spell of drought they are sometimes the first sign of a change.

At times, especially in summer, some of the middle clouds are drawn up into little heads like miniature cumulus; they often rise from a flat base, and the little heads gleam white in the sunshine. When such turret clouds, as they are called, are seen coming from a southerly or south-westerly point they are an indication that thundery conditions are approaching from the south-west.

ORNAMENTAL

# The Story of a Dress

## by LORRAINE TIMEWELL

Our dress was designed in England. The
scissors point to the North, where the
finest fabrics are made. Across the Channel
lies Paris — a city of silk. Uniting
the fashion centres of London and Paris
is a current of industry and needlework.
We send them woollens, they send us silk.

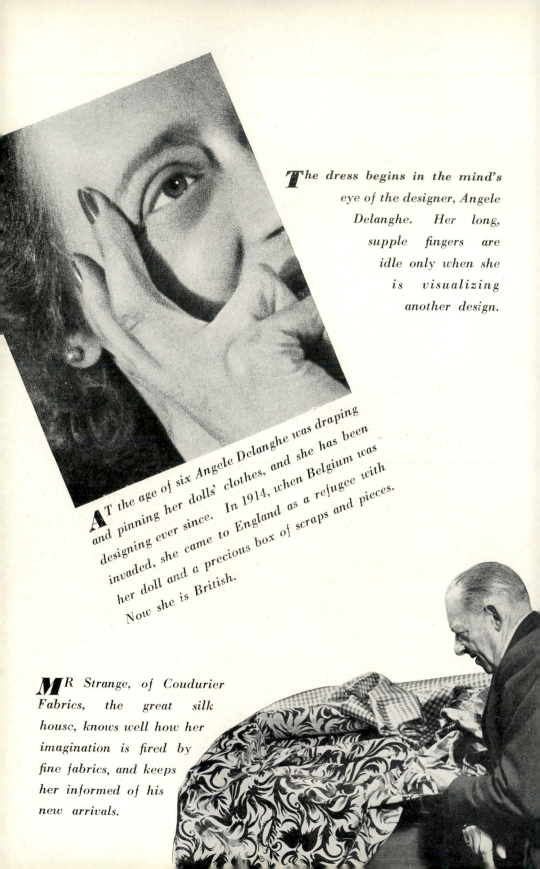

*The dress begins in the mind's eye of the designer, Angele Delanghe. Her long, supple fingers are idle only when she is visualizing another design.*

*A*T the age of six Angele Delanghe was draping and pinning her dolls' clothes, and she has been designing ever since. In 1914, when Belgium was invaded, she came to England as a refugee with her doll and a precious box of scraps and pieces. Now she is British.

*M*R Strange, of Coudurier Fabrics, the great silk house, knows well how her imagination is fired by fine fabrics, and keeps her informed of his new arrivals.

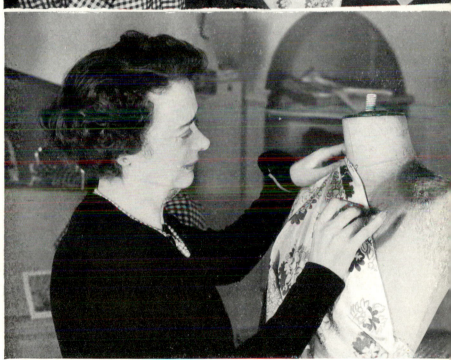

IN a tiny room she works with the selected fabric straight on to the dummy, its shoulder scarred with pin-marks. In picture one, she is concentrating her mind not on the checked silk, but on the floral printed silk lying on the table by Smuts the cat. She knows exactly what she wants to do with it, and in picture two begins to drape and pin. It is a fine silk in a pale oyster white, with burnt rose and grey outlined flowers scattered over it.

**W**HEN the model has been assembled by Delanghe, it goes to the fitter in one of the workrooms, who cuts a pattern in 'toile' from the original. Then, under her supervision, the dress goes into the hands of the young sempstresses. In the picture above the moment of judgment has arrived. Miss Garner, the fitter, is taking the completed model to be tried on by a mannequin and viewed by Delanghe.

AUDREY Kenney, the mannequin, with her head in a bag, is helped
  into the dress. The bag protects the fabric from lipstick and powder,
and protects also her new ' hair-do.'

*T*HE date for the showing of the collections for each new fashion season is decided by agreement amongst the various designers, or couturiers. In London, they are known as the 'Big Ten'—the Incorporated Society of London Fashion Designers. Their present President is Norman Hartnell, and Delanghe is one of the 'Ten.' The eve of the collection finds the models facing their most formidable audience—the people who made them. The dress whose story we have been tracing (it has a name now, 'Madame Butterfly') passes the critical inspection of the staff. Then the clients arrive on the important day.

*T*HIS is what they see: the soft feminine grace of 'Madame Butterfly,' which resembles an old oriental painting in the lines of the drapery, and has a short kimono-type sleeve.

**T**HEY also see 'Madame Butterfly's' 44 companions, including its opposite number, 'Gleneagles.' Some of the models are never again seen in England: they go to the United States and elsewhere abroad.

AND what next? The fabric manufacturers, the button makers, the fashion-supply companies, the printers, the Press, the fitters, the sempstresses, the secretaries, the telephonists have all been involved in the life of 'Madame Butterfly,' the demure navy and white checked afternoon dress (left), which we saw being designed on the stand, and their companions. Well, Angele Delanghe is looking abstracted. 'I am thinking of the next collection,' she says. And so it begins all over again.

# The Farmer's Job

## by *ADRIAN BELL*

### *wood engravings by Eric King*

SAID a farmer nearing his eightieth year: 'I think farming all day, and I dream farming all night, and if I had my time all over again I'd be a farmer.' He added, with a twinkle in his eye, 'and I reckon I could teach these young 'uns a thing or two.'

I don't know whether this is true of other trades. Does the motor manufacturer dream of his motor-factory; does the cotton-spinner dream of cotton-spinning, the miner of the coal-seam, the sailor of the sea—as lovingly, as longingly, day in, day out, all the days of his life? The sea-farer seems to like to settle down far from the sound of the sea. The engineer can so far forget his engineering as to put his heart into a game of golf. But the peculiar thing about the farmer which, I think, distinguishes him, is—he is a man without a hobby.

Engineers may talk about this or that. Farmers together always talk shop. At market, yes, but also in drawing-rooms, in trains, at weddings. One wrote to me from the turret of his tank while waiting to go into the battle of Alamein—about farming.

But the farmer, too, is an engineer. An engineer of the infinitely variable. A field is a piece of engineering. A well-farmed field is a masterpiece of timing. My first impact with farming long years ago was a journey I took in a slow old car with a farmer whose pupil I became. Much of the scenery was beautiful; but my friend stopped the car once in a blank, flat landscape and said: 'Look—what a picture!' It was fifty acres of barley. 'The best bit of barley I've seen this year.' A monotonous expanse, but he saw the art that lay behind it. Later, the country improved again: the fields glowed with poppies, and held patches of cornflowers like reflections of the sky. 'Poor old land—wouldn't have it as a gift,' was his comment.

Later I came to see the country like that. And how much more interesting a journey became from that view. Yes, however beautiful the light on the hills, and the sweet, snug valleys under blossom, and the wildness of the wilderness, the sight of well-farmed land is fundamentally more exciting: there you touch nature and human-kind together: it is the sinews of life.

The modern farmer must be as practical to a decimal point as the engineer: and he must have the sensibility of an artist. He must dream and he must act. He must make poetry out of arithmetic.

There are two distinct phases to the farmer's day: the hours of from 5 till 5, when he is a vital part of the working machine of the farm—arms, legs and burdened back. Then the hours from tea till bed-time, when his men have gone home, and he can walk round quietly, alone on his farm. That is when he can proportion his thinking again to the whole picture, which has become distorted by the seemingly burning importance of the job he has actually been on that day.

IT IS VERY NECESSARY, this readjustment of focus. A farmer can be too busy: it is not just a question of putting one's back into it: one must put one's imagination into it, too. The farmer must make time to take time off. Time off for a day's holiday, which does not mean a day at the seaside, but a day spent at a farm demonstration or agricultural show or a tour of an experimental farm. Even though many of the things he sees are not applicable to his own farming, he gets from these occasions a sort of mental uplift: his vision is rekindled.

This is very important, because the innumerable details and petty accidents of a farming day can worry a man to despair. He hasn't, you see, a roof over his job nor firm ground under his feet. Once a man lets his vision drown in the quagmire of daily routine, he is done. He might as well pack up and sell out. But those days off smooth away the mistakes and the irks, and he sees the thing whole again. He starts, in his mind, afresh. And although to the outward eye his farming does not seem to be much different from what it was, yet this or that little idea which he picked up sticks: alterations are made in small ways, and his farm evolves —not into a model of any of the demonstration farms, but into something quite individual to the conditions of his soil and layout, and quite his own.

The present is a most arduous but also exciting time for farmers. Formerly everything was governed by folk knowledge and tradition. Now it is directed by science. Formerly in any single district there was but one way of keeping cows: now there are half a dozen ways.

I am just old enough to have experienced both sorts of farming; and to any who think that the poetry has gone out of farming with the advent of new methods and new machines, I would say that the inspiration (that is not too strong a word) derived from the application of modern scientific method is beyond anything that came from rigid obedience to the old commandments of the four-course-shift—albeit it was done with those beautiful horses.

THIS IS A transitional age, nowhere more so than in farming. Here are a few of the problems of the modern, or rather transitional half-modern, farmer's day.

If it is winter, he awakes in what might be midnight, but his clock says 5 a.m. The time taken to drink a cup of tea contains many thoughts. The sound of rain on the windows governs them; for even winter farming is not a matter of routine; it is, as always, an allocation of priorities. Not a question of what is the next job, but which of the six jobs needing to be done is the most urgent?

In his mind there is a sort of double column of jobs—one column for dry weather, the other for wet. He must be able to switch his team quickly from one job to another—otherwise a lot of hanging about and busy-seeming idleness. His mind must be a store-house of innumerable small details of repair and maintenance, noted when this or that machine was put away after the summer: now is the time, or there will be half a sunny day's delay four months hence.

The farmer's eye must never sleep; he must see an implement or horse or cow every time he looks at it as though he is seeing it for the first time even though he has worked with it daily for a dozen years. Half his time is taken up in saving hours by spending five minutes.

His first thought on entering the cow-shed is, as it has been day after day for five months in the year, 'Oh, for electricity!' It is a wish as regular as the rattle of his match-box. Even if you have never had it in your cow-shed, electricity is—today—a thing you never get used to being without.

A yellow flame illumines the whitewashed cow-shed: you try to get the glass chimney on before the draught blows it out, and succeed at the second or third attempt. Spit on the match-ends; always spit on the match-ends about the farm: a naked flame looks like the devil himself among straw yards. Even if the match is quite out, black-headed, spit on it: it becomes a superstitious act, like throwing salt over your shoulder.

Now milking. In our fathers' days we just milked cows; today we produce clean milk, tuberculin free. There's a vast difference. It takes much longer: you wash the cows; you brush the cows; you examine each udder and the first milk from each teat individually. The buckets of milk are taken straight through to the cooler, after being weighed and the weight of milk recorded on a sheet opposite the name of each cow. Yes, it takes longer; but it is vastly more interesting.

I know the old way, too. Two rows of cows back to back, a narrow passage-way between; the floor littered with straw last week and no cleaning up since. Pails, empty and full, stand in the middle way dangerously near the backs of the cows. The farm cat comes and balances itself on the edge of a full pail and has a good drink (to wash down a meal of fresh-killed rat); the milkers sit milking, reminiscing or exchanging village gossip, as they watch the cat drinking.

We are more concerned today with daily yields and feeding formulae than with the old humanities of village life. 'Do you remember that time when——?' They were great reminiscers, those old hands. But as to discussing the feeding of the cows they were milking—well, it was a subject which did not admit of discussion; the RIGHT WAY had been determined by their fathers, and it was impertinent to question it.

As for wanting accurately to measure what a cow gave, there was something almost impious in the suggestion. The usual recommendation of a cow was 'she gives a pailful'—omitting to state what size of pail.

Milking plays a large part in the modern farmer's life. The early routine, seven days a week, is a tie; and yet it is so much more interesting the modern way, that one hardly grudges the early winter rouse-up. There is always the anticipation of how are they going to yield this morning? If you have a herd which you have bred yourself, scientifically, you always look forward to seeing them again, even since last night.

THE FARMER'S MIND is thus filled with two things as he prepares the mangers: his whole breeding and feeding policy plus the general layout of his premises. Can a few steps be saved one way or another and the

time shortened?  That is the background of his mind.  At the same time his eyes must be seeing that all the tie-up chains are laid right: that two doors of the cow-shed are shut before the third (which admits the cows) is opened.

It is easy, thinking of general matters, to get caught napping over a detail.  If everything is right, the cows will come in and go each to her place, dividing away to the left and right as in the figure of a dance.  It is pretty to watch.  But let some detail be not as it was yesterday. . . . One day we nailed up salt licks in front of each manger; the cows came trotting in, reached their mangers, saw the salt licks—something fresh—recoiled in panic.  The cow-shed became like Bedlam.

A new window was put in the old dark stable.  The horses were terrified, especially Prince, whose manger was opposite.  I ought to have foreseen, ought to have seen, with horses' eyes, not a window there but a flashing square where before had been familiar gloom.  We had to curtain the window with a sack for weeks.

BEFORE ANYTHING IS UNDERTAKEN the farmer must rehearse it in his mind's eye to the last detail, searching for possible snags.  Before he sows roots on a certain field in the mellow conditions of spring, he must be thinking of how he is going to cart them off that field in the possible quagmire of late autumn.  It is difficult mentally to telescope the seasons; difficult to visualize the approach to some stacks as a quagmire when the ground is baked hard.  Yet that may be when the threshing-machine will need to get to them.

The thought required in the siting of stacks alone is considerable. It is quite easy for the straw from the threshing of one pair of stacks to block the approach to another. It's like a game of chess: the stack that stood end-ways on has to all appearances taken a jump forward and sideways, and there you are—check! No, your barley stacks must go somewhere else.

When you see a farmer walking about in the corner of a field in summer looking as though he has lost something, that may be what he is doing —playing a kind of chess with imaginary blocks of corn and straw.

It is like generalship: the campaign is finished and the stubble fields are empty in the mind's eye before the first day of March. Only generalship with this difference: you do not know whether the weather will be friend or foe. One prepares for it to be a treacherous ally at best.

But though the ardour is greater, modern conditions have taken much of the worry out of the sky, and out of the market. In the fickle conditions of the hay and corn harvests of last year, the Air Ministry's 8 a.m. district weather forecasts were a blessing beyond price. Cocked hay is half made and half won. The cocks, well built, are shower-proof: yet before the hay is safe to stack, they usually need to be broken out, the hay scattered to have a few hours' wind and sun on it. In that state, a sudden storm can ruin it.

Formerly the decision to break out cocks of hay was fraught with anxiety. Now, the farmer listens to the district forecast as he has his breakfast. I ruled my harvest days by it last year, breaking out a whole field of hay-cocks before a horizon boiling with black clouds, simply because the forecast said 'Fair, with bright periods,' while old Tom shook his head and thought I was mad. But, towards the end of that harvest, even old Tom began to ask, 'Well, what does the wireless say this morning, master?'

Formerly, too, the farmer used to have to spend much time worrying about prices, attending markets, watching dreary processions of cattle sold, simply to keep abreast of current fluctuations, so that when he had something to sell he would know how to deal with the buyer. What a waste of time that was!

Oh, yes, I know—the abundant humanity of the market-place and all that; but how much more worth-while the time spent at scientific demonstrations and trials of new methods of production, and how much more fruitful the conversations which one enjoys there.

At last the farmer has guaranteed prices fixed well in advance. Better still, he has produced his own organization for the marketing of milk, the Milk Marketing Board. The individual farmer's job is production, not salesmanship; and the amount of latent energy released for the technique of production by these measures can hardly be exaggerated. How often, formerly, a farmer would earn a pound doing a deal at a market and lose five by not being at home attending to his farming.

ALTHOUGH THE farmer's job is much more arduous than formerly, the compensation for that is that he is much more heart and soul in it. I have seen great changes. The young farmer is less of the country play-boy than he used to be. You will find him more often on his tractor than on his hunter, and his mind is occupied with the fascinating problems of modern techniques.

Why, though, is his job more arduous than formerly? Because formerly a farm was a dairy farm or an arable farm; it produced milk or corn: full time jobs each of these. Now it produces both: two full-time jobs in one. In addition it produces sugar-beet, which is equivalent to having a double root crop, always the most laborious crop on the farm. And again I would emphasize, dairying is not just milking cows: it is producing clean, germ-free milk by modern methods.

Take an average farmer, one who farms about a hundred acres. There are himself, a man, and a youth; that is his labour force. By the time he has milked his dozen cows, cooled the milk, sterilized the utensils, swilled down the cow-shed and fed the young stock, his grandfather who farmed only for corn would have been afield with his horses and harrows for three hours. So a quarter of the day is gone before the land can claim the modern farmer's full attention. How is this time going to be made up, seeing that it took the older farmer a full day's work six days a week to keep up with his cultivations? And the modern farmer must grow more, not less, crops than his grandfather—there is no bare fallow in his rotation today, and sugar-beet is added to the list. There is only one way—by the use of the tractor.

I remember, formerly, four men employed in drilling corn, and five horses: one man to drive the horses, one to steer the drill, one to walk behind watching the corn, and the fourth with two horses harrowing in the corn behind the drill. Today the farmer, possibly leaving his man to finish off in the cow-shed, hitches the drill behind his tractor and harrows behind the drill, and away he goes and does the whole operation in one, by himself.

By afternoon milking-time he has caught up with the ghosts of his ancestors trudging across that field, and if there is a little yet to be done, he can spare his man to finish it, while he and the youth go to the milking. The job done, instead of the long process of feeding, grooming, and getting-in of hay for five horses, one motor engine is simply switched off.

AFTER MILKING, after his tea, he looks out and sees the weather fine, the land in beautiful working condition. So he mounts his tractor again, and, dragging crab-harrows behind him, works another five acres down to a seed-bed ready for drilling tomorrow, before he has his supper. So now

he has outstripped the ghostly four men and their five horses at the arable work and produced thirty gallons of milk as well in the day.

The modern iron horse never tires: the fatigue is all on the man. But these are exigent times. The man, unlike the horse, is working under his own will; it was not uncommon in the old days for horses to be worked to death.

The same applies to ploughing. Formerly ploughing went on from harvest time till the New Year, half an acre a day, wet or fine. The modern farmer is ploughing in September and October till ten o'clock in moonlight. But then he is done: the upturned furrows lie exposed to the action of sun and air and frost till springtime.

WHAT THEN OF THE HORSES? Well, modern farming is a holiday for horses. Never have horses had such a comfortable life. On his hundred acres the farmer will have two, besides his tractor. One horse is useful for occasional carting of hay, straw and fodder to the cows, for horse-hoeing and raking and pulling the light seed-harrows.

What about the other?   He is young, he is frisky and needs plenty of regular hard work to keep him in order.   But there is only work for him sporadically; and that is bad, because, though he is frisky, his muscles are not hard, and after half a day's hard pulling he is like a fat man who has run a mile to catch a train.   Why then does the farmer keep this second horse, who costs a pound a week for keep?   To be quite truthful the farmer keeps him for just the same reason that one touches wood : this is a transitional age, and he has an uneasy feeling that there might come a freakish season when the tractor would not operate on the land, so he could still plough with his horses.   A sort of 'you never know' feeling. It is difficult after centuries of horse-work to feel quite sure that the horse is dispensable.   Talk to any farmer and the chances are he will tell you he has at least one horse that hardly does three weeks' work in the year.

That freakish season came : it was 1946.   Water stood among the stooks.   I said to my two fat horses, 'You will have to work this summer.' I fetched out the old harvest wagon, a hundred years old.   They could hardly pull half a load of sheaves : the narrow wheels cut into the stubble. I tried the tractor, pulling the trailer that was one year old.   The broad twin pneumatic tyres kept on the surface of the ground and supported big loads home.   That was one illusion dispelled.   The same with the ploughing : the tractor did it, despite the conditions; the horses were dead-beat in half a day.   So now we know.

OTHER AIDS WE HAVE.   An electric Little Boy Blue, for instance.   Not again will self-made men begin their reminiscences, 'My first job was herding cows on the common at 6d. a week for Farmer Bull.'   Unfenced road verges, village greens, banks, all provided a useful addition to the summer grazing.   The fact that they were not fenced did not matter; there were always plenty of children with nothing to do but make daisy chains who could be sent to keep them within bounds.   A single electrified strand of wire now does that duty, while the children are at school, studying to be citizens.

Actually the electric fence has made a science out of that old haphazard keeping of cows on bits of waste-land.   It is the science of controlled grazing, whereby one piece of sward may be fed intensively, then rested, rather than the cattle be allowed to wander over whole acres and trample as much as they eat.   It has made possible arable-dairying as a fine art, whereby green crops may be grown on unfenced fields or portions of fields, and the land ploughed up for corn again directly.   The electric fence is perhaps the most notable invention for food production in our time.

Formerly every village had its proportion of half-wits, sad result of immobility and interbreeding. These were the hewers of wood and drawers of water. The yoke and pails were seldom off their shoulders. These happily have almost died out. Piped water-supplies to dairy and fields have taken their place.

What of the farm buildings? Old timbered barns and byres beautify the landscape. But these also are tools of a man's trade, and in that light are today inconvenient and embarrassingly permanent. We have to tinker with them and adapt them as best we can. Oak beams and concrete, corrugated iron and old pantiles somehow contrive a working partnership in this era of transition. The lofty barn was built to house sheaves of corn which were threshed by hand on the middle floor. Now all that loftiness is empty, only the floor space occupied; yet many implements have to stand out of doors for lack of roofage.

AND WHAT, AMID all this engineering to fit nature's seasonal system into a human system of food production—what of the beauties of nature? Does the farmer see the first primrose? Has the nightingale music for his ears? Does his heart leap up when he beholds a rainbow in the sky? Or does it not? Does he ever see a cow as a cow, or only as a beef type or a dairy type? I confess I have at times (particularly during the war) been so busy that whole seasons have passed me by, and I have not noticed one flower fading and another coming into bloom. I have hardly regarded the seasons as seasons at all—but only for the work due to be done in them. Spring was not so much nature's upspringing as the word of command to me to jump to it.

And yet—and yet as I look back I know that nightingales were singing in the coppice as I spread manure in the field hard by; that primroses were staring at me in primal innocence out of the ditch from which I was trying to extricate the tractor. Curiously enough, the little clods that were jostling under my harrows on a March morning brought to my mind the hopeful happy feeling we usually associate with the sight of early flowers. Our minds are indeed preoccupied; yet I think we imbibe these things through our pores. Because the farmer is not outside nature, he is in it, at grips with it. Spring comes to him with its hope deepened into something like fear: will he fail to meet all that it demands of him? He does not end where his limbs end, but where his farm ends: a stack uncovered to the rain, tender corn exposed to frost—they are his back bare, his fingers frostbitten. Work, worry, hope, fear—he becomes absorbed in his job, absorbed into it. What he does, he is.

# Cyprus Holiday

## by *RAYMOND MORTIMER*

WHERE I want to make a holiday. Macassar, Malacca, Macao, Yucatan; any archipelago in a sea that is not cold; any city that I have not visited that is rich in monuments of the pre-industrial age. Alas, most of these are out of reach, and I am not one of those who can expatiate on places they have never seen, their imaginations fired by vicarious voyaging. Let me choose rather an island I have visited, though so unthoroughly that it remains a mystery, an island I liked and disliked, the birthplace of Aphrodite and of the cauliflower.

Cyprus is smaller than either Sicily or Sardinia, a little larger than the combined counties of Norfolk and Suffolk. It has the shape of the arm upon a signpost, hanging below Asia Minor and pointing to Syria. Flying has brought Cyprus as close to us as the Riviera is by train. You can breakfast in London, sleep in Athens (or alternatively in Cairo), and be in Nicosia for luncheon the next day. The return fare, by the Athenian route, is just over £100.

Before the recent War, Cyprus was conspicuously cheap—I should say 'inexpensive,' since this euphemism is favoured by the class of retired Englishmen who found the island an asylum where they could live in ease upon their pensions or their savings. (Envious tongues have baptized the little port of Kyrenia 'The city of dreadful knights': not having met any of these, I suspect calumny.)   Prices have trebled, yet Cyprus remains cheaper than Egypt, Syria, the Lebanon or Greece.   Though its name, according to Gibbon, 'excites the ideas of elegance and pleasure,' it is hardly to be recommended to those who are exigent of luxury or fine cooking.   The hotel at Kyrenia is said to be excellent; the Acropole at Nicosia I found modestly agreeable.   At Famagusta I stayed in a more pretentious place such as I resent: while I ate unappetizing, inappropriate, would-be English dishes like steak-and-kidney pie, a saxophone and a piano sought to distract my attention, and nobody dreamt of answering the bedroom bell.   In the other towns the hotels with few exceptions are, I gather, of the order that Baedeker describes as 'variously judged'—which means that there can be only one opinion about them.

Meat and eggs are plentiful; the oranges are the best I have eaten; fish is rare, for the Cypriots—how strange in islanders that consider themselves to be Greek—are not seafaring, and you may look from the coast for hours without seeing a sail.   The shops are pathetically dismal; the imported goods in the shop-windows look shoddy; lace, sponges, fleece-lined slippers seem almost the only local products—oh, and pots, beautiful pots with geometrical ornament.   (These are some four thousand years old, and they cost only a pound or so.)   I suppose I must add that carobs, asbestos and copper are valuable exports, copper indeed taking its name from Cyprus, *cuprum aes,* unless it is the other way round.   The climate is ideal in spring; and a mountain, over 6,000 feet high, Troodos, offers ski-ing in winter and freshness at midsummer.

AND NOW FOR WHAT MAKES Cyprus interesting.   It is a Mediterranean island that has become a British colony after a history unsurpassed in variety and legible in the monuments it has deposited.   If you are not interested in history, you will miss the chief point of Cyprus: there are islands at least equally beautiful much nearer home.   (Most of what I have to say about its past has been lifted, let me gratefully confess, from *Historic Cyprus* by Rupert Gunnis, a guide-book exemplary in its thoroughness, clarity and occasional unobtrusive humour.)   Pharaonic Egypt, Assyria, Persia, the Ptolemies, Rome, Byzantium, Haroun al Raschid, Richard Coeur de Lion, the Templars, the French family of Lusignan, Venice and Turkey have preceded the British in the possession of this dangerously attractive land. The admirably kept museum at Nicosia reflects this stratified past, and I know of no museum with a greater number of curious objects in proportion to its size. The meeting in Cyprus of diverse cultures gave birth to mongrel artifacts that would be very puzzling if one did not know their *provenance*. Unluckily the digging has been usually most unscientific; and the richest collection of Cypriot art is in New York.

The two chief ancient Greek sites appeal to the imagination chiefly by their natural beauty. Salamis shows here and there, among its sand dunes, overgrown with wattle and giant fennel, the remains of Roman forums and temples, and of a vast Byzantine basilica; but nothing, not one stone, of what was once a great Greek city. Here is opportunity for excavations, enormous in extent. Vouni, an acropolitan palace superbly placed on a headland facing north, has pavements and walls, but not a column standing. The remains of a hammam testify to the unGreek luxury of Cyprus, where kings survived, seven of them, into the classical age.

The principal pride of Cyprus is Famagusta, a city hardly less picturesque than its history. In 1191 Cyprus was seized, not unjustifiably, by Richard Coeur de Lion, who celebrated in Famagusta his nuptials with Berengaria of Navarre. He sold the island almost at once to the Templars, who resold it with equal promptitude to Guy de Lusignan, a member of the Poitevin family who had made themselves kings of Jerusalem. This was the period, so stimulating to the romantic imagination, when adventurers from Western Europe, some of them simple country gentlemen, founded dynasties through the Eastern Mediterranean. Lesbos was Genoese, there were Catalan Dukes of Neopatras, Lombard Barons of Euboea, Roman Counts of Cephalonia, French and Flemish Princes of Achaia, Venetian Dukes of the Archipelago.

The Lusignans ruled Cyprus for three centuries, and Famagusta became proverbial for its luxury, the medieval equivalent of Corinth, Sybaris or Capua. In 1489 through the marriage of Caterina Cornaro with the penultimate Lusignan, Cyprus became Venetian, the easternmost bastion of Christendom against the Turks. Cristoforo Moro, governor of Famagusta, is thought to have been the original of Shakespeare's Moor; and part of the fortifications is still known as Othello's Tower. After a siege of nearly a year, Famagusta fell to the Crescent in 1571. The great cathedral was turned into a mosque, the city dwindled into a village, forgotten save as a desolate spot to which the Sultan might occasionally exile some offender. The British took over the administration of the island from the Turks in 1878, and annexed it in 1914.

A number of French Gothic churches, in various stages of disfigurement and dilapidation, survive mournfully in the fortified Venetian *enceinte*

at Famagusta, which is a monument of military architecture rivalling in perimeter and preservation Carcassonne and Aigues-Mortes, Avila and Ragusa. If a few squalid modern buildings were replaced by gardens, this would become one of the supreme masterpieces of the picturesque. (I should like also to train cascading roses and other creepers over parts of the churches to replace the carvings they have lost.) Instead, there are vile schemes for wrecking the noble site with layerage installations. Already the aspect of the Sea Wall is spoiled by sheds, and there is now talk of a new customs-house and quarantine buildings and I know not what other abominations.

The Royal Fine Arts Commission has, alas, no voice in Cyprus, and since so few in England have seen Famagusta, it is less likely to be embellished than further destroyed. Remembering the prodigality with which Fascist Italians restored the beauties of Rhodes, one blushes for England. We are sometimes a wretched advertisement for democracy.

Though Nicosia, the capital of the island, is also surrounded by Venetian fortifications, an exact circle with snake-head bastions, these are comparatively small and unspectacular. Within them again is a great church, purely French in style, resembling Rheims. This is now a mosque: a *mihrab* to show the direction of Mecca has been built in the South transept, the tracery of the windows has given place to the perforated gypsum favoured by the Turks, a gallery with grilles offers seclusion to the seraglio of the Governor, a minaret soars incongruous beside the three-portalled façade. Bare, altarless and whitewashed, the church is still beautiful, reminding one of Holland and the paintings of Saenredam. These Gothic mosques are as it were an Islamic requital for Cordova Cathedral, in which Mass is sung among the largest forest of horse-shoe arches that the world contains.


I LIKED NICOSIA, liked it immensely. Instead of the desolate grandeur of Famagusta, it offers animation and *Gemütlichkeit*. The walls contain a labyrinth of narrow streets, one of them aptly named after Ariadne. The buildings are of golden stone and most of them pleasingly Turkish, with balconies, heavy eaves, green shutters and often good ironwork. A market some seventy years old, I imagine, reveals to what graceful use cast iron could once be put. I doubt whether either the Cypriots or the British officials have woken up to the exceptional charm of this little capital: already a few disastrous 'modernistic' buildings have been allowed to jostle and overlook their decent neighbours. Even the bungalows in the outskirts, many of them built in this century, have a surprising charm. It is only during the last decade that vulgarity has begun to spread. Since we British impose our rule upon Cyprus, why not be tyrannical enough to impose severe restrictions upon buildings, as the French so triumphantly have done in Fez? While this would not make us much more unpopular, it would strengthen our defence when our rule faces the verdict of history.

Coming to Cyprus from Europe, you will be struck by its orientalism. Geographers include it in Asia, and you notice mosques and *turqueries*, pi-dogs, camels and that curious smell, compact of spices and frying-oil, which tickles the nose alike in Marrakesh, Stamboul, and Shiraz. Even the currency is inconveniently exotic, nine piastres to the shilling, so that what we call 1s. 6d. is 1s. $4\frac{1}{2}$d.

Fresh from Egypt, on the other hand, as I was, one is struck chiefly by what is Western. The standard of life is startlingly superior to anything in neighbouring Asia, Africa or Eastern Europe. No sign of the blind, the syphilitic, the famished, the ragged or even the barefooted; the villages are clean, though the mud-brick buildings require to be made weather-proof with some sort of plaster and enlivened with whitewash. How constantly, and often amusedly, some incongruity reminded me that I was, for the first time, in a British colony! If I had found a Lady Bountiful in Majorca opening a flower show or the ephebes of Taormina bowling at the nets, I could hardly have been more taken aback than at the spectacle of policemen, with only a few words of English, clothed in the familiar dark blue; of carob-shadowed letter-boxes protruding the cypher G.R. & I.; of olive-hued boys playing football in the moat with, tightly attached to their heads, those mean school-caps which ushers have designed to identify their charges. If some of the streets are named after Dionysus and Euripides, others pay homage to Mr Gladstone and Kipling. (My Acropole Hotel was in the *hodos* of Tennyson.) Whereas in London I smoke Cyprian cigarettes, in Famagusta I had difficulty in finding any, though every other shop was stocked with Player's and Woodbines.

UNWILLINGLY I MUST SAY SOMETHING about the politics of Cyprus. The movement in favour of *Enosis*—union with Greece—is undoubtedly strong. The leaders of the Right and Left are united in nothing save this demand, each side looking forward to liquidating their opponents when we leave. The Turkish minority alone is openly anxious for us to remain. Whether in their hearts a majority of the islanders would in fact welcome *Enosis*, I do not know. (After only a week in the island, how could I form an opinion?) Though Cyprus has been in many ways a neglected corner of the Empire, it is conspicuously more prosperous than Greece, as well as more orderly and better administered. Though we have not given the island the irrigation that would multiply its wealth, much has been done for afforestation and agriculture, and relief has been given to the peasant from usurers, who in consequence are now among the most ardent and conspicuous champions of *Enosis*.

Nationalism, however, has become throughout the world a force as

irrational and fanatical as religion in the Dark Ages: it is arguable that everywhere most men prefer self-government to good government. Born a little Liberal, I have lately found my enthusiasm for self-determination cooling into a sad, cynical acceptance of its inevitability. The great nineteenth-century Englishmen who propagated the ideal of nationalism took it for granted that a nation, when given its independence, would practise toleration. Racial and religious persecution was a thing of the past. This assumption now seems grotesquely ingenuous.

So far from toleration spreading into Asia, it has been confined in Europe to a narrow strip running from the North Cape to the Riviera, and even in France it is menaced. An independent India seems promised to massacres on a magnificent scale—which at least will replace famine and epidemic disease as a solution to the problem of over-population. An independent Egypt is likely to prove uninhabitable for its non-Moslem citizens. I suspect that many, if not most, Greek-speaking Cypriots, as well as all the Turks in the island, would have enormously more to complain of under Greek rule than they have now. The only peoples who are good at politics are those which don't take them too much to heart. In Greece, on the other hand, politics have become the hashish of the people. They get lots of fun from the drug, but how it enfeebles and brutalizes that vigorous and delightful race.

I DO NOT ARGUE THAT such considerations necessarily justify us in retaining the colony. It is likely, however, that the Cypriots would be wise to try for ten years or so autonomy within the British Empire before committing themselves to the mercy of the warring politicians in Athens. The British may be patronizing and self-righteous: at least they are not corrupt, cruel or intolerant. (I found Communist journals, filled with attacks on British rule, freely on sale in Cyprus.) For my part, I cannot feel sure that we shall be making the world a better or happier place if we depart. But one might as usefully argue with cholera as with nationalism. If we remain in Cyprus, it will be because we believe it strategically important.

The desire of many Cypriots to get rid of us does not show itself, so far as I know, in any rudeness or even stiffness towards English visitors; and while these islanders are an uncommonly murderous people, they seem to use their quick knives only on one another. Those who wish to pursue the higher studies graduate in Athens, for there is no university in Cyprus. The energies of the richer class are concentrated upon business or politics: I, at any rate, did not have the luck to meet there anyone comparable with the so intelligent, amusing and sophisticated Greeks who make Athenian life so agreeable.

G

The resident British incline, I fancy, to be regrettably—perhaps not inexplicably—colonial in their attitude towards the Cypriots, which is one reason why I recommend the island as a place to visit rather than to inhabit. Did I feel at moments something disquieting, even sinister, behind the curtain of beauty, resulting perhaps from some thirty centuries of alien and often oppressive rule?

The monastery of Bel Pais rises in my memory to dispel any such superstition. I have nowhere else seen Northern Gothic in so luxuriant a Southern setting. Though the cloisters and dormitories of the old Premonstratensians are largely ruined, the church remains, and a noble, vaulted refectory. Flowers exuberate everywhere, and what a grandeur of situation, on sharply sloping ground with the mountains immediately behind and a celestial view of the Mediterranean a few miles down the hillside! Springs and rivulets enrich the foreground with a poetic lushness: everywhere a profusion of orange-trees, olives, carobs, young wheat. Shelley in *Epipsychidion* imagined just such a paradise. And a few miles along the coast is Kyrenia, white houses curving above a toy harbour with a massive ancient fortress controlling it—the general effect very North African. I felt even a rush of affection when I discovered on the waterfront an elderly Englishwoman in a topee seated on a folding stool with her box of watercolours, one of the last survivors of the mettlesome race I used to meet a quarter of a century ago in the *pensions* of Granada and Assisi, discussing which picturesque church or corner of the city-wall they should select as foreground to a Winsor and Newton sunset.

I WANT TO GO TO CYPRUS again: there is so much I had no time to see. Though I did visit the little church of Asinou, its walls entirely covered with Byzantine paintings, I missed the vast Monastery of Kypko, with its picture by St Luke which no eye has been allowed to see since the sixteenth century. (A one-man show of the evangelist's *oeuvre* would be of considerable size and absorbing interest.) I missed the house built for the Government by Rimbaud, which is said to look like a shooting-lodge in Perthshire. I missed Paphos, the home of Aphrodite, where the sea still intricates a vast lace of the foam from which in her nacreous conch the goddess rose.

Perhaps I may hope to repair these omissions. For Cyprus has one advantage which I have not mentioned. It is in the sterling area. By the time this paper is published, a pleasure-hating Treasury may have further interfered with our freedom to contrive an occasional, urgently needed escape to olive-yards and the Central Sea. But in March, 1947, when I made my raid on Cyprus, one could take there as much money as one liked, or rather as much as one had.

# Lapland  Holiday

## by  F. SPENCER CHAPMAN

EFORE the war I was a schoolmaster and a bachelor, and on two occasions during the school Easter holidays I visited Lapland : now I have neither of these excuses to spend April abroad, but some day I hope to take my son (not yet a year old) to Lapland for his first Polar expedition.

My main reason for choosing this remote corner of Europe was that, as a member of Gino Watkins's two expeditions to Greenland, I had a haunting desire to return to the Arctic, and I discovered that in a single month and at a cost of about £25 I could spend a fortnight some hundreds of miles north of the Arctic Circle experiencing all the vicissitudes of Polar travel in the happy company of an unspoilt and primitive people—the nomad Lapps.

On my first visit, in 1935, I went with a single companion who, like myself, was prepared to travel hard—in every sense of the word. We left South Shields on the night of April 2 in S.S. *Venus*, and the following morning, in spite of a nor'westerly gale, we breakfasted in Bergen, and caught the train to Oslo, which we reached on the morning of April 4. After two hours, spent in feverishly buying our skiing and camping equipment, we entrained again and were soon in Sweden. We travelled third class and had brought our own food, but as we carried li-lo air mattresses and sleeping-bags, and the train was fairly empty, we had two

99

tolerably comfortable nights and fascinating days watching the scene becoming increasingly Arctic as we sped northward. At last, about midnight of April 5–6, we reached Kiruna, already more than a degree north of the Circle, in less than half a week's travelling from Newcastle.

This was as far as our plans had been laid. Indeed, when we left England we had intended to go on to the railhead at Narvik, but had got out at Kiruna on the advice of a Swedish acquaintance we had made on the journey north. From here we meant to cross the north-western corner of Finland and make our way to any one of the several ports in the extreme north of Finmark (the most northern district of Norway), where we would pick up the weekly mail boat to take us back to Bergen.

Certainly we were not tied down by too rigorous planning. As we could not afford to drive in state in reindeer sledges, we knew that we should have to travel on ski—though my companion was not yet proficient in their use; but we were not certain whether we should follow the sledge which we might hire to carry our gear, manhaul our own sledge, or carry all our possessions in rucksacks on our backs. Nor had we made up our minds whether we should sleep in the tent we had brought, follow the local custom of bedding down in the snow after wrapping ourselves up in reindeer-skin robes, or rely on staying with the Lapps or making use of the rest-houses called *fjeldstue*, which were alleged to be found every fifteen miles along the main routes. It all depended on the relative cost.

We spent four days at Kiruna collecting local knowledge and the final items of our equipment, and on the morning of April 9 left by bus for Karesuando on the Swedo-Finnish border, seventy-five miles to the northeast. The road lay between banks of snow five feet high, and on our way we saw our first wild reindeer, as well as ptarmigan, snow-bunting, and the ubiquitous magpie.

That night—a short half-night of about four hours—we saw a display of aurora far finer than any I had seen in Greenland. Then we saw Finns and Lapps actually driving reindeer, and it looked so romantic, so efficient, and withal so easy a mode of progress that we then and there determined that at all costs we must hire or buy a reindeer for ourselves and drive it northwards on a compass course until we met the Arctic Ocean. After all, there were several ports to make for—Alta, Hammerfest, Vadsö or Kirkenes, and if we missed one we could surely find another.

At Kiruna we had been warned of sub-zero temperatures, of savage wolves and bears, and of the danger of being immobilized by a sudden thaw which would make sledging impossible and rot the ice on the rivers; we were told that without guides we should never find the *fjeldstue* or the way from one village to another. But we were prepared to discount

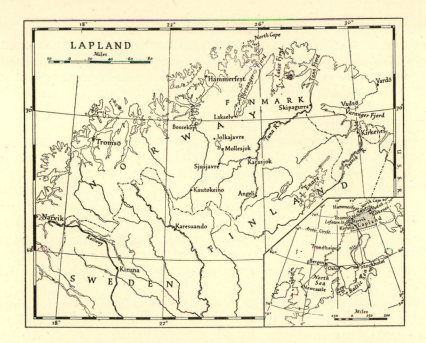

all this if only we could drive our own reindeer like Father Christmas and like these fascinating gnome-like little Lapps.

At Karesuando, accordingly, we bought our reindeer—for 100 kroner (£5)—from an old Finn, called Isak, after whom we named our purchase. This man was on his way home to Kautokeino some fifty miles further north, and a condition of the transaction was that we should accompany him and at the same time learn to drive.

We also bought a ramshackle sledge which would carry the 150 lb. of gear we had accumulated—tent, eiderdown sleeping bags, li-los, windproof suits and fur boots, primus stove and cooking pots, and rations for a fortnight, consisting of pemmican, butter, oatmeal, biscuit, sugar, and chocolate, also skiing and photographing equipment.

At midday on April 11 we left Karesuando in a blizzard. Driving reindeer did not seem so difficult after all, and three days of sledging over barren undulating country with fir trees in the valleys and scanty willow scrub on the higher ground took us to Kautokeino.

This journey taught us a good deal about the people and the country but not, as we very soon discovered, how to drive reindeer. When we were with our guide, Isak's halter had been tied to the back of the sledge in front, which contained a lichenous moss, the reindeer's staple diet, and as a consequence he pulled like a husky; also he was going home. But once we were on our own Isak took full advantage of our inexperience, and it was often a full hour before we could get him harnessed up in the morning.

Although he was very small (seen with the diminutive Lapps, reindeer look quite imposing, but in fact they are little more than three feet high), he was very full of life in the early morning and used to rear up and lash out with his sharp hooves. Coming in from the side, we would then wrestle with him and throw him on the ground; then one of us would sit on his head while the other pulled the sledge into position.

Even then he would leap sideways out of the shafts and, running to the end of his rein, would watch us with lowered head and large melancholy eyes. Luckily we had been careful to buy a hornless reindeer (at this time of the year they were beginning to shed their horns), otherwise Isak would have been more than a match for us.

The reindeer is controlled—or not—by a single rein which is attached beneath the chin to a light halter. To make him go to the left you pull the rein, and if you shake it he may go to the right; but there is no way of stopping him and—what is worse—no way of making him start if he does not want to.

First thing in the morning he would dash off at furious speed, but once this initial burst of energy was expended he would stop dead and only start again if one of us went ahead and hauled on the rein while the other pushed behind the sledge yodelling and making hunting cries. It was not long before we realized that, except as an emergency ration of meat, Isak was not really a very good investment.

From Kautokeino our next objective was Karasjok, a large Lapp centre another seventy miles north-east, and as we had to pull or push Isak most of the way, this journey took us the best part of a week. The only consolation was that, as we were in Finmark, we were able to sleep in comfort on birch-twig mattresses in the excellent *fjeldstue*, except one night when we lost our way in a snowstorm and had to spend the night in our tent.

As a rule there were plenty of other travellers on the way—all Lapps —and, though we could speak only a score of words of their language, we had only to say 'Karasjok?' and sweep an arm round the horizon to be put on the right track. The Lapps were friendly but strangely shy and aloof. Our efforts to drive Isak, however, soon broke down their reserve and they would laugh till they fell down in the snow.

The men wore delightful clothes of reindeer skin and gay coloured cloth with wide embroidered belts and four-pointed hats which, in the Karasjok style, were stuffed huge with eiderdown. The women, who hated being photographed, wore tight bonnets, long flowing dresses of blue cloth and scarlet scarves.

At Karasjok, where there was deep soft snow among the pine trees, the ordinary sledge on runners was outnumbered by the *pulka*, which resembles a small keeled canoe with an upright stern to support the back.

The *pulka* is attached to the reindeer by a single padded trace which passes between his hind legs, and the harness is gaily decorated with scarlet, yellow, and green.

In the early morning, when the animals are fresh and full of moss, they either dash round in small circles or set off at an impetuous gallop, often skirting fir trees so narrowly that in avoiding them the passenger leans too far to one side and overturns the sledge. The *pulka* has to be balanced like a bicycle and the single rein is tied round the driver's wrist, so that when he is thrown out in the snow he will not lose his reindeer.

But once the animal has settled down to a hand gallop it is a most delectable means of progression and, being so low in the snow, one has a great sensation of speed. Unfortunately Isak would have nothing to do with a *pulka* and, jumping over the trace, would face the impotent driver with lowered head.

April 21 was Easter Sunday, and all the Lapps went to church in their gay clothes, many of them arriving in their *pulkas* from outlying villages. Two days later we left Karasjok, having sold Isak with glad hearts but at great financial loss.

As it was impossible in the time to procure or make a really lightweight sledge, we sent most of our gear by horse-sledge to meet the boat at Hammerfest, while we set off on ski for Kirkenes carrying all we needed for the journey in rucksacks on our backs. Our route lay up the Tana river to Angeli and then across the huge island-scattered lake of Enare and down the Pasvik river to Kirkenes, where we hoped to pick up the boat.

On the third day—or rather night, for the snow was now too soft to travel in the daytime—we had just reached Lake Enare when the temperature suddenly rose and it came on to snow huge wet flakes. We could see nothing, and our ski balled up so that we could hardly move them. We were still a hundred miles from Kirkenes in a trackless waste of soft snow or melting ice, and we realized that we should be lucky if we ever got there.

Our only hope of catching the boat was to retrace our steps and, travelling night and day, to follow the Tana river to Skipagurra, where our map showed a motor road, then to go by car forty miles east to Vadsö where we could pick up our boat. This we should just be able to do by hiring relays of horse-sledges down the frozen Tana river.

On April 29 we reached Vadsö in plenty of time to catch the *St Swithin*, which came in next day. The voyage to Bergen was six and a half days of sheer joy. We went round the North Cape, called at Hammerfest and Tromsö, took the passage inside the Lofoten Islands, and stopped at Trondheim, where we saw redwings nesting in the churchyard of the

magnificent Norman cathedral.   On May 7 I was back in my classroom
ready to start a new term.


IN 1939 I SPENT another school Easter holiday in Lapland.   This time
the two adults of the party were accompanied by ten boys between the
ages of fifteen and nineteen.   In the light of experience gained on the
former expedition I made certain changes.

In the first place there would be no more Isaks.   We would take
Nansen-type lightweight sledges and, wearing ski, would manhaul them
ourselves.   If we fell in with a Lapp cavalcade and could hitch our
sledges on to the spare reindeer they usually had running free, so much
the better.   Secondly, as the coastal boats left only once a week from the
northern ports, while the trains for the south ran daily from Kiruna, we
would plan the journey the other way round, going straight up by sea
from Bergen to Hammerfest, then sledging southward to Kiruna.   A great
advantage of this would be that we should save several days by being
able to prepare all our gear—much of which would be bought at Oslo—
on board ship instead of wasting precious days at Kiruna, as we had done
in 1935.   A disadvantage was that we should be travelling into warmer
weather and might expect difficult snow conditions as we moved south.

This time also, as I was responsible for inexperienced boys and could
therefore afford to take no unnecessary risks, the equipment had to be
much on the lines of a Polar expedition—double pyramid tents, heavy
eiderdown sleeping bags, grenfell-cloth windproof suits, and full rations.
The unfortunate result of this was that we were grossly overloaded and
that the expedition cost rather more per head in spite of experience
gained in 1935 and the travel concessions granted to a larger party.

I might add that the members were not chosen for their experience or
toughness: I took any reasonably fit boy who could persuade his parents
to spare him for the holidays and put up £30.

I intended to disembark at Hammerfest, proceed to Lakselv at the
head of Porsangerfjord by boat and lorry, then to sledge some 300 miles
via Karasjok and Kautokeino to Karesuando, whence we would catch
the bus to Kiruna.

All went well until we reached Hammerfest, where we learned that the
road to Lakselv was still blocked by snow.   This meant that we had to go
by boat to Bossekop at the head of Alta fjord and start the journey from
there, as a result of which the first few days of manhauling, before we had
got used to this purgatorial means of progress, attractive only in retro-
spect, were over a low range of hills.   Luckily, just as we were being
forced to the expedient of relaying the overloaded sledges one at a time,

we were overtaken by an empty horse-sledge driven by a friendly Norwegian who at once offered to tow our sledges to the top of the hill. On the long descent on the south side we were able to ride our sledges; indeed, they went so fast that it was almost impossible to control them, and the wide, well-waxed hickory runners slid easily over the frozen surface of a lake to the *fjeldstue* at Jolkajavre, where we spent the night.

After a day's rest here the weather changed for the worse. It came on to snow and thawed so much that the snow balled up on the runners of the sledges so that we could hardly move them. It was midnight before we reached Mollesjok, the next hut, and the boys needed another full day to recover their strength. The going was now so bad that it was clear we should have to miss out Karasjok and go straight down to Kautokeino. Reindeer were unobtainable in this area, so, accompanied by the only boy who was a good skier, I went on to Karasjok to make arrangements for some reindeer to meet the party at Sjusjavre, about fifteen miles south of Mollesjok. The two of us skied about a hundred miles in forty-eight hours, but as we travelled at night and slept during the day the going was quite good.

From now on we at least had enough reindeer to pull our gear, while the party followed on ski, and sometimes there were enough for all twelve of us to ride precariously in *pulkas*—a cavalcade, including our guides, of about twenty sledges.

The journey from Bossekop to Kiruna took us about a fortnight, and this just left us time to spend two days in both Stockholm and Oslo before we caught the boat home from Bergen.

NEXT TIME I GO to Lapland I shall, unless time is no object, do the journey from north to south, but I shall go as far as Vadsö by boat so as not to miss the North Cape which, perhaps from an early attachment to Longfellow's ballad, has always seemed to me one of the most romantic of the more accessible places in the world. I shall take really light sledges and loads so that each man can pull his own gear and hitch it—and himself—on to a reindeer when available. I shall not take any camping equipment: I shall rely on sleeping in the excellent *fjeldstue* or in Lapp houses or tents; and I shall take only the barest minimum of food, as one can nearly always buy reindeer meat, rye bread, and milk.

To travel hopefully is better than to arrive. Some people pursue the analogy still further and say that to plan an expedition or to look back on it is even better than carrying it out. But for myself I would infinitely rather do a thing than write or read or think about it: already I am longing to leave my desk and hear the reindeer bells and see the Northern Lights once more.

# South of France Holiday

## by DILYS POWELL

T must have been the first week of July, 1947, that the diving-stage was towed out into the bay at Saint Raphaël and left there, dipping and rolling, with the flag of the Sporting Club flying over the high board. Up till then the high spirits, the Mediterranean energy of athletic visitors and residents had found outlets agreeable indeed, but modest.

There were, for instance, the pedalos, little two-seater paddle boats, painted red and white, brilliant in the sun, and spanking along under the motive power of four human legs, bicycling. You could take out a canoe if you liked; or the bolder equilibrists pushed themselves round the mole on water-skis. A corner of the beach was occupied in the late afternoon by the gymnasts. 'Hup!' they cried gaily, hoisting one another about, perching uncertainly on each other's shoulders, handstanding and somer-saulting and forming uneasy pyramids. Then, exhausted, they sat in knots by the dressing cubicles; or joined in the game, favoured by a few of the girls too, of banging a football back and forth over a high net; or ran to fling themselves into the lazy water.

For, of course, the sea was the thing. Everybody went in: the proud, beautiful swimmers; the girls holding their bare heads a little out of the water, but coming ashore with dark or yellow hair dripping just the same; the naked babies shrieking in the frothy verge.

All day a score of little boys ran and jumped and dived into the shallows from a platform of concrete and rock, the remains perhaps of a jetty: all day, from morning, when the streets were still cool and empty, and the waiter still had not finished carrying the chairs and the sunshades to the hotel terrace across the promenade; from midday, when the holiday families had packed towels and bathing trunks into striped holdalls and gone home to eat and sleep; to evening, when mushroom shadows lay on the sand yards away from the parasols which cast them, and old ladies in wrinkled stockings shuffled out to gossip on the public benches.

One of the small fry had found a sport more delicious even than the round of running, jumping and clambering back to start again. With goggles, a tube to breathe by, and a baby harpoon, the child swam endlessly under water, peering for fish to spear: indifferent to the bathers, the divers, and the practical jokers who poured water down his breathing-tube. His elders played the game too, but with smarter tools. Gradually, as we looked, from the hundreds a few single figures began to detach themselves: the physical aristocrats of the beach. We came to recognize, for instance, the tall golden man in white trunks with his crest of corn-coloured hair; the youth burnt black by the sun, black shoulders, black chest, black thighs; and the splendid boy in emerald trunks with the aquiline features, the praxitelean curls, the graceful arrogant movements. These three went hunting, one by one, for Mediterranean fish. They walked down to the sea with the harpoon gun and the mask, goggles and breathing-tube in one; then we would see, out in the bay, the trail of the swimmer, the wake of thrashing feet, and the tube mysteriously gliding, like a periscope ; later the golden hunter, perhaps, would stalk past with a string of spiny fish.

Fine sport for a strong swimmer, and recommended by Monsieur Saquet, our host at La Cigale: 'I shot three fish, big like this, before breakfast this morning!' he would tell us as we wandered off to the beach.

When we arrived at Saint Raphaël we felt at first, watching the to and fro of the bathers, the careless parade of umber backs and bellies, that we were ill-equipped to join, however modestly, in the public fun; we must, we said, find some private corner, along the coast, perhaps, towards the point with its porphyry islands, past the eastern promenade which the Germans blew up, and there expose to the sun a few inches of our mauve northern bodies. The Hotel-Restaurant La Cigale, which, in the best traditions of French comfort, is a restaurant first and a hotel afterwards, stands on the corner of a street leading down to the promenade. To the right, the promenade runs the short length of the new town to the Casino; opposite is the Reserve, a bandstand and ballroom combined. A band plays in the Reserve for tea-dances, then after dinner turns itself into an orchestra with soloists and executes, on the terrace, songs about the Boul' Mich' and the Place Pigalle, and spirited imitations of Popeye; later in the night it goes underground again and beats it out eight to a bar, and any visitor to La Cigale capable, after a day's air, sun, food and drink, of wakefulness, might hear into the small hours a dull persistent stomping. Beyond that he might catch the rumour of the sea; for there it is, just across the road, scarcely bothering of nights to creep a yard or two over the gritty oaten sands.

Near enough for us to walk across the promenade from the hotel, down the steps, and into the water in one breath. We went for a trial swim and came back to sit on the verandah of the Reserve and drink cold sweet orange juice.

The beach, in the last days of June, was not crowded, not by English standards. Fifteen or twenty striped parasols, in the small curve between the children's jetty and the mole where canoes were drawn up for hire, shaded the family groups: the father and the boys in black or coloured trunks, the mother and the girls in flowered miniature drawers and tiny bodices which covered their bosoms and left ribs and waist to turn the

colour of rosewood.  The rest of the bathers stretched in the open sun.
New arrivals glistened with oil; the light was in a mood to flay without
warning, for the sparkling water, the small wind from the bay gave a
deceiving sense of cool.  The sands burned the feet.  But the bathers
walked carelessly as salamanders: the lovely girl with fair braided hair
and the magnificent body of a hetaira, the squat fellow with a bicyclist's
calves, even the beach photographer in his white belted jacket and shorts.

The few English visitors—no more than a dozen at a time in all Saint
Raphaël—were inclined to shrink from the embrace of the sun.  The
middle-aged pair from the pension came down to the water in bathing
wraps; the Englishman with his French wife steamed all day in a shirt
and pullover, and his two little daughters, their childish shoulders taking
on as days passed the tint of a pale paper bag, paddled in coolie hats.
The rest of the world yielded itself.  Not only to the sun, the sea, the
air; but to a kind of relaxed good humour.

An etiquette, we noticed, was observed.  On the promenade, in the
gossiping before dinner or in the eddying, chattering dusk hour, everybody
stared, though without rudeness ; the girls in their printed frocks and white
sandals were conscious of the men's eyes, the boys, their physical confidence dimmed in shirts and trousers, eyed every passing woman.  But
on the beach, indifference.  Nobody looked at the beauty with the long
sun-gilded thighs and the bare ochre belly.  All the superb half-naked
young creatures were as if clothed in modesty; the very extravagance of
flesh nullified the meaning of the body.  And by the same acceptance
the elderly, the ugly and the eccentric went unregarded.  An old lady
with long white hair and the ruins of an exquisite figure came every afternoon to bathe, to comb her hair in the sun and lie on the sand.  An old
gentleman with a Mosaic beard took off his boots and went for a solitary
swim.  Not a head turned.  On the beach you could be as private as you
pleased.

It was not long, then, before the nonchalance of the French put us to
shame; we, after all, were the ones who were staring.  And it was not
long before the hesitations of the new arrival gave place to the assurance
of the old hand: a transition helped by the graceful good manners of
everyone round us.  We established ourselves in a corner of the beach in
the narrow sheltered stretch beyond the children's jetty.  The white
parasol by the rocks, word went round, had been appropriated by the
English couple; the beach attendant, his powerful body suffused with
summer, ran to adjust its shade for us each morning.  Soon, so well
recognized was our claim, to pay for it was obviously regarded as an
extravagance; the attendant with his friendly marine growl would have
liked to wave away our thirty francs.

When we came back after our siesta the sands were more crowded than in the morning. Girls and boys had come out of their offices, no doubt, and women had finished the day's housework. But nobody had taken the deck-chair, and the rush mat under the parasol was unoccupied. By afternoon the water had no trace of chill. We swam, lay shading our eyes from the sun, and swam again. At last we rubbed off the sand, gathered up our unread books, and went to collect the deposit on the hired towels. 'At your service!' cried the smiling woman by the barricade of lemonade bottles: 'Till tomorrow!'

Tomorrow came with more sun, more sea, more intensification of physical happiness. The spring of effort, too tightly coiled, gently unwound. And the southern heat gave the feeling of richness and abundance which in itself is repose to the pinched northerner. The sense of luxury was, perhaps, illusory; France in the summer of 1947 was not living through easy times. But at least there was no false luxury: no deceiving the eye with palaces. Saint Raphaël is not for the sophisticated wealthy. The French, rediscovering in the absence of the foreigner their own playgrounds, send here the middle classes, people who ask of a holiday not display but comfort.

Just as we had on arrival felt unequal to the insouciance of the sands, we shrank in the first days from the size of the meals. Or rather our stomachs, trained to the aridities of the English kitchen of the nineteen-forties, panicked at the sight of so much oil, so much butter, so many eggs, steaks and cutlets.

Still, we had asked for it. We had chosen to stay, not at one of the large hotels, but at a modest place which took pride in its cooking. La Cigale has probably no more than fifteen rooms; these have running water and what else a reasonable man may ask: they are clean, airy and comfortable enough for all the purposes to which a Continental bedroom may be put. For the rest, the hotel does not squander its energies on lift-boys, clerks and decorative attendants, but concentrates on good Provençal food, lovingly cooked and served by waiters who look as if they wanted you to enjoy it. We were there, in fact, to eat well: all the opportunities were before us; only the flesh was weak.

For a few days we admired the sagacious French, who, nosing out what we had guessed to be the best and cheapest meals in Saint Raphaël, ate through the terrine de campagne, the bouillabaisse, the entrecote and the fresh raspberry melba. We were, we knew, in no physical condition for such exploits. We came in from the beach at midday under the spell of an incomparable indolence, and ordered, from the menu at 225 francs, about 9s. 6d., baked eggs with chicken's liver, cold ham, a salad, fruit and lager. The eggs tasted of butter, the ham had the texture of ice cream, there was good olive oil in the salad and the peaches had ripened in the sun of Fréjus.

Next day, one of us, no matter which, asked for more eggs, and at the end of the meal our host, with a genial essay in dictatorship, sent over two raspberry melbas. We grew experimental. With such cooking, we said, we should like to try everything; let us choose now and then from the card of the day and pay the difference between the cost and our pension terms. Monsieur Saquet, whose figure and temperament suggested a similar adventurousness, beamed and replied that we should order from whatever card we liked and pay the same. We drank white wine and rose from our host's own vineyards, occasionally changing to a pink called, from its colour, Onion Peel; once or twice we ventured on a bottle of Old of the Isles, a heavy, powerful, sweetish wine, in the manner of the Cretan red, described in the menu, simply, as marvellous.

As our appetites grew we spent much time over the various bills of fare, weighing the comparative merits of omelette with truffles and ham and eggs, tournedos and Bresse chicken roasted on the spit; but not more time than Monsieur Saquet himself, who might be seen any night strolling across the promenade to read, with justifiable satisfaction, his own composition pinned up at the entrance to the sea terrace. ' *At the Cigale one can regale*,' it declared. '*A menu at 125 francs (quick meal) served on the sea terrace. The menu at 225 francs herewith. Our gastronomic meal at 450 francs (marvellous). The great card with fine specialities. In a Provençal setting ! One gives oneself a treat !*'

True enough : we did give ourselves a treat. Lest the identity of the day's menu at midday and in the evening should cramp us, our host would visit us at table and suggest some private variant: 'For lunch,' he would say, 'you ate hors d'oeuvres and veal. For dinner, if that would please you, I can arrange a melon, a langouste, or, if you prefer, a mixed grill in the manner of Uncle Tom.' And there would be a little round melon, sweet as honey, and a delicate crustacean; or perhaps, if after the day's air and exercise we were bold, a dish of bouillabaisse, with bony rascasse in the thick rich soup.

The days slid by in a joyful routine. At half-past eight the chamber-maid bustled through the bedroom to put the breakfast tray out on the terrace ; the sun was already creeping round to look in through the window, and there would be a scurry to save the butter from melting. About midday, after the morning's bathe, the newspaper-seller picked his way across the sands, advertising his approach by blowing a small tin trumpet; over lunch at the cool table by the window we studied the news of the national bicycle race, the Tour de France, still in its first days and due to last another three weeks. There was a temptation, after bathing again, after brushing the salt from the hair and dressing, to eat too many cakes, too many ices, at the tea-room; or you could spend the half-hour before the apéritif looking at the shops, buying cigarettes and fruit for breakfast, speculating on what manner of audience might visit the municipal cinema on a warm light June night to see a piece of American fiction about the German attack on Russia.

We drank vermouth and soda flavoured with lemon at the bar of La Cigale, then ate our dinner sitting outside on the pavement. Life fluttered past us in the dusk: family parties walking and murmuring, a pair of young girls larking and waiting for the appearance of their heroes the band players, a woman in the fashionable short trousers getting out of a car with a mastiff, a waiter on his night off smiling at us as he went by with his hands in his pockets. The dogs ran from side to side of the promenade, gambolling and sniffing at one another's rumps: poodles, terriers, pekinese, alsatians, mongrels.

We watched; chatted a little with Monsieur Jean, the *maître d'hôtel*; greeted the fair-haired Madame Saquet with her shy dignified air; until it was time to drink a brandy in the Reserve and listen idly to the band, or have a fling at the Casino. Once we saw a visiting circus: a one-night stand with clowns, acrobats who doubled with the dancers, and a herd of wild animals composed of two plump docile ponies; but that was an excursion into the frenetic life of pleasure which could scarcely be repeated.

The diving platform crowned the gaiety. We did not see it arrive, but one day we got up, rubbed our eyes, looked out over the aloes and the prickly pear which fringed our terrace, and there it was, pitching and swaying in the bay. That morning we eyed respectfully the procession of sporting types scaling the steps to the high board and, a little hesitantly from so mobile a starting-point, launching themselves through the bright air.

The spectacle, pretty though it was, cast at first a private shade over what we had come to think a model for communal playgrounds. Everybody, we understood now, could join in the riot of sun and food. But everybody could not enjoy a dive from the stage of the Saint Raphaël Sporting Club; there was something from which we were shut out. On the beach the daily pleasures went on. The party under the next-door parasol, two stout middle-aged women, a man in glasses and a hairy character in a sun-hat, were holding hands in the water and bobbing up and down in a ring; one of their children, a disagreeable infant addressed in wheedling or exasperated tones as Jo-Jo, feeling himself unattended, was howling and kicking a beached canoe. 'Leave that bark tranquil!' cried a little boy, hurrying up, shiny from the sea. One of two olive-skinned girls, self-consciously smart with their smooth black hair, their coral lips and their identical egg-yolk sun-suits, was sparring with an admirer. 'Go away!' she cried, piercingly. 'You get on my nerves, you are insupportable!' In the shadow of a rock a woman no longer young, with fine fierce features and a vast frizz of golden curls, was kneeling up and dotingly combing the hair of her companion, a dark man with the insolent warning look of a film gangster. The athletes teetered on the diving-board and sprang.

Suddenly a roar, the composite voice of bathers and watchers, went up from the beach. The diving-stage, overweighted with swimmers, rocked this way and that by impatient figures swarming up to the high board, heeled; righted itself; heeled again; and overturned. As it went over the divers, like frogs disturbed, plopped off in all directions. The sea boiled for a few moments; then the stage could be seen placidly bobbing bottom up. Its somersault had entangled a canoe in what might be called the rigging, now submarine. But the bathers were safe. Splashing and shouting, they swam back to their mischievous toy.

There was a conference; the swimmers gesticulated, the canoists sat swinging their legs. Boys and girls on the promenade got off their bicycles to look; the newspaperman forgot to blow his trumpet; the photographer stood on the rocks pointing. The divers clustered on one side of the stage and put their weight on it. The thing swivelled to an angle of forty-five degrees and sank back; the crowd laughed. Morning mounted to midday. Pedalos and water-skiers collected; solitary figures lying face down, paddling spreadeagled on white-painted floats, went to get a view. The divers shoved and struggled. At last there was a heaving of the water; the stage upended itself, hesitated for a second or two, then slowly swung over. The divers thrashed away out of reach; then as, dripping, the diving-boards and the flagpole rose into the air, the brown bodies turned and approached once more. Soon they were clambering aboard again and flinging themselves, sprawling a little, from the high board.

So it was that the Sporting Club became, not a private pleasure, but part of the popular amusement. Like the rest of the watchers on the beach, we came to look to the diving-stage for entertainment. The gymnasts tumbled on the sands, the little boys shrilled and wriggled at the jetty, the nonchalant beauties rolled their bathing drawers a little further down over their golden hips. We lingered a few days more, drawing out the mornings and the evenings as best we could. The town was sparkling when we left: sparkling with light and heat and fun. At the corner of the street we turned to look at the beach and the bay. The child was still fishing with his harpoon and his tube; the English family still sat under their parasol; the girls still came running in with dripping hair.

And the diving-stage? The diving-stage, of course, surrounded by an excited crowd of swimmers, canoists and water-skiers, was floating upside down.

# Fair and Frail

## *by EDWIN SMITH*

**E**nglish pottery and porcelain is the theme of the pages that follow. The mixing and baking of clays to make objects of delighting ornament and utility resemble in many fundamentals the mixing and baking of doughs by an oven-tending housewife, and the important difference between porcelain and pottery might be paralleled in homely but not inaccurate metaphor as the difference between bread and pastry. The fusible nature of the mix, the higher temperature of its baking, the ability to take and retain greater delicacy of shape; such characteristics are shared by porcelain and pie-crusts, together with a translucency when held against light. Since china, sometimes almost surprisingly, is inedible, this translucence is the readiest means of distinguishing porcelain from pottery which, like bread, is opaque.

Like the staple commodity to which we have compared it, pottery is indigenous to all countries and civilizations, but porcelain was for some eight centuries produced only in China. In 1709 a German alchemist discovered the secret of its manufacture whilst attempting to make gold—and for his royal master, who was thereby enabled to found the first European porcelain factory near Dresden, it was only a little less fortunate than if he had succeeded. In England a patent for the process was taken out at Bow in 1744, but the earliest English piece known originates from Chelsea, dated 1745. Important early factories were also at Derby and at Worcester, where the Basket and Stand illustrated above, from the Victoria and Albert Museum, were made about 1770.

*Staffordshire earthenware pipe (1760) from Fitzwilliam Museum.*

orcelain figures, now shelved in cabinet or
museum, were first intended as a decora-
tion for the dining table—a more durable
development of the sugar-paste figures and
centre-pieces that once stimulated the eye of
the affluent diner. Bow, which produced the
elegant rustic above; Chelsea, the figure on
right; and Derby, from whence comes the
'Africa,' all in the 1760s, were the principal
places of their manufacture.

Pottery figures, though their material and spirit are senior, developed concurrently with their porcelain counterparts, sounding in cottage parlour a coarser echo of the pleasures on the rich man's table. The numerous potteries of Staffordshire were the main source of these wholly native gems, from whence the ageless 'Battle for the Breeches' (c. 1825), the pair of Lovers (Burslem 1825) and the lovely smaller figure on the left (c. 1745). Examples on both pages from the Fitzwilliam Museum.

The merit of English porcelain figures is high, yet they yield to those of Dresden, upon imported originals of which our own were often modelled. In pottery, however, as in this rough-cast Bear-jug (1740), and particularly in stoneware, of which the Horseman (c. 1730), from the Victoria and Albert Museum, and the Lovers on a Bench (c. 1745) from the Fitzwilliam Museum, shown opposite, are classic examples, English figures are in their sense of simple form and humour unique and unsurpassed. Even the Victorian Staffordshire figure, of which three examples are shown above, is in its period unparalleled.

*Fitzwilliam Museum*

Our noted fellow-feeling for the small and dumb is reflected in the many figures of animals and birds, which are in both mediums among the most successful and original native products. The subtle realism of the Bow porcelain owl (opposite) from the Victoria and Albert Museum, and the robust formalism of the Staffordshire pottery owl-jug from the Fitzwilliam Museum (right), make an enlightening contrast, each so eloquently expressive of its medium. The Chelsea tureen (c. 1755), below, whose lid so ingeniously lifts by the ears, is full rabbit size. Lady Schreiber, who donated this splendid piece, in a monumental collection of porcelain, to the Victoria and Albert Museum, records in her journal that the vendor 'only asked £5 for it and took £4.'

The stoneware owl-jug (c. 1746), with its pie-crust piping, wittily reminds how close to the baker's is the potter's oven. The Spaniel (1760), the Cockerel (1745), the Cat (1745) and the lower Owl (1760) are all Staffordshire pottery from the Fitzwilliam Museum.

This rich array of 'crocks,' old with some modern, pottery with some porcelain, though all but entirely for liquid utility is as richly decorative as a case of well bound books.

*Derby porcelain plate (c. 1790), landscape by Boreman.*

*Copeland pottery plate (mid-19th cent.).*

*Longton Hall (Staffordshire) porcelain plate (c. 1755).*

*Chelsea porcelain dish (1755).*

*Burslem pottery plate (c. 1830) by Enoch Wood.*

*Longton Hall (Staffordshire) porcelain fruit-dish (c. 1755).*

All plates from Victoria and Albert Museum.

*Bow porcelain tureen and stand (c. 1765) in the Victoria and Albert Museum.*

*A porcelain inkstand (1860), from the Chamberlain factory of Worcester. Fitzwilliam Museum.*

SUSAN'S FAREWELL.
*Adieu she cry'd, and wav'd her Lily Hand.*

Illustration in copper-plate engraving and etching and the production of fine
pottery and porcelain were contemporaneous. In these transfer-printed
pieces, a Liverpool pottery jug from the Fitzwilliam Museum and two porcelain
cups, the two mediums are expressively united. The picture is transferred from a
print taken from the copper plate in enamel—usually of black, as in these three
examples, but sometimes in red, brown or purple.

**R**ockingham, source of the large vase above, was the last English porcelain factory established and the only one in England associated with royal or aristocratic support; it produced from 1826 to 1842. The small vase, above, is Derby porcelain (c. 1765), the Bottle, below, is Worcester porcelain (1815), all from the Fitzwilliam Museum.

In origin and intimate service, tea and porcelain are closely connected, and early English tea-pots in that medium, like the one of Lowestoft (c. 1765) below, are often free copies of Chinese originals. Even designs of European character—the Liverpool cup and saucer (c. 1760) below, and the Staffordshire lustre pair (opposite page, below)—lack handles *à la Chinoise*.

The Worcester factory, which produced the tea-service partly shown above, c. 1775, apparently made no figures, but its articles of domestic utility are among the loveliest in English porcelain. The porcelain jug (opposite page, lower left) is ascribed to the Lowdin factory of Bristol (c. 1755). In Staffordshire pottery are the two tea-pots (c. 1750) at the top of the opposite page and the lustre jug (c. 1800) below them. Examples on both pages from the Victoria and Albert Museum.

The objects examined in this much-omitting glance at pottery and porcelain are of high merit, some are works of art, but few are works of rare genius. Indeed, any healthy society would produce as a matter of course their contemporary equivalent. In the century that has elapsed since such objects ceased to be made, sharp-edged time, the museum and the antique dealer have swept them from common or even polite everyday use, and no creative hand has been helped to replace them. Like the 'joke mug,' above, the beer is now gone and ugly toads remain. Such work of today as would well compare with even the humble, but wittily formal, Victorian 'Rockingham-ware' boot bottle and the leg vase, below, is rare, unrepresentative, and generally unregarded. What shall we leave that will be greeted with pleasure and coveted in the junk-shops of tomorrow?

# London Pubs

*by NATHANIEL GUBBINS*

*drawings by Laurence Scarfe*

SUPPOSE the first London pub was a Roman wine-shop where veterans of Caesar's conquests bored each other to death with tales of old campaigns. In the London pubs now veterans are doing much the same.

After the Roman wine-shops came the Saxon hovels where they drank honeymead out of the decorated horns of cattle; then came the Norman wine-shops, the taverns of the Middle Ages, the inns and ale houses of the centuries roughly between the fifteenth and the nineteenth, and finally the glittering public-house full of polished glass and metal and mahogany which appeared in the prosperous and vulgar period that marked the second half of Queen Victoria's reign and attained its full glory in the golden age of the upper and lower middle classes between the coronation and death of Edward the Seventh, known to one and all in every bar in England as Teddy.

The modern pub, affectionately called 'the local' by regular customers, is the anaemic child of those friendly, hearty, red-blooded gin palaces, where the landlord was a character with handlebar moustaches and brilliant check waistcoat decorated with fabulous gold watchchain and seals; where the barmaids were full-bosomed, bold-eyed and sharp-tongued, always dressed in black with their hair piled high in nets and their fingers shining with jewels; and where gin was a penny a nip and twopence a double, beer twopence a pint in the four-ale bar, and a cut off the joint and two veg followed by a sweet and cheese and biscuits was anything between sixpence and a shilling, and was sometimes given away free to attract custom.

Now the beer is anything from tenpence to one shilling and sixpence a pint, according to the kind of beer it is and the kind of bar you drink it in. Gin and whisky is priced according to the nerve of the landlord and your ability to pay. The cut off the joint and two veg is rare now and much more expensive, though it is still the most satisfying meal in London.

And most of the publicans are not 'free' like their fathers and grand-fathers. Only a few own their own pubs, with the freedom to buy liquor and food where they like according to their own judgment and their customers' tastes. The great hand of monopoly has grabbed most of the licensed premises, so that the characters with their check waistcoats, their straw hats worn indoors and outdoors in summer and curly brimmed soft hats worn indoors and outdoors in the winter, have become either tenants who are obliged to buy all their liquor from one brewer (the owner) or managers who are nothing but neatly dressed clerks with no personality whatever and without even the right to order their own catering in food.

Whatever may have happened to the landlords, the customers of London pubs have not changed a bit, except that at least half of them are women. At one time only women who were social outcasts went into pubs, but since the two wars women of all classes (you wouldn't know the social outcasts from the others) jostle men at the bars, buying their own rounds of drinks, swallowing pints of beer and increasing the general shortage of spirits.

Nor, unless there has been complete reconstruction, is there any change in the layout of pubs. There is always the saloon bar where the best customers are served. They are the people who wear collars and polish their shoes. They might be tradesmen, bank managers, clerks, book-makers, commercial travellers, lawyers, idlers with money to burn, or even journalists. Almost every class in the country except workmen, char-women and belted earls use the saloon bar. The belted earls use the Carlton Club.

With a few exceptions there is always the public, or four-ale, bar used by the workmen, the charwomen, the newspaper sellers and all those who never wear a collar or polish their shoes except on Sundays. Should one of these untouchables enter the saloon bar by mistake he or she is greeted with a shout from the landlord,'Not this side, please,' and goes humbly and without protest to the place where he or she belongs. This bar is called the 'four-ale' because the ale sold there was once fourpence a quart.

Nobody knows why it is also called the 'public' (the whole place is a public-house, isn't it?), unless it is because the bar is usually wide open for anybody to see the lower classes in their cups, whereas the saloon-bar customers are protected from the vulgar gaze of the four-alers by little frosted-glass windows on swivels, which can be opened if the best people want to go slumming with their eyes, or closed to hide them from the rabble, leaving only their better-dressed stomachs visible between the bottom of the little windows and the counter.

There is also the private bar used mainly by nervous women and secret drinkers. It is also known as the 'jug and bottle department,' where jugs and bottles are furtively filled with beer.

In the saloon bar there is the best furniture, with a brass rail to rest your feet on as you lean elegantly with one elbow on the counter. Around the walls there are the glittering mirrors advertising somebody's beer or spirits in letters of gold. In the bar where the best customers drink there are hung the best pictures, 'The Stag at Bay,' Highland Cattle, King Edward (Teddy is still the publican's favourite royalty) photographed at various ages from infancy to full manhood in shooting cap or white topper at Ascot, the late Admiral Earl Beatty (the publican's favourite sailor after Nelson), football and cricket groups looking muscular and self-conscious, bowling groups looking happily drunk, and the inevitable 'Dignity and Impudence,' a coloured print of a big, patient doggie looking tolerantly down at a small, cheekie doggie . . . nostalgic pictures, unchanged for thirty years, of a prosperous age of plenty now probably gone for ever.

In the saloon bar there is also a good red carpet, and serving there is the best-looking barmaid available. The best customers must have the best of everything.

In the four-ale, or public, bar, where the beer is cheaper, there is no carpet on the floor. There is sawdust. It is sometimes called 'the spit and sawdust.' There are no pictures on the walls, unless they are the cheaper advertisements for somebody's beer. There is no furniture but wooden benches and a few kitchen chairs, often without backs. Normally a barman serves behind the counter, but if it is a barmaid she is the kind the saloon bar doesn't want. She is usually elderly and severe, ready to 'come the acid' with anybody who doesn't mind his Ps and Qs, just the sort to keep the mob in its place if it gets out of hand on a Saturday night. You feel she has seen better days in the saloon when commercial travellers made dates with her and has gradually come down in the pub world till she is now nothing but a beer puller in a bar where sex appeal is considered too good for the customers.

But only a short time ago the four-ale bar, despite its lack of elegant furniture and barmaids, had one advantage of the saloon and the private. It had the dart board all to itself.

Darts is a game of great skill which at one time was as exclusive to the working classes as was polo to the non-working classes. Its All-England final is still played with great ceremony at the Horns, Kennington, as important to darts as the Oval or Lord's is to cricket, or Madison Square Garden is to boxing in America.

To win a game you must throw your final dart into a space two and a-half inches by three-eighths of an inch from a distance of nine feet. If you miss it more than once in a game between experts you are almost certain to lose, which means that you, or your side, buys the drinks. Experts hardly ever miss more than once. Some hardly ever miss at all.

When only experts played it was safe to be in the same bar during a match. You could sit within a foot of the board without running the risk of losing an eye. Then the trousered women of Chelsea and Bloomsbury descended on the dart boards in the four-ale bars. Slumming was such fun and so democratic. The polite experts made way for them, gallantly giving up their evening's enjoyment. But when the trousered women began throwing darts all over the place, everybody made way for them. They cleared a bar quicker than a hired chucker-out.

Soon after that it was anybody's game. People played it in clubs and private houses and finally in the lordly saloon, where it competed in popularity with pin-tables and where they had better darts and boards, as they must have the best of everything.

The four-alers still have one advantage left. They are not too proud to belong to the slate clubs, the sick clubs (instituted long before national insurance), the holiday and the Christmas clubs. They pay their sixpences and shillings every week to the landlord, who saves their money and shares out in hard times and holiday times. They trust him implicitly, and their trust is justified, for to be a fully licensed man you must first have a character as spotless as a bishop's. Moreover, he makes them pay subscriptions for their own sake, and often pays himself if they can't afford it. He gives them sound advice, knows all about their families and asks after the children. They may not go to church often but he is their shepherd and they are his flock.

In the private bar there is usually a threadbare carpet which, like the four-ale barmaid, has spent the best years of its life in the saloon. There are a few genteel chairs, but if there are any pictures they are never noticed, for the secret drinkers, the nervous women and the porters of flats who don't want to be seen drinking by the residents tippling behind the little frosted-glass windows, never look anywhere but at the middle distance, asking for their drinks in mutters and whispers as if they were thoroughly ashamed of themselves, and guiltily stuffing bottles and flasks into pockets and bags.

This sense of shame when drinking intoxicating liquor is almost universal among the English lower middle classes, and is responsible for the fact that some of the bigger pubs have several private bars where people who have 'come down in the world,' little old ladies who fancy themselves as 'impoverished gentlewomen' and all who feel superior to those in the four-ale bar and not on easy terms with some of the flashy talkative customers in the saloon, may even avoid each other and occasionally drink in complete solitude.

The bombing of London suspended this exclusive spirit to a certain extent.  Common danger brought the classes together, and four ale-ers were allowed in the saloon without hearing the cry of 'Not this side, please.'  But the day after the last all clear had been sounded and nobody wanted to tell anybody (who would listen) of a narrow escape, they all went back to their proper places as if nothing had happened.

The feeling of guilt when drinking also makes the slogan 'Guinness is Good For You' the most subtle advertisement in the trade.  If you can persuade an Englishman that his weaknesses are good for his health you can sell him anything.

What do the people in pubs talk about?  In all the bars but the private bars, where they hardly say a word, they talk of racing, cricket, football, dogs, the weather and food.  Food as a general topic of conversation has become as popular as the weather, which is also bad.  They talk, too, of politics without bitterness, quoting their favourite editorials as if they had thought up all the arguments themselves.  In later stages of intoxication they will sometimes touch on religion, revealing a deep desire for spiritual comfort which the churches have failed to give them.  In the saloon they tell each other clean, unfunny stories if women are near, and dirty, unfunny stories if they are not.  In the four-ale bar, where the real Cockney wits drink, they don't have to rely on the commercial traveller's repertoire of second-hand jokes.  Their acid observations and lightning come-backs are spontaneous.

But in any saloon bar in London you will find an elderly character who always occupies the best seat in the corner, who maintains a non-stop monologue about himself, his friends, his family and food from opening time to closing time.

There are London pubs patronized by special people, like the one in Mayfair where gentlemen's gentlemen gather, taking the names of their employers and introducing each other as Lord Smith, or the Marquis of This and the Marquis of That.  There are the market pubs which open at five a.m. instead of the normal eleven a.m. and close when the market closes early in the afternoon.  Such is the confusion of licensing hours that there are pubs closed on one side of the street while those on the opposite side are open.

There are pubs with strange names, like The World Turned Upside Down, in the Old Kent Road, with its fifteen bars, its pin-tables, its radio and its young blondes, natural and unnatural, drinking their double whiskies like old topers.  There is the old and famous Elephant and Castle at Newington Butts, said to have been named in celebration of the discovery in 1714 of the skeleton of an elephant in a gravel pit, though the elephant with a castle on its back appears frequently in heraldry and was once the crest of the 500-year-old Cutlers' Company.

There are many Dolphins, corruption of Le Dauphin, or eldest sons of the kings of France, many Cocks, Cocks and Bottles, and even a Cock and Bull, most of them dating from the cock-fighting days; many Chequers, shield of the Warrennes, kinsmen of William the Conqueror; many Angels, like the one at Islington, sometimes named in honour of Saint Michael, the Archangel, and a large number of houses named Adam and Eve, with an inn sign showing the arms of the Fruiterers' Company.

There is The Man With a Load of Mischief, its sign showing a man bearing his wife, a monkey and a magpie on his back; the Noah's Ark, showing the crest of the Company of Shipwrights; the Hole in the Wall, which was once in Chancery Lane and got its name from a hole in the wall of the debtors' prison through which prisoners received gifts, and there is the Goat and Compasses, which most people think is a corruption of God Encompasses Us. But according to Sir Gurney Benham, an authority on heraldry and inn signs, there is not a word of truth in it. The Goat and Compasses was a beckoning sign to thirsty shoemakers and builders. The arms of the Company of Cordwainers (shoemakers) were three goats' heads. The carpenters' sign contained three compasses. In the days of wooden houses carpenters were builders. And there you have it.

Sorry to put you right.

# They Lived in Albany

## by CYRIL RAY

### drawings by Philip Gough

'YOU know the Albany—the haunt of bachelors, or of married men who try to lead bachelors' lives—the dread of suspicious wives, the retreat of superannuated fops, the hospital for incurable oddities, a cluster of solitudes for social hermits, the home of the homeless gentleman, the diner-out and the diner-in, the place for the fashionable thrifty, the luxurious lonely, and the modish morose, the votaries of melancholy, the lovers of mutton chops. He knoweth not western London who is a stranger to the narrow arcade of chambers that form a sort of private thoroughfare between Piccadilly and Burlington Gardens, guarded at each extremity by a fierce porter, or manmastiff.'

It is Marmion Savage writing, introducing the hero of his unjustly forgotten novel, *The Bachelor of the Albany*. The scene is sketched in whilst Mr Spread makes his rather circuitous way from his lodgings in Suffolk Street, along Pall Mall and up St James's Street, to call on Mr Barker, the 'man of much worth and more eccentricity, who was now growing grey in a small set of chambers in the Albany, where he led the life of a bachelor and a cynic.' Mr Spread is dressed for his West-End

walk in an ample blue body-coat
with gilt buttons, a buff waistcoat
and grey trousers; and observes in
the course of it, through his ponderous eye-glass, a political friend
dropping down to Brooks's, a caricature of Lord Brougham in a shop-
window, and a pretty woman 'on
her wicked way to expend her husband's dear-earned cash in shawls
and ribbons at Swan and Edgar's.'

Yes; it is a novel of the eighteen-
forties—the scene might be one of
those fresh, bright, London litho-
graphs of Shotter Boys's. It was in
1847 that Marmion Savage wrote
his Peacockian leg-pull of the
Oxford Movement, turning his
Albany bachelor, in the course of
it, into a 'nervous husband and a
rather fidgetty father.' A sad end
(save that there is no taking Savage
too seriously) for the first fictional
character to take up residence in
Albany.

(The first, that is, that I intend to
recognize. I live in Albany myself,
and I prefer to ignore the impudent
letter dated 'Albany, August 10,
1845' and signed 'your most obeajnt
Survnt, Fitz-James de la Pluche.'
Did Savage's Mr Barker know,
one wonders, when he took his
rooms in Albany, that he would
have James Plush as a neighbour,
Mr Thackeray's jumped-up foot-
man from Berkeley Square? Perhaps, though, he would not have
minded, would have observed
merely, in his ironic way, that
odder people were riding into
unlikelier places on the buffers of
the Railway boom.)

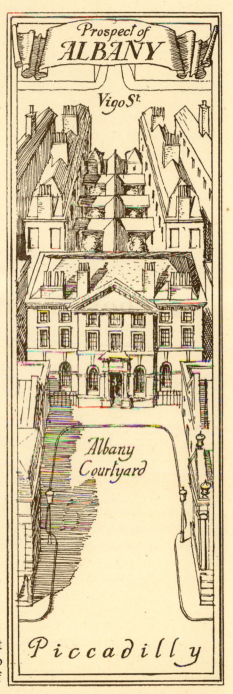

Fitz-James de la Pluche apart, Albany was acceptable enough. Lord Brougham, whose caricature was round the corner—his caricature was everywhere: what could he expect with a nose like that?—could be seen in Albany in person. Mr Macaulay was there, too, in E 1, working on his history, and observing to a friend that his address was one 'which no younger son of a duke need be ashamed to put on his card.' And at a mere ninety guineas a year, which is less, dear reader, than one pays today.

Young Mr Gladstone had been and had gone, after six Albanian years of trying to decide between Church and Law; it was more than thirty years since Lord Byron had written 'Lara' in Lord Althorp's rooms in 'the mansion,' that more sumptuous quarter of Albany at the Piccadilly end, once the Duke of York and Albany's town house, through the gardens of which the enterprising Mr Copland had built his private alley-way of bachelors' chambers. And it was forty-odd years before Mr Barker arrived in Albany that Mr Thomas Coutts had put up the money for those extensions and their covered way, 'the rope-walk,' to 'oblige His R.Hs.'

SO WE FIND, that bright frosty forenoon in 1847, an Albany already respectable and well-established. Respectable enough, in spite of Byron, and yet . . . and yet . . . There had been that odd affair of Rosina Bulwer's being forcibly removed, a screaming fury, from her husband's rooms—the same rooms that Byron had had—and from the august corridor of 'the mansion.' A mere matter, said Bulwer's friends, of her finding two tea-cups on Edward's tray—the second tea-cup waiting for Frederick Villiers. But it became, in the words of the venomous Rosina, 'I went to visit my husband in his rooms, which he kept so as to have undisturbed communion with the Muse. I found the Muse in white muslin seated on his knee.'

A slander, both on the author, wrestling with *Rienzi*, and on Albany, but a memorable enough phrase to be largely responsible, perhaps, for that faint aroma of raffishness that hangs around Albany throughout nineteenth-century fiction, mingling with the sedater airs that surround Gladstone and Macaulay and many a ponderously respectable Victorian aristocrat.

And it may be due to Rosina that Mr Barker's nearest fictional successor earns himself a thrashing in his rooms in Albany and the eighth chapter of the fourth book of *Our Mutual Friend*. But no; Fascination Fledgeby is too much to saddle on to poor Edward and Rosina. Too much, indeed, for Albany to remember without a shudder; we have his creator's word for it that he was 'the meanest cur existing

with a single pair of legs.' He is best left as Jenny Wren left him, after she had peppered the wounds left by Alfred Lammle's cane, writhing on his bed in his Persian cap and his Persian dressing-gown and crying 'Oh! how I do smart!'

Leave him, for Albany has more engaging scamps than that to boast of. None more engaging, to me, than A. J. Raffles, for it was in the first sentence of the first story about that most professional of amateur cracksmen, most accomplished of amateur cricketers, that I first came across Albany. 'It was about half-past twelve when I returned to the Albany as a last desperate resort.' What an excellent opening that is! And how evocative of place and class and—undesignedly—of period that first page; the baccarat-counters, the night fog coming through the open window, the Sullivans in Raffles's preferred cigarette-case, the 'one of his innumerable blazers' for which the very finest slow bowler of his decade had discarded his dinner-jacket.

To some it is Holmes and Dr Watson that summon up most surely the London of the years between the jubilees; the foggy, gas-lit streets, the clop and clatter of hansom-cabs. But there is a universality about the Holmes stories, as about other classics, that transcends period; a minor work can be a more precise and detailed guide, as Surtees is than Dickens. And—Baker Street, in any case: pooh! Give me Raffles and his Bunny. They lived in Albany, in the heart of it.

IT IS ALL DETECTIVES now; we have no heroes on the other side.   And
of contemporary detectives only Roger Sheringham that I know of lives
here, except for a dim character in a Phillips Oppenheim story that I can't
pin down.   Life is too short to search the canon.   One wonders how Lord
Peter or Mr Campion could have kept away from Albany—or any of those
other smooth and ever-so-cultivated young men that the women novelists
run up.   But it is better so; they'd be exacting neighbours to live up to.
Such cellars we'd need, such libraries, such dictionaries of quotations.

By modern standards, of course, Raffles is no hero, and could hardly
be classed as on the 'other side' from our pet detectives.   No killings, no
floggings, no sex, and precious little drink.   Though he must have taken
an occasional hock and seltzer; I should have looked that up.   (It is
curious, incidentally, that there have been no fictional killings here; a
body could lie for years without discovery in the blind-ended narrow
gully that divides Albany from Burlington House.   There may be
skeletons there now, for all I know, of who knows what ornaments of
the Regency.   But none flung there by an author.)

No, Raffles was a mere thief, though he stole from some of the best
addresses in England, for those were the days of country-house cricket.
And his own address was not, if I may say so, undistinguished.   One of
Albany's historians has heavily rebuked Raffles's creator for taking
liberties with the sacred buildings: the old lag Crawshay drops from
Raffles's window on to the roof of a cab in a side street: there are
apocryphal side doors in addition to the Piccadilly entrance and the North
door in Burlington Gardens; there is an office and—crowning horror!—
a clerk to show empty rooms to casual callers.   Some of which is
impossible and some unspeakable.   But for myself, I do not share Harry
Furniss's sense of outrage: Raffles is the most lovable of the men who
have lived here in books, and Albany shall be arranged the way he wants
it, even to a convenient side street where a ghostly growler waits for ever
for his shadier friends.

It is a jump of thirty years or so from Fascination Fledgeby to A. J.
Raffles.   (A short jump for the social changes that divide the age of
Dickens and Surtees from that of Hornung and Conan Doyle ; I doubt
if we have seen as much since 1917.)   But Albany was not, in the mean-
time, uninhabited.   The great scene of Besant and Rice's *The Golden
Butterfly* is played out there, in Lawrence Colquhoun's rooms.   Such
names they had, in the 'seventies !   For it is Victoria Cassilis, Lawrence's
former wife, that slips in at night, leaving her cab in Burlington Gardens;
the husband who so nearly surprises her is called Gabriel; below are the
rooms of Sir Richard de Counterpane and opposite are those of young
Lord Orlebar, where he entertains 'a few friends connected with the
twin services of the army and the ballet for a little cheerful supper.'

There is still, you will notice, about Albany in fiction, that element of aristocratic goings-on.

A dramatic scene, that in Colquhoun's rooms, and half-a-dozen years later an equally dramatic one in old Mr Scarborough's, when he chose to tell his eldest son, Captain Mountjoy Scarborough of the Coldstream Guards, that he was illegitimate, that he would never inherit Tretton Park, that the post-obits with which he had subsidized his gambling would never be honoured. It was in May 1882, in the last few months of the author's life, that the readers of Trollope—not, perhaps, quite so multitudinous as they had been—first met in the pages of *All the Year Round* that determined old pagan, Mr Scarborough, in his rooms in Albany. An earlier Trollope character, the Lord Lufton of *Framley Parsonage*, had led a quieter life here.

But one of our most distinguished residents was still to come—ten years after the last posthumous instalment of *Mr Scarborough's Family*, and fifteen or sixteen years after Victoria Cassilis had confronted Lawrence Colquhoun with 'Remember—you shall never marry Phillis Fleming! Not if I have to stop it by proclaiming my own disgrace!' It was almost, indeed, the age of Raffles, when, on May 27, 1893, the curtain rose at the St James's Theatre on 'Aubrey Tanqueray's Chambers in the Albany—a richly and tastefully decorated room, elegantly and

luxuriously furnished; on the right a large pair of doors leading into
another room, on the left at the further end of the room a small door
leading to a bedchamber.   A circular table is laid for a dinner for four
persons which has now reached the stage of dessert and coffee.   Everything in the apartment suggests wealth and refinement.   The fire is
burning brightly.'

It is into these rooms that the lady who is to be the second
Mrs Tanqueray comes, at eleven, as unexpectedly as Lawrence
Colquhoun's Victoria: at eleven—after dinner!—strong stuff in the
theatre of half a century ago.   And this, moreover, was Albany's first
appearance on any stage.

But it was to get a 'mention,' and at the same theatre, in less than two
years' time.   For on February 14, 1895, Mr Allan Aynesworth, playing
Algernon, takes up for the first time one of Mr George Alexander's cards
—he had already, you will remember, been reading Mr Alexander's
private cigarette case—and reads from it, 'Mr Ernest Worthing, B.4, The
Albany.'   And the explanation followed, 'Well, my name is Ernest in
town and Jack in the country, and the cigarette case was given to me
in the country.'   Which explained everything, as Algernon points out,
except for the fact that Jack's small Aunt Cecily, who lives at Tunbridge
Wells, calls him her dear uncle.

It was very proper that Oscar Wilde should settle his most charming
character in Albany, for Albany was the easternmost boundary of his
London.   That at any rate was what he once told a passer-by who asked
the way to Curzon Street.   'I am pleased,' he said—or so the story goes
—'that I should be asked to direct you to so eminently desirable an
address.   Personally, I am unacquainted with any part of London east
of Albany.'

Oscar enjoyed many last words—when Whistler was not about—
but not the theatre's last word on Albany.   In our own time, on Christmas Eve, 1943, in the days of the little blitz and of 'any gum, chum?'
Mr Terence Rattigan, himself a resident, opened his refresher course
on Albany, which ran in Shaftesbury Avenue until a year ago.   It was
early in the first act of *While the Sun Shines,* that the astonished Air-
Corps lootenant woke up from his all-night jag with:

'Pardon me—where am I?'
'You're in my chambers in Albany.'
'What are chambers?'
'Flat!  Apartment.'
'What's Albany?'
'It's a sort of block of chambers—apartments—off Piccadilly.'

\*     \*     \*     \*     \*

'Say, I hope I didn't disgrace you.'

'Oh, no. The porters are very discreet. They've been used to putting people to bed for well over a hundred years. Lord Byron lived here.'

'Did he now? Isn't that something? It is kind of old-world, this place, at that.'

And soon Lootenant Joe Mulvaney was telephoning Spike, 'I slept in the same bed as an earl . . . No, not a girl, stupid, an earl! E-a-r-l, earl . . . Hell, no, I wouldn't fool you, Spike. . . . Because he says he's an earl . . . Well you got to believe a guy when he says a thing like that . . . No, they don't wear crowns . . . Doesn't it slay you? . . . Well, he's young . . . you can too be an earl when you're young. Remember Little Lord Fauntleroy? . . . you're a disbelieving son of a bitch . . . A place called the Albany . . . sort of old-fashioned apartments, only the apartments are called chambers . . . Wise guy. . . . Listen, Lord Byron lived here . . . Lord Byron . . . No, he's dead, you ignorant bastard. Don't you know anything except how to drive a B.17?'

An earl, you see, and a young earl at that, and all tied up with the popsy Mabel Crum on his wedding-eve. Even one's neighbours go around perpetuating that Albany legend of high life and low living. Mr Rattigan himself, a hard working dramatist, is a more representative Albany resident; one forgives him only for the fun one gets out of Mabel Crum, Joe Mulvaney, and Able Seaman the Earl of Harpenden.

There have, though, been authors who have housed characters here not so young as Lord Orlebar, not so complicated in their love-lives as

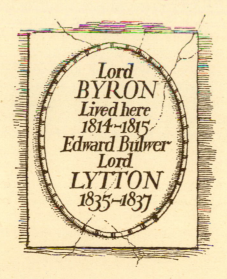

Lord Harpenden, more upright than Raffles and more likeable than Fascination Fledgeby. The man's man, Maitland, for instance, in that very early short story of John Buchan's, in whose 'ugly rooms in the Albany . . . you never saw such a collection of whips and spurs and bits.' There was more to Maitland than that, though, and he was the hero, in every sense, of the twenty-odd year old John Buchan who wrote *Fountainblue*. Lord John Roxton, too, the explorer of Conan Doyle's *The Lost World,* who took his journalist friend Vigo Street way, 'through the dingy portals of the famous aristocratic rookery,' to those rooms that 'mingled the luxury of a wealthy man of taste and the careless untidiness of the bachelor'; furs, rugs, an Oxford oar and a Leander, foils, gloves, rhinoceros heads, and the lovely Louis Quinze table scored with the marks of glasses and cigar stumps. Conan Doyle and E. W. Hornung were brothers-in-law: the one did better for Lord John in the way of pictures, with a 'sensuous Fragonard, a martial Girardet, and a dreamy Turner' among the sketches of boxers and ballet girls, than the other did for Raffles, for whom reproductions of *Love and Death* and *The Blessèd Damozel* must serve to prove that 'there has always been a fine streak of æstheticism in his complex composition.'

And it is in Prescott's rooms in Albany that the young Michael Fane of *Sinister Street* 'was immeasurably aware of the life of London that was surging such a little distance away; but in this modish cloister he felt that the life he was aware of could never be dated, as if indeed were he to emerge into Piccadilly and behold suddenly crinolines or even powdered wigs they would not greatly surprise him. The Albany seemed to have wrung the spirit from the noisy years that swept on their course outside, to have snatched from its heart and in the museum of this decorous glass arcade to have preserved it immortally, exhibiting the frozen palpitations to a sensitive observer.'

ONE FICTIONAL RESIDENT of Albany lived, so to speak, in real rooms. Arnold Bennett, who had stayed in Edward Knoblock's rooms, G 2—they had collaborated in *Milestones*—put the G. J. Hoape of *The Pretty Lady* in the same set, carefully described, and among the same furniture. 'He had furnished his flat in the Regency style of the first decade of the nineteenth century, as matured by George Smith, "upholder extraordinary to his Royal Highness the Prince of Wales." The Pavilion at Brighton had given the original idea to G. J., who saw in it the solution of the problem of combining the somewhat massive dignity suitable to a bachelor of middling age with the bright, unconquerable colours which the eternal twilight of London demands.'

That was in 1918—there are few better pictures of the London gaieties of the first Great War, of the last days of the Empire Promenade, than *The Pretty Lady*—and G. J. Hoape was ahead of his time, as Knoblock must have been, in his taste for Regency. Though nowadays we collect from that brief period rather more elegant and portable pieces than Knoblock did; when his furniture came up at Sotheby's only eighteen months or so ago it fell flat—mad though we all are for Regency—as the heaviest Regency style of all—exactly, indeed, as Bennett described it : 'the clash of rich primary colours, the perpendiculars which began with bronze girls' heads and ended with bronze girls' feet or animals' claws, the vast flat surfaces of furniture, the stiff curves of wood and of drapery, the morbid rage for solidity which would employ a candelabrum weighing five hundredweight to hold a single wax candle, produced a real and imposing effect of style; it was a style debased, a style that was shedding the last graces of the French Empire in order soon to appeal to a Victoria determined to be utterly English and good; but it was a style.'

A style indeed. Knoblock's furniture would have done for those mansion chambers in which Cosmo Hamilton put his dandy of the 'sixties, the Marquis of Alresford of *The Aunt of England,* a novel based on the play that was produced at the Savoy in 1935. Cosmo Hamilton knows his Albany, for he, too, lived here once, and Alresford, dundreary whiskers, stringless eyeglass and all, also lived in real chambers, the

K

famous A 14 set in which had lived Lord Desart, Mountstewart Elphinston, Lord Kinnaird, and Lord Lowther. It is on three floors and one of its rooms is that in which the Duke of York—before he sold Albany House to Copland—would entertain among his other friends his brother, the Regent himself, and hold cockfights, the feathers fluttering and the claret-sodden oaths re-echoing against the lofty ceiling and among the massive limbs of Regency bucks and Regency sideboards.

Is any fictional resident of Albany a match for those real-life beefy bounders in solidity and character? Not many. . . . Not Mr Barker, the progenitor of them all, for he is a peg, an argument, rather than a character in the round. Raffles, perhaps, and G. J. Hoape, though G. J.'s pleasures were so furtive: the pretty lady's, Christine's, flat was in Cork Street, and she came only once to Albany. . . . And Fledgeby and James Plush, we have agreed, are best forgotten. Myself, I have a weakness for Mr Rattigan's Lord Harpenden and Mr Compton Mackenzie's Prescott. Not for themselves, but because in their respective rooms Lootenant Joe Mulvaney and Michael Fane, each in his own way, caught something of the spirit of the place. Not that fictional naughtiness, that notion of Albany as a rookery for rogues and rakes, but the spirit that moved Mulvaney to recite—almost unconsciously—'We'll go no more a-roving,' because it was Byron's, who had lived here, and he had slept where Byron had. The spirit preserved in this 'decorous arcade,' 'exhibiting the frozen palpitations to the sensitive observer' who was Michael Fane.

'ON THE N. SIDE of Piccadilly,' says Muirhead's Guide, 'is Sackville St, long notable for being without lamp-posts. Next, on the same side, is the *Albany,* styled simply "Albany" by the quidnuncs. . . .' The style is recent, and 'quidnuncs' is delicious. We quidnuncs who live in Albany and drop its 'the,' we who live here now, in an Albany still bomb-scarred and shabby, we too—I like to think—may catch the spirit of the place. But we are writers, many of us, actors and actresses and the like, in a world of hard work and high taxation; none of us can hope, I suppose, to reflect that more gracious and more gallant spirit. Only one of my neighbours have I seen do that: that exquisitely, Edwardianly, dressed peer who at eighty-two offered to drop by parachute with food for occupied Jersey, whose victoria and pair, in 1942—the very middle year of the war—could be seen being walked round the courtyard of Albany, all of a sparkle and a shine: coachwork, harness, the horses' coats, and the coachman's cockaded top-hat.

# LONDON ASPECTS

## Eight Drawings by Francis Gower

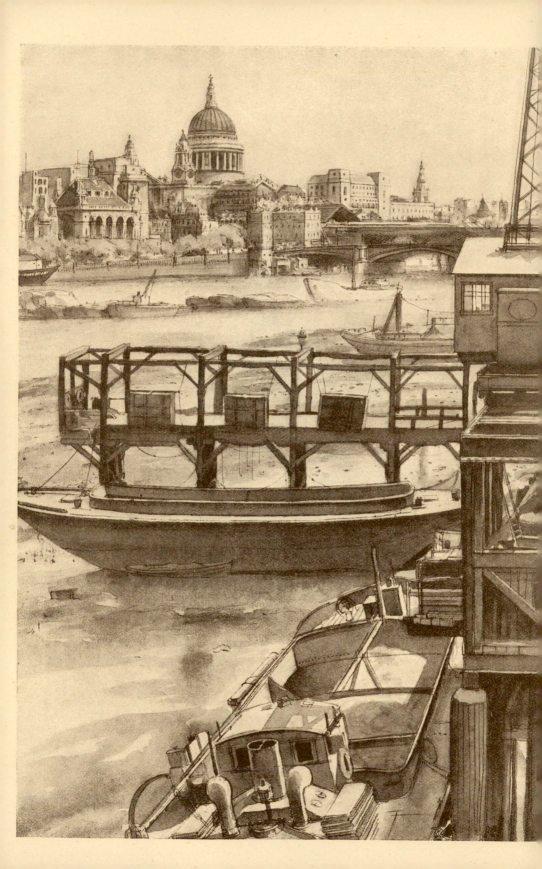

# Exhibit "A"

### by R. C. HUTCHINSON

### drawings by Ronald Searle

N the Army you meet the pleasantest men alive and you lose them; as soon as your friendship is established they get posted away and are never seen again. The other kind—the ones who waste everyone's time on courses with verbose and fatuous questions, the bullies, the bores, the bad hats—always come round again in the swirl. It was therefore no surprise when, after two years' merciful separation, I found 8064119 Dubb, W., taking care, according to his lights, of the Trans-Iranian railway.

We had left Ahwaz in the evening. The rear coach in which I travelled had been loaded higgledy-piggledy with warlike stores and other goods having, I suppose, some relation to the war—telephone switchboards, typewriters, boxes of coffee and (Heaven knows why) women's shoes—leaving only two carriages for passengers. One of them I shared with three friendly people of most agreeable manners, a little Hindu captain from Mysore, a lieutenant from Kansas, gigantic in person and good humour, and the elderly Iranian Minister for Regional Settlements; the captain's servant was in the other one, with a lance-naik of the Indore Infantry and some Persian civilians. Somewhere near midnight my uneasy dreams were penetrated by the notion that we had stopped and started to drift backwards, and I woke fully to find that we were standing still.

On that line at that period nothing a train did could be called unusual. The others were snoring; I happened to be in the worst stage of sandfly fever, which is a piffling disease but does not seem so when you have it, and there was no evident reason for me to move; but when nothing had happened for about forty minutes I was sufficiently puzzled by the stillness to stir myself and get down on the track. At the forward end of our coach my torch revealed a broken coupling; there was no sight or sound of the rest of the train.

In the brake-van at the rear I found a smell of opium and a Persian brakesman asleep on the floor; from the polite but rather discursive speech he made me before going to sleep again I gathered that the Deity had personally broken the coupling and that appropriate action would be taken by the railway authority in due course. When I returned to the carriage the opinion of my fellow-passengers, sitting in total darkness, seemed to be roughly the same. Captain Sivaji remarked that all Persians were lazy rascals. What, the lieutenant asked, could you expect in this sort of goddam country: why, in Kansas they'd have had a relief engine back and hitched on to us half an hour ago—not that couplings ever did break in Kansas. It was God's will, but a very great misfortune, the civilian said in his promiscuous but graceful English: it was absolutely essential for him to get to Tehran by next evening, and he hoped that the railway authorities would realize this. Did I know anyone among the railway authorities, he circuitously inquired, who would accept a small honorarium for hurrying the coach towards Tehran? These jerks, the lieutenant continued, could do what they liked with their goddam railroad, but if they didn't deliver the carcase of Lieutenant Oswald D. Oldenveld at Tehran some time before next sundown there would be all hell to pay and then some.

Presently I heard him sleeping again and Sivaji followed him. The Minister stayed awake, uttering little cries of agitation and despair. My own inclination was to curl up in my corner and rely on someone discovering, not too far up the line, that the train was a coach and a brake-van short. But at that time the R.E. had only just started to take over the virtual operation of the railway; native railwaymen might regard the loss of a coach or two as immaterial; and my reasons for wanting to get on with the journey were urgent enough to make me climb down once more and start to walk along the line.

I went some distance, more than a mile perhaps, always thinking that

I should come upon some post in another hundred yards. It was the enterprise of a fool—Heaven knows how far I might have walked—but I was rather lightheaded from fever, and there is a Providence which cares for fools. At the time it seemed quite natural when the cutting opened and I distinguished a small stone building beside the track. It showed no evidence of life, but a faint light leaked from the door of a ramshackle hut behind. I thumped on this and went inside.

The hurricane lamp burning dimly on a table showed immediately the evidence of British habitation: an S.M.L.E. rifle lying half-stripped on a trestle-table, webbing equipment on the drip-stove, familiar pin-ups. The stale air had English cigarette-smoke in it. But the bundle I tripped over cursed me in clear Italian and a second, when I prodded it with my toe, rolled over to reveal the face of a Kurd.

'British here?' I asked this man, and in time he got himself erect and went over to a third cocoon which I had not noticed. This, very slowly and with a wealth of oaths, unwound itself; became by degrees a man standing at something approximating attention; displayed, as I turned up the lamp and brought it nearer, features of dreadful familiarity.

I said just now that Fate looks after fools. Yes, but in a way of her own. Open-handed, she had cut short a crazy pilgrimage of what might have been twenty miles and given me a station. (Station? I didn't know, I don't know now.) She had supplied the outfit with what I most needed at that time and place, a man of my own speech. And then, with a sickening turn of humour, she had let that man be Dubb.

A very sleepy, a much surprised, a feebly grinning Dubb. *The* Dubb, once bane of an overworked C.S.M.'s existence and of mine, the C.O.'s recurring nightmare, a permanent blot upon a good battalion's reputation, immortal and incorrigible, the dim and dirty, the effeminate and sloppy, the one and only Dubb. Unchanged: with uneven strands of thick, straw-coloured hair falling about his eyes and neck, a golden stubble on what passed for his chin, the butt of a cigarette lodged on his right ear, his flabby lips parted in apologetic and canine acquiescence: the same bow-legged stance, his over-long, thin arms hanging as limply as of old. Feeling the sensations of nightmare I uttered the time-honoured imbecility, 'Hullo, Dubb, what brings you here?' and got the answer it deserved:

'Well, you see, sir, I got taken on a draft, that was when you was gone on leave, sir. Come on one of them troopships—feedin's somethin' awful on them, sir. Make y' a cup of tea, sir?'

Yes, I could do with that.

He called laconically, 'Abdul! Char! Bucky-upoh!' and the Kurd went into action with a spirit stove. 'Got put on a sort of a railway job,' he added to me.

From the War Office downwards some organization had been required to remove 8064119 Private Dubb, W., from a camp near Bridlington to where he stood now; to collect and equip the man, handle his documents, provide him with the trains, the ship, the convoy, the food he disapproved of. Of this Dubb knew nothing. He had been there, and now he was here. That was all. And it seemed to me a pity.

'Listen,' I said, 'if you're a railwayman nowadays you may be able to do something for me. I've lost a train.'

He clicked his tongue. 'Time and again I've missed trains myself, sir.'

'Not missed it—lost it. The train's gone on and left my coach behind —down the line there. Coupling broke.'

He clicked his tongue again. 'What train would that be, sir?'

'Well, it left Ahwaz at 8.24.'

'But there isn't a train at that time, sir.'

'Whether there is or there isn't, there was. And it must have passed through here about an hour ago.'

'I didn't see no *train*, sir,' he said, as if I were inquiring about a herd of giraffes in top hats and crinolines.

'Whether you saw it or not, I want to get it back,' I told him. 'Or rather, I want to get a locomotive. Can you get on to Dorud or somewhere and tell them what's happened?'

He thought it most unlikely that he could get on to Dorud. But there was, he confessed, some sort of a telephone in the office ('only it's a Persian job, if you see what I mean') which was meant to connect him with Dusaband. ('Only the sergeant there, he don't much like being called up at this hour.') I dismissed the sergeant's sensibilities, and Dubb, till then in shirt and pants, produced a grimy bush shirt and drill slacks from under his bedding and put them on, adding a battered topee: the temperature at that hour and altitude must have been below freezing-point, but there had been a Command Order that summer dress was to be worn from the first of that month, and this particular order Dubb had chosen to carry out. I noticed with horror that the arm of the crumpled shirt was dignified by a lance corporal's stripe. We took the lamp and crossed over to the stone building, where an aged Persian in some kind of railway uniform was snoring on the office desk.

'Did you see a train go through, Ammid?' Dubb asked him.

The Persian made the noises of one disturbed in sleep.

'He says he didn't see no train either,' Dubb told me reproachfully.

'Get on with the job,' I said.

He knelt on a form and addressed himself to an apparatus of the kind one's son makes after reading *The Boys' Own Book of Indoor Games and Hobbies*. I cleared a part of the table behind him to sit on, and while he laboured the memory of his transgressions passed before me like a documentary film: While On Active Service being absent without leave, losing by neglect one respirator, anti-gas, damaging through neglect one rifle, neglecting to clean his billet, being late on parade, appearing on parade 'in a filthy condition, sir.' And ah, God, if C.S.M. Barnett could have seen the 'office' we were in now! In my experience the British soldier on a lonely job becomes exceptionally tidy; isolation somehow promotes self-esteem and a care for the small decencies of living. To this, as to every other rule, Dubb was the exception. Railway schedules mixed up with *Picture Posts*, Company Detail and letters from home, boots and pullthroughs and disintegrating socks were scattered about the room in a chaos suggesting the tenancy of orang-utans.

'Goin' to have a bit of a tidy-up tomorrer,' he remarked, as if he felt my thoughts through the back of his neck. 'Only you can't seem to get no cleaning stuff.' (In what past life had I heard those words?) He went on cranking the machinery. 'Ullo . . . ullo . . . ullo. . . .' He pushed the topee still further back, lit the cigarette stub and got into a more comfortable position. I recalled that in civvy street he had been a baker's roundsman and as he sat now I could picture him half asleep in his van: how often, I wondered, had he set out in the morning without the bread and been obliged to go back for it? 'Somethin' wrong with the wire, I shouldn't wonder. There is, more often than not. *Ullo . . . Ullo. . . . .*'

The door towards the line opened. My friends had grown bored or anxious, perhaps they had found the carriage too cold, and here they were, Sivaji's bearer and the lance-naik as well, all rubbing their frozen hands and muttering and blinking. A few flakes of snow followed them into the room. 'Is this where we get any action?' Oldenveld wanted to know. There was action from the Kurd, who had brought in the tea; he disappeared and returned smiling with the Italian prisoner, the kettle, two mugs, five N.A.A.F.I. cups and a couple of mess-tins: not in the War Office itself had I seen so much tea being slopped about. For another ten minutes, but with less visible optimism than the priests of Baal, Dubb went on cranking and ullo-ing.

The Minister for Regional Settlements approached me with diplomacy: I fancy he had a 500-rial note crunched in his hand and with the smallest encouragement would have slipped it into mine.

'You will make him understand, if you please, that my business is impotent? There is vitality for me to reach at Tehran. Please, yes!'

'That's what he's telling them,' I said.

I had rather lost interest. While the rest were frozen I was sweating, and things in the crowded room were starting to float and bob. 'Action,' Oldenveld was saying again and again. 'I don't want any more char, I want action!' while the Kurd and the Italian stood in line with the Persian railwayman, holding fresh cups and equably smiling.

'Dubb!' I said. 'Is there any back door to this place? I mean, is there any road to it, any vehicle, donkeys?'

It took him a few moments to get out of the trance in which his own voice had wrapped him.

'There's nothing only the truck the old Wog got, along by the quarry. You never saw such a thing. Had it for a contractin' job, makin' the railway. Dirty? Strewth! Fallin' to bits. The Wog ain't clean himself, neither.'

'I don't mind about the Wog. Where could he take us if he could take us anywhere?'

'Well, there's nothing like what you'd call a road. A track, you might call it. Get washed away whenever the floods come. Join up with the Ammydam road in the end—if it keep goin' at all, see what I mean. Sometimes it do and sometimes it don't. I could see the bloke for you, sir, only he's not a bloke that goes in for night work. Might be eighty by the looks of him. Not much more left of him than there is of the truck.'

'Rout him out!' I said. 'Tell him the Prime Minister of Persia requires him to report instantly with truck. But first put on your greatcoat—it's snowing.'

'Well, if you don't mind, sir, I cleaned the buttons on Sunday, sir. I wouldn't like to have them out in the snow, if it's all the same to you, sir.'

'All right. Only buck up!'

Sivaji, who was shivering all over, poor fellow, furiously ordered his bearer to shut the door which Dubb had left wide open and then, turning to Oldenveld, resumed the gentle and cultured voice in which he had discoursed to me on Shelley and Keats from Ahwaz to Andimeshk. 'You see, it is always the same. The Persians are a poor race, but they build for themselves a great railway-line and it works. The English come, the Persians are pushed out of the way—and then nothing works. The train breaks in half. The signalling apparatus will not function any more. What do the English do? Nothing. "That," they say, "is the affair of the Persians" ' (he turned one sympathetic eye upon the Minister) ' "—what are native peoples for but to remedy the results of our own inefficiency!" Of course, I'm not talking about any gentleman present,' he added courteously. 'Once the English were a strong race; they were cruel and treacherous, but they were virile, self-reliant. Do you find such Englishmen now?'

Of the article he referred to only two samples were in the vicinity: one had sandfly fever and the other was Dubb. I decided not to join in the discussion.

'Now these,' my friend continued, turning his head, 'what have the English done, what will the English ever do for them?'

Guiltily following his glance, I found there were three more souls in the room than I had realized—I had not seen them come in, or particularly noticed them on the train: three children, Bakhtiari by the look of them; barefoot, each clothed in what we should call a nightgown, dark grey with many seasons' dirt, and probably nothing else. Children? Two were toddlers; the third was perhaps fifteen, but there was not the slightest doubt about her condition and it looked to me as if her time was close. While her sisters hung whimpering to her skirts she was talking in a scared, persistent fashion to the porter, who presently made a decorous approach to the Minister. The Minister turned to me.

'You will excuse, please, the man says the female says she must reach to her grandmother in Tehran. The grandmother will be appalling with anxious, and there is high vitality for medico treating in Tehran. For me also there is largest vitality to reach to Tehran.'

'Poor little bees!' Oldenveld said.

'It is of no interest to the English,' Sivaji commented very gently, with just a quarter of one eye on me, 'whether the little girl gets to Tehran or whether she dies.'

I was saved from the duty of answering the Minister by the sound of three ear-splitting explosions. They were followed by a noise like that of a reaper-and-binder, of several reaper-and-binders working together, which grew until the little building shook with it and then petered into silence. Dubb reappeared.

'Very sorry, sir, couldn't make the ole bloke hear me. Had to do a bit of scroungin'—borrowed his truck. Thought you might like to go

down to the Ammydam road, sir—might pick up a convoy down there.'

I told him I was not up to driving on a mountain track I didn't know, at night and with this bug on me.

'Drive you m'self, if it's all the same to you, sir.  Antonio, here, he can mind this joint.  There ain't nothing in it now the phone's packed up, he's only got to keep a tally on the trains, an' there won't be none of them, most likely.  Only take an hour, sir.'

I put the matter to the others: they could stay where they were and wait for something to happen, or they could take a chance on reaching the main road and picking up some kind of transport which might get them on to Hamadan.  They went outside and surveyed the truck, an affair of Detroit origin and some 30-cwt capacity, with local improvements: it was perhaps fifteen years of age, and looked as if a tap from a hammer would cause it to fall into quite small bits.  Was this soldier an efficient driver, the Minister inquired.  This soldier had won prizes for driving, I assured him.  Was the road perfectly safe?  Perhaps a little rough by Tehran standards, I said.  They were still debating while Dubb coaxed the engine into a new convulsion, and then they decided to go.

'Got one of the side lamps goin',' Dubb told me with satisfaction. 'Manage with that, I reckon.  Headlamps been pinched—blokes round these parts got no notion of right and wrong, sir.'  Then, 'Oy!' he suddenly said.

The Minister had taken the spare seat in the driver's cab.  Dubb said 'Oy!' once again and made a gesture with his thumb.  The Minister sadly but without protest moved himself to the back.  In a casual fashion Dubb picked up the eldest Persian girl, placed her in the comparatively comfortable seat, dumped the toddlers on and about her and wrapped the whole bundle in an Army blanket.  'Do best hold on at the corners—the truck ain't what she was,' he advised the passengers at large; then relit his cigarette, spat, pushed his topee further back, took his seat and let in the clutch.

My recollection of that journey is fragmentary and dream-like.  As the truck, leaping and plunging, hurled us about like dice in a box I had glimpses of a cliff-face coming straight at my eyes, of vertical drops which seemed to start directly below our wheels.  Sometimes I found myself on top of Sivaji, who crouched face-downwards on the floorboards, sometimes my head knocked against his bearer's or against the sharp shoulder of Oldenveld, who was gasping 'Gorrer-*mighty*—would *you* say—*gorrormighty*!'  Huddled and bouncing like a ping-pong ball, the Minister too seemed to be in prayer.  Occasionally I caught sight of Dubb's head turned towards me and through the shattering din I once or twice caught his voice: 'Road want something done to it . . . bit of a close one, that was!'  When this confused experience had lasted through most of eternity the truck gave a sharper twist than any which had gone before, nose-dived, sprang up again and went into a starboard list which brought Sivaji on top of me and my own face within inches of the ground. Like that it came to rest.

'Sorry about that, sir,' I heard Dubb say. 'Weren't really fit fer the road, this truck, brakes are U-S. Better climb out the other side, sir. Bit of a drop there is, this side.'

That was correct: beyond the side-board of the truck there was a foot or less of slatey rock; beyond that the Hamadan road, 150 feet below.

'Pity we couldn't quite make it, sir,' Dubb said.

Yet we seemed, in a fashion, to be under a lucky star; for when we had done the remaining half-mile of hairpin bends on foot and reached the main road there were lights approaching: a convoy of 10-tonner Mack-Diesels, a dozen or perhaps twenty of them, grinding steadily through the narrow pass. That was as far as our luck went. Oldenveld stood as far out in the road as he dared, bellowing at one after the other; we waved, we pleaded, we imprecated. In the light I flashed from my torch I had glimpses of the faces of Indian drivers, dutiful, impassive. Not one of them would stop.

We sat down on the boulders which lined the road, and presently that shapeless, toneless voice of Dubb's was in my ears again: 'Very hard to make anything stop—they think it's tribal blokes trying to hold 'em up, the way they do, sir. Not without we was to put something big in the road, a bit o' rock like that you're sittin' on now.'

The rock weighed, at a guess, four and a half tons. I said: 'You can, if you like. Not me.'

A little later he was climbing up the cliff, taking a short-cut back to the truck; he had, I supposed, forgotten his cigarettes or his pay-book.

'What a country!' Oldenveld had started again. 'Trains run when they like or don't if they don't like. Break in half and no notice taken, no complaints and no action. Look at this road, now: back where I come from——'

'My country,' said the Minister, 'is one of high misfortune. We have an industrious that is second to nobody in the world. We have an aspiration of the highest and up to date, we work, we struggle, we labour. Always the foreigner come to put down and destroy. Today I have business of the highest vitality. I ask only for the train or the auto to take me to Tehran. In the train I have the part which does not go. In the auto is the driver which does not stop.'

By way of example, a second convoy went by.

At least the snow had passed, leaving the sky clear. Around us, as the light broke, there grew a scene more fabulous than any I had witnessed in four continents: a giants' chamber of receding and overtopping walls hewn out in every shape that the most diverse body of sculptors might conceive, in boldly slanting planes, in fluted bastions, gothic verticals, extravagant arabesques; and as these turned variously from black to smoky grey, from grey to silver and reddish brown, a vast steeple of snow which overlooked them all was catching from the hidden sun a film of delicate mauve which passed to vermilion, to deep rose, to the subtlest green and then to flaming gold. Exhausted as I was, I drank from this stupendous and tranquil mystery of light an enchantment which lasts till now. I said sleepily to the Minister:

'If it had nothing else, your country would at least possess a beauty which defies all comparison.'

'It is capital that we do not possess,' he answered without looking up. 'Without capital a nation can do nothing. And without a vehicle I cannot reach at Tehran.'

'The Indian driver does not stop,' Sivaji was saying—and I thought again how beautiful his soft and delicately modulated voice was—'because the soul of India has been submerged. When Indians are free, there will be none, I say not one, who will ever pass by a needy traveller.' And a few minutes later he was saying, 'That is what the English philosophers themselves have preached, the great law of charity towards those in distress; preached, but never practised—because the soul of the English themselves has been atrophied by the lust for power and wealth.'

'Just one little, little morsel of action,' Oldenveld murmured, half asleep, 'give me for the love of old Abe one tiny particle of action!'

In the steadily lightening scene a new and more abrupt change took place. The truck which had brought us, just visible from where we sat, had looked like a permanent part of it: at the very lip of the precipice she had lain on her side, reposefully, like those who have died honourable deaths. But now she stirred, hesitated for a moment as a nervous diver does, and then in a series of strangely agile somersaults plunged down on to the road. A boss of granite which she struck in her descent came after her like Mary's lamb; and when the cloud of dust had settled, the roadway, which for all its roughness had been clear of major obstacles, was neatly barred across by six or seven tons of twisted steel and rock. Presently Dubb was at my side.

'Sorry about all them boulders, sir. Never thought all that stuff would come down—I jus' tipped the old truck over with the jack and I thought she'd fall by herself. Still, it makes a road-block all right, don't it, sir?'

'Yes,' I said, 'it makes a road-block. It makes a road-block which it will need twenty or thirty men to shift. Putting it another way, you've blocked the road for perhaps three days. I am supposed to be in Qum in a few hours' time, this gentleman who is a member of the Iranian Government has the most urgent business in Tehran, so has the American officer, and the captain here. All those important appointments have been finally knocked on the head. And apart from throwing the whole Aid to Russia convoy programme out of gear that's all the difference your little act has made.'

'It's these kids what's bothering me,' Dubb said with a trace of unhappiness, nodding towards the three Persian children, who lay on the roadside huddled together and asleep. 'That big one, she's in a bad way. Should've reported sick days ago, if you ask me. Still,' he said more cheerfully, 'those lorry blokes won't go past without stopping any more.'

If there was any difficulty in following his reasoning it was removed by the appearance of a truck which came swaying and bouncing towards us at 35, lurched round the bend and stopped at the barrier in a long, zig-zag skid. It was a truck similar to the one which now lay in wreckage on the road, and not—to the casual eye—in much better repair; on it, somehow, were heaped not fewer than forty people, very old men, cripples, women with babes in arms, children of all ages, as well as chickens, goats, and at least one donkey foal. ('Come from Curbeller, most likely,' was Dubb's comment. 'Go there for their religion. Rum, if you ask me.') These slowly, and with no trace of annoyance, disentangled themselves from the truck and fell into groups at the roadside, where some stood amiably gossiping and some lay down to sleep.

Our next visitor was of a rather different cast.

His vehicle was probably of the same horse-power, but with seats for only four: an American saloon with the bows of a submarine and headlamps like aero engines, immense, immaculate, and stinking of cash; and the uniform of its single passenger—the pressed and spotless tunic with its splendid epaulettes and several rows of decorations, the burnished high boots—made me feel as Dubb might have felt if he had been granted the power of feeling, a ragamuffin of the seediest type. Hardly less point-device was the driver, who left the car with its nose to the tail of the pilgrims' truck and came to me.

'Colonel Ustusov wishes to speak to you, Major.'

'Although I am rather troubled with fever, I should be most happy to see the colonel.'

'He wishes you to come to his auto.'

'I await the colonel with the greatest eagerness,' I said.

In the end he came: a colonel in fairly unreliable humour; and with the others grouped about us we held converse through the interpretation of the driver, whose shaky American was helped out by rapid and admirable French. Rapid, but hardly rapid enough; for although our talk lasted for some forty minutes, and Ustusov kept the bowling almost entirely to himself, that length of time hardly sufficed for all that he apparently needed to say. Like the others, Ustusov had business in Tehran; but this

was business compared with which the business of the others was mere
foolery; in brief (and he was by no means brief) the successful prosecution
of the war depended entirely on the early if not the immediate arrival of
Colonel Ustusov in the capital.  He was being held up by incompetent
management of the roadway.  The British were responsible for the
roadway.  I was the only British officer present, and I was therefore responsible for removing the obstacle to his passage: my
failure to have done so already was characteristic of a British incom-
petence and deliberate obstructionism with which Ustusov was painfully
familiar.  The whole matter was going to be reported to the colonel's
G.O.C., to the British G.O.C. North Persia Area, to the British Embassy.
The report would unquestionably be transmitted to Moscow and from
there, with observations at the highest level, to London. . . .
   With the sun already high enough to be a burden, the fever running at
high voltage through all the veins between my stomach and temples, I

was unequal to these civilities, or even to keeping fully awake. I offered the man, from time to time, a cigarette; I spoke of my profound admiration for the Army he represented; and I remarked, in the end, that if he could find a force of a hundred able-bodied workmen for removing the obstruction I should be happy to give the necessary orders.

'Only,' I said, and the driver translated, 'to the best of my knowledge and belief there are not as many as six men of that kind within a hundred miles of us, unless they be Lurish tribesmen who would shortly settle the matter for us both by removing the tyres of your car and then cutting all our throats.'

And there I was extremely wrong. Where the road showed again half a mile ahead and at a higher level I saw what I took to be mirage of a kind common enough in those parts and particularly at that hour of the day: the semblance of a long, straggling line of men coming towards us on foot. But Dubb was never an ingredient of mirage, and the foremost of this party, as it approached, was unmistakably Dubb: behind him, ragged, acquiescent, smiling with all the seductive charm of their race, the male population (I should have said) not of one village but of two or three, with the usual cohort of children trailing after them like the tail of a kite.

It was a moment not without drama: even Ustusov was smitten with silence. But Dubb himself was unequal to the central rôle. Unkempt and repulsively dirty, hands in pockets, a cigarette stuck to his underlip, he was wandering along with an invertebrate, civilian slouch that violated the whole, long, proud tradition of the British Army. When he reached the barrier he merely stopped and caught the aged man who came just behind him by the arm; made two gestures, one with his thumb at the débris, one with his chin towards the ravine which lay below the road; and with that, washing his hands of the whole affair, sauntered on to stand with his back to the colonel and continue his talk with me.

'Blokes what used to work on making the railway. Told 'em this was a government job, "Shah makee muchee trouble," I said—that's right, ain't it, sir—these blokes do have a Shah?' Then, musingly, 'Hard on them kids, all this, ain't it, sir!'

It was at this point, when Ustusov had not yet recovered his rhetorical powers, that I saw no further advantage in struggling against the weariness which fever and a sleepless night had laid upon me. I got down beside the boulder on which I had been sitting, made a pillow of my greatcoat and let my eyes fall shut.

When I woke, perhaps an hour later, I saw Ustusov holding a conversation of gestures and polyglot phrases with the men who had shared my carriage. His driver had returned to the car. It was not hard to guess that my friends were trying for seats; I noticed that the Minister was fingering his notecase in an idle fashion and I thought I could detect between his face and the colonel's profile an incipient understanding. That was no affair of mine, and it seemed a little improbable that Ustusov liked me well enough to choose me as a passenger. I slipped away quietly and went up the road to the block.

A miracle had been achieved there. The ruined truck appeared to have been sheared in half, a part of it was down in the ravine and already there was a passage some four feet broad. With the shifting of one giant boulder, on which a score of men were shoving and sweating now, the space would be wide enough at least for Ustusov's car to get past. I looked about for Dubb and found him talking to the colonel's driver.

'. . . Tehran, British hospital,' I heard him say with the loud and pedantic emphasis that the ignorant use for the insane. '*British* hospital, comprenny?   Then—drive H.Q. and wait for colonel.   Got savvy? Colonel—say—you—go—quick.   No stop.   Muchee speed—colonel's orders—savvy?'

The grunts and excited cries of the improvised labour force were increasing in volume: with some cunning they were using a member from the truck's chassis as a lever, they had the boulder rocking and then toppling.  It turned half a somersault, they shoved the truck's tailboard in to prevent it falling back, and with the fury that Persian labourers can show on their best days a dozen of them hurled themselves against it. It rocked and toppled again, they swarmed upon it afresh, in four seconds more it had completed the second somersault with half its base projecting over the outside edge of the berm.  With a certain dignity, a sense of occasion, the elderly foreman walked up to it alone and pushed it with his hands.

'Mind, muchee quickee!' I heard Dubb say, and then all sound was hidden by the boulder's crash into the ravine.  Ustusov's car shot forward, scattering the workmen from the six-foot gap they had so stalwartly cleared.  The seat beside the driver was empty; but when I glanced into the rear compartment I just caught sight of the puzzled faces of three small Persian girls.  Hearing the first of Ustusov's yells emerge from the engine's roar, and wishing, for reasons purely of prestige, to avoid the spectacle of an Allied officer tearing a British soldier limb from limb, I allowed myself to disappear among the crowd.

Twenty minutes later, when I returned circumspectly to the spot, the gap had been widened by another two feet; the driver of the pilgrim's truck was cranking his engine and the pilgrims were laboriously piling themselves on board.  I glanced about for any recognizable remains of Dubb and saw him standing beside the driver's cab, displaying a weak and foolish grin as he shoved a 100-rial note in the pocket of his bush-shirt.  The spare-seat in the cab was occupied by the Minister.  I called out, 'Dubb, come here!' but evidently he failed to hear me. He ambled round to the back of the truck, where I saw a hand come out with another 100-rial note: immediately above the hand, and packed like the heart of a lettuce in a tight cluster of dark and grimy faces, the defeated, resigned and reluctantly grateful face of an Allied colonel.

As the truck rattled away Dubb continued the desultory conversation with me which seemed to have gone on all through my lifetime.

'Couldn't have you in with all them Wogs, sir—dirty lot, they are, you don't know what you might pick up. There'll be the E.L.S. truck coming up in less than half an hour now, proper driver an' all, you'll be all right an' hotsy-totsy on that, sir. Bit of a squeeze to get 'em on that truck,' he said reflectively. 'Easy enough, them three Indians, it was the Yank what took up all the room.' He broke off to shout at the working party, who after their latest effort had fallen into somnolent chatter. 'Oy! Shah say Work—muchee quickee! Make all road hotsy-totsy for Major-sahib!' And then to me again, 'Well, if you don't mind, sir, oughter be gettin' back now. That Antonio might be gettin' all mixed up on the job, them Eye-Ties don't have no idea how to organize. Got to get the Wogs on at tidyin' the billet—have to keep at 'em, you know, sir, blokes what've got no notion of civilization. Honky-tonk, sir!'

With the ghastly topee slung on his arm he gave me that deplorable jerk of thumb to cheek which was the best salute we had ever managed to teach him; once more relit his cigarette and, leaving me to think what I should say to D.A.D. Claims about this business, shuffled off, bareheaded in the now ferocious sun, five-feet-three-inches of ineradicable contempt for the King's Regulations, to begin the twenty-mile tramp back to the place where he supervised His Britannic Majesty's affairs.

Ronald Searle

# The Major of Hussars

## by H. E. BATES

THAT summer we lived in the hotel on the lake below the mountains, and Major Martineau, the Major of Hussars, lived on the floor below us, in a room with a eucalyptus tree on the balcony.
The weather was very hot and in the sunlight the lake sparkled like crusty golden glass and in the late afternoon the peaks of the Blümlisalp and the whole range of the Jungfrau glistened in the fine mountain air with fiery rosy snow. The major was very interested in the mountains and we in turn were very interested in the major, a spare spruce man of nearly sixty who wore cream shantung summer suits and was very studious of his appearance generally and very specially of his smooth grey hair. He also had three sets of false teeth of which he was very proud: one for mornings, one for evenings, and one for afternoons.
We used to meet the major everywhere: on the terrace, where lunch was served under a long pergola of crimson and cream-white roses and from which you got a magnificent view of the snowcaps; and then under the dark shade of chestnut trees on the lake edge, where coffee was served; and then at the tram terminus, where the small yellow trams started

their journeys along the hot road of the lake; and then on the white steamers that came up and down the lake, calling at all the little towns with proud peeps of the funnel whistle, several times a day. At all of these places there was the major, very spruce in cool shantung and always wearing the correct set of false teeth for the time of day, looking very correct, very English and, we thought, very alone.

It must have been at the second or third of these meetings that he told us of his wife. 'She'll be out from England now any day.' And at the fifth or sixth that he told us of his false teeth. 'After all one has several suits. One has several pairs of shoes. All excellent for rest and change. Why not different sets of teeth?' It did not occur to me then that the teeth and his wife had anything to do with each other.

Sometimes as we walked along the lake we could see a figure marching briskly towards us in the distance.

'The major,' I would say.

'It can't be,' my wife would say. 'It looks much too young.'

But always, as he came nearer, we could see that it was the major, sparkling and smart and spruce with all the shine and energy of a younger man. 'Sometimes you'd take him for a man of forty,' my wife would say.

Whenever we met on these occasions we would talk briefly of the major's wife; then of the lake, the food, the delicious summer weather, the alpine flowers, the snow on the mountains and how we loved Switzerland. The major was very fond of them all and we got the impression, gradually, that his wife was very fond of them, too.

'Ah!' he would say, 'she will adore all this. She will simply adore it.' His correct blue eyes would sparkle delightfully.

'And when do you expect her?'

'Well,' he would say, 'in point of fact she was to have been here this week. But there seems to have been some sort of hitch somewhere. Bad staff work.'

'I hope she'll soon be able to come.'

'Oh! any day now.'

'Good. And oh! by the way,' I said, 'have you been up to the Jungfrau yet? The flowers are very lovely now on the way up.'

'The Virgin?' the major would say. 'Oh! not yet. I'm leaving all the conquest of that sort of thing till my wife gets here,' and he would laugh very heartily at the joke he made.

'It's just as well,' I said.

But the next day, on the steamer, we saw the major making a conquest of the girl who brought the coffee. She had a beautiful Swiss head, with dark coiled hair, and she was wearing a very virginal Bernese bodice in black and white and a skirt striped in pink and blue. She was very young and she laughed very much at whatever it was the major was saying to her. On the voyage the major drank eight cups of coffee and ate four ham rolls. There was so much ham in the rolls that it hung over the side like pink spaniel's ears, and the major had a wonderful time with his afternoon false teeth, his best pair, champing it in.

'The major is conquering the Jungfrau,' I said.

'You take a low view of life,' my wife said. 'He's alone and he's simply being friendly.'

'Queer how he doesn't notice us today.'

It was true that the major did not notice us; he did not notice us in fact for two days and I wondered if I had said something to offend him. But when at last we met him again under the chestnut trees at noon, with a glass of lager at his table in the shade, he seemed more friendly, more sparkling and more cheerful than ever. The yellow beer, the cream shantung suit and the gleaming white teeth were all alight with the trembling silver reflections that sprang from the sunlight on the water.

'Any news of your wife?' we said.

'Coming today!'

We said we were very pleased. 'What time?'

'Coming by the afternoon boat. Gets in at three.'

He looked at the lake, the roses on the terrace, the blue-grey eucalyptus tree shining on the balcony of his room and then at the vast snows towering and glistening beyond the lake. 'I can't tell you how she will adore all this,' he said. 'I can't tell you.'

'I'm sure she will,' we said. 'You must be very excited.'

'Just like a kid with a toy!' he said. 'You see, I came out first to arrange it all. Choose the place. Choose the hotel. Choose everything. She doesn't know what she's coming to. You see? It's all going to be a great surprise for her.'

'Don't forget you have to conquer the Jungfrau,' I said. 'The soldanella are wonderful above the Scheidegg now.'

'Of course,' he said. 'Well, I must go. Perhaps you'd join us for an *apéritif* about six? I do very much want you to meet her.'

We said we should be delighted and he went singing away up to the hotel.

'Your remark about the Jungfrau was very pointed,' my wife said.

'I saved it with the soldanella,' I said.

'Anyway, be careful what you say tonight,' she said.

FROM THE LOWER TERRACE we could watch the steamers come and go. The afternoon was very hot and we stayed under the dark shade of the chestnut trees to watch the three o'clock boat come in. Among the hotel porters with their green and plum coloured and scarlet and brown caps and uniforms the major stood out, in cool spruce shantung, as a very English, very conspicuous visitor on the quay.

When the white steamer came up the lake at last, tooting in the hot afternoon air, the major had taken up his stand in front of all the porters, by the water's edge. I got up and leaned on the railings of the terrace to get a better view.

The steamer came swinging in with a ring of engine-room bells, with six or seven passengers waiting by the gangway.

'There she is,' I said.

'Where?' My wife had come to stand beside me.

'The lady with the green case,' I said. 'Standing by the captain. She looks about the major's age and about as English.'

'She looks rather nice—yes,' my wife said, 'it could be.'

The steamer bounced lightly against the quay and the gangway came down. The hotel porters adjusted their caps and the passengers began to come ashore. In his eagerness the major almost blocked the gangway.

To my astonishment the lady with the green case came down the gang-way and went straight past the major, and the porter from the *Hotel du Lac* raised his green and gold cap and took the case away from her. The major was looking anxiously up the gangway for the figure of his wife, but in less than two minutes all the passengers had come down. When the steamer moved away again the major was standing on the quay alone, still staring anxiously and still waiting for the wife who had not come.

That evening we went down to the terrace for the *apéritif* with the major. 'For goodness' sake don't make that joke about the Jungfrau,' my wife said. 'He'll be in no mood for that.' The five o'clock steamer had come in but the major's wife had not arrived.

'It's his joke,' I said. 'Not mine.'

'You twist it round,' she said.

On the terrace the major, dressed in a dark-grey suit and with his evening false teeth in, had an appearance of ebullient gaiety. He had a peculiar taste in drinks and drank four or five glasses of Kirsch because there was no whisky, and after it he did not seem so tired.

'Met a friend in Paris,' he explained to us. 'Amazing coincidence.' He kept waving a rather long telegram about in front of us. 'Hadn't seen this friend for years and then suddenly ran into her. Of course it's only a night. She'll be here on Thursday.'

Three weeks went past but the major's wife did not arrive. The best of the roses by that time were over on the terrace and long salmon-scarlet lines of geraniums were blooming there instead. In the beds behind the chestnut trees there were purple petunias with interplantings of cherry-pie and in the hot still evenings the scent of them was delicious against the cool night-odour of water. 'It's a pity for her to be missing all this,' we said.

Now when we met the major we avoided the subject of his wife. We went on several excursions to the mountains, and sometimes on the steamers the major was to be seen on the first-class deck champing with his false teeth at the spaniel-eared ham sandwiches and drinking many cups of coffee. As he talked to the Swiss girl who served him he laughed quite often. But I did not think he laughed so much. I thought in a way he seemed not only less happy and less laughing, but more alone. He had stopped making explanations and I thought he seemed like a man who had given up hoping.

AND THEN IT ALL began again. This time she was really coming. There had really been some awful business of a hold-up about her visa. It had taken a long time. It was all over now.

'She'll be here on Sunday,' the major said. 'Absolutely certain to be on that boat that gets in at three.'

The Sunday steamers were always crowded, their decks gay with Swiss families going up the lake for the day, with tourists going to Interlaken. The little landing stages at the lake-side resorts were always crowded too. There were many straw hats and Bernese bodices and much raising of caps by hotel porters.

So when the steamer arrived this time there was no picking out Mrs Martineau. Crowds of Sunday holiday-makers stood on the steamer-deck and pushed down the gangway and more crowds stood on the quay waiting to go on board. Under the trimmed lime-trees of the quay-side restaurant the Sunday orchestra was playing and people at little gay white tables were drinking coffee. It was a very simple, very laughing, very bourgeois, very noisy afternoon.

On the quay the major waited in his bright afternoon shantung suit, with his best teeth in.

'There she is,' I said.

'You said that last time,' my wife said.

'You can see her waving, and the major is waving back.'

'Several people are waving.'

'The lady in the grey costume,' I said. 'Not the one with the sun-glasses. The one waving the newspaper.'

At the steamer rails an amiable, greyish Englishwoman of sixty was waving in a nice undemonstrative sort of way to someone on shore. Each time she waved I thought the major waved back.

'Anyway,' my wife said, 'let's go round and meet her.'

We walked up through the hotel gardens and across the bridge over the stream that came down and fed the lake with green snow water from the mountains. It was very hot. The sun-blinds in the hotel were like squares of red and white sugar candy in the sun, and in the hot scented gardens under the high white walls almost the only thing that seemed cool was the grey eucalyptus tree growing on the balcony of the major's room. I had always rather envied the major the eucalyptus tree. Even the steamer whistle seemed stifled as it peeped the boat away.

'Now mind what you say,' my wife said. 'No references to any jungfrau.'

'If she's that very English lady with the newspaper I shall like her,' I said.

Just at that moment we turned the corner of the kiosk that sold magazines and post cards of alpine flowers, and the lady with the newspaper went past us, arm in arm with another English lady carrying a wine-coloured parasol.

My wife did not take advantage of this situation. At that moment she became, like me, quite speechless.

Up from the landing stage the major was coming towards us with his wife. She staggered us. She was a blonde-haired girl of twenty-five, wearing a very smart summer suit of white linen with scarlet cuffs and revers with lipstick of the same colour. I do not know what it was about her, but even from that distance I could tell by the way she walked, slightly apart from the major and with her head up, that she was blazingly angry.

'A Jungfrau indeed,' I said.

'Be quiet!' my wife said. 'They're here.'

A moment or two later we were face to face with them. The major had lost his habitual cool spruceness, I thought, and looked harassed and upset about something and seemed as if he would have gone past us, if possible, without speaking.

Instead he stopped and raised his hat. His manners were always very correct and charming and now they seemed painfully so.

'May I present Mrs Martineau?' he said.

Across the narrow roadway the orchestra on the restaurant terrace was playing at full blast, with sour-sharp violins and a stinging trumpet. Mingled with the noise came the sound of guitars played on the steamer as it drew away.

We both shook hands with Mrs Martineau and said we were glad to meet her. She smiled at us in a politely savage sort of way and the major said:

'Had an exhausting journey. Going to get her some tea and let her lie down.'

'Not exhausting, sweetheart,' she said. 'Just tiresome.'

'I thought you said you were exhausted, dear.'

'I did not say I was exhausted. I am not exhausted.'

'Sorry, dear, I thought you did.'

'You shouldn't think,' she said. 'I am not exhausted. The last thing I am is exhausted.'

I could see by the way she looked over her shoulder at the restaurant orchestra that she already hated the place.

'Perhaps you will join us this evening for an *apéritif*?' the major said.

We said we should be delighted but Mrs Martineau did not speak and together, walking apart, she and the major went on to the hotel.

'Oh! dear,' I said.

'You sum up people so quickly,' my wife said. 'Too quickly.'

'I didn't say a word.'

'Then what was behind that oh! dear?'

I really didn't know what lay behind that oh! dear. It may have been that Mrs Martineau was very tired; it may have been that she was one of those women who, though young, get fretful and unsociable and angered by the trials of a journey alone; it may have been that she was a person of sensitive temperament and ear who could not bear without pain the terrace orchestras of Swiss Sunday afternoons. I did not know. I only knew that she was less than half the major's age and that the major, when he walked beside her, looked like a sorrowful old dog that had been beaten.

'They didn't say any time for the *apéritif*,' my wife said. 'Or where.'

It was about six o'clock that same evening and it was still very warm as we went downstairs.

'The major always has his on the terrace,' I said. 'We'll wait there.'

We waited on the terrace. The red and white sun-blinds were still down, casting a rosy-yellow sort of light, and I asked the waiter to pull them up so that we could see the mountains. When he raised the blinds the whole range of the Jungfrau and the Blümlisalp shone, icily rose and mauve above the mountain-green waters of the lake, and in the gardens below us the flowers were rose and mauve too, tender in the evening sun.

It always seemed to me that you could sit there on the terrace for a long time and do nothing more than watch the changing colours of the lake, the flowers and the mountains.

'The major's late,' I said.

From across the lake the smaller of the white steamers was coming in, and as it came nearer I could hear once again the sound of the guitars that were played by two Italian Swiss who travelled on the lake every Sunday, playing gay little peasant melodies from the south, earning a glass of beer or a coffee as they played on the boat or the cafés of the landing places.

The sound of the guitars over the water was very gay and hungry-sweet and charming in the still air.

And then suddenly as we sat listening to it the major came hurrying down.

'So sorry.' He seemed agitated and begged several times that we should forgive him. 'She'll be down in a moment. Waiter! Very exhausted after that journey. Awful long way. Waiter—ah! there you are.'

The major insisted on ordering drinks. He drank very rapidly and finished four or five glasses of Kirsch before Mrs Martineau came down.

'I've been waiting for hours in the lounge,' she said. 'How was I to know?'

'Let me get you something to drink,' I said. 'What will it be?'

'Whisky,' she said, 'if I may.'

'There's never any whisky,' the major said.

'Good grief!' she said.

I got up. 'I think it'll be all right,' I said.

I walked to the end of the terrace and found the waiter. The hotel had a bad brandy that tasted spirituous and harsh like poor whisky, and I arranged with the waiter to bring a double one of that.

When I got back to the table my wife and Mrs Martineau were talking of the mountains. My wife was trying to remember the names of those you could see from the terrace, but she was never very clear as to which they were.

'I think that's Eiger,' she said.

'No,' the major said, 'that's Finsteraarhorn.'

'Then which is the one with pigeons on top?' she said, and I knew she was trying to avoid the question of the Jungfrau. 'It has bits of snow on all summer that look like white pigeons,' she explained.

'You can't see it from here.'

'The one straight across,' the major said, 'the big one is the Jungfrau.'

My wife looked at me. Mrs Martineau looked very bored.

'There's a railway goes almost to the top,' my wife said. 'You must really go up while you're here.'

I knew the major did not think very much of climbing mountains by rail. 'I don't think you'd find it very exciting crawling up in that cold little train.'

'Oh! don't you?' Mrs Martineau said. 'I think it would be awful fun.'

'No sense of conquest that way,' the major said.

'Who wants a sense of conquest? The idea is to get to the top.'

'Well, in a way——'

M

'Oh! don't be so vague. Either you want to get to the top or you don't go.'

I said something very pointed about the mountain being called the Jungfrau, but it made no impression on her.

'Have you been up there yet?' she said.

'No,' I said, 'we're always meaning to go. We've been as far as Wengen, that's all.'

'Why don't we all go up together?' my wife said. 'I think it would be lovely.'

'Marvellous idea,' Mrs Martineau said.

'It means being up very early,' the major said. 'Have to be up by six. Not quite your time.'

'Don't be so rude, sweetheart,' she said.

'Anyway, you'll be tired tomorrow.'

"I shall not be tired. Why do you keep saying I'm tired? I'm not tired. I simply don't know the first thing about being tired and yet you keep saying so. I can certainly be up by six if you can.'

I could see that she was very determined to go. The major drank three more glasses of Kirsch and looked more than ever like a beaten dog. The sound of the guitars came faintly over the lake and Mrs Martineau said, 'What is that ghastly row?' and we ended up by arranging to go to the Jungfrau the following morning and then went in to dinner.

The train to Jungfraujoch goes very slowly up through lovely alpine valleys rich in spring and summer with the flowers of the lower meadows, violet salvia and wild white daisy and pink lucerne and yellow burnished trollius, and peasants mow the flowery grass in thick sweet swathes. There is a smell of something like clover and butter in the bright snow-lit air. As the train goes higher the flowers by the track grow shorter and finer until on the slopes about Scheidegg there are thousands of white and pale mauve crocus, with many fragile purple soldanellas, and sharp fierce blue gentians among yellow silken anemones everywhere about the short snow-pressed grass.

As we rode up in the little train that morning under the dazzling snow-bright peaks the major was very interested in the flowers and kept asking me what they were. He was quite dazzled by the blueness of the gentians and kept saying, 'Look at that blue, darling, look at it,' but I had never seen anyone quite so bored as Mrs Martineau. As we climbed higher and nearer the snow until at last the air was white with the downward reflection of snow-light from the great peaks above, the powder on her cheeks, too heavy and thick for a young girl, looked scaly and blue and dead, and the scarlet of her lips had the flakiness of thin enamel wearing away.

'God, I simply loathe tunnels,' she said.

Above the Scheidegg the train goes into the mountain and climbs darkly and coldly inside, with funereal creakings and clankings every yard or so, for several hours. Mrs Martineau was furious every yard of that cold gloomy climb.

In the half-darkness she said she could not think why the hell the major had not told her it was this kind of train.

'I did tell you,' he said. 'I said it would be no fun.'

'You said absolutely nothing of the kind.'

'My dear, indeed I did. Did you expect the train would climb outside the mountain all the time?'

'How the hell did I know what to expect, if you didn't say a word.'

'I said——'

'The whole trouble is, sweetheart, you haven't a clue.'

'It isn't far to the top, anyway,' he said.

'It seems a hell of a way to me!' she said. She looked terribly restless and shouted something about claustrophobia.

So we climbed up in the cold gloom of the tunnel, with Mrs Martineau growing more and more furious, exclaiming more and more of claustrophobia, and all the time calling the major sweetheart more often, as her anger grew. In the queer unworldly coldness of the clanking little train it was hard to believe in the pleasant heat of summer shining on the lake below. Mrs Martineau shivered and stamped her feet at the halts where we changed carriages, and in her white and scarlet suit, with her scarlet lips and her white lambskin coat thrown over her shoulders she looked like a cold angry animal pacing up and down.

But if she hated the journey up in the wearying little train under the mountain, she hated even more the hotel at the terminus on top.

The hotel was bright and warm and flooded with the brilliant sunlight of high places, snow-sharp as it leapt off the glacier below. There was a pleasant smell of food, and the menu said *potage permentier* and escallops of veal with spaghetti. But Mrs Martineau said she was height-sick and did not want to eat.

'In any case I loathe spaghetti!' she said.

'All right, dear,' the major said. He had been quite gentle in an almost frightened way, under the most trying circumstances in the train. 'Have the veal alone.'

'I'm not so frightfully fond of veal, either. I'm not hungry.'

'Try it, dear.'

'Why should I try it if I hate it? Why should I eat if I'm not hungry?'

The major looked terribly embarrassed for us and did not know what to do.

'Well, can't you get the waiter, the manager or something?　At least we could order a drink!' she said.

The major sent for the manager.

The manager was a very pleasant fat man with glasses who was amiably running about the large pine-wood dining-room with two or three bottles of wine in each hand.　There was a great popping of corks everywhere and in the high alpine sunlight, with the smell of food and pine-wood and sun-warmed air, nothing could have been more pleasant than to eat and drink and talk and watch that amiable man.

In a few moments he spared the time to come over to us.　The major explained how Mrs Martineau did not like the menu.　Wasn't there something else?　he said.

'It would mean waiting,' the manager said.　'The veal is very good.' He pronounced it weal instead of veal.

'She doesn't like veal.　What else could you do?'

'It would mean waiting.'

'Isn't there a steak or something?' Mrs Martineau said.

'A steak, yes.'

'All right, dear, if you'd like a steak.'

'Or I could do you a *fritto misto*,' the manager said.

'What is that?' Mrs Martineau said.　'What is *fritto misto*?'

The manager explained what *fritto misto* was.　I am exceedingly fond of *fritto misto* myself; I like the spaghetti, and the delicate morsels of fried meat of various kinds including, as the manager said, the small tender escallops of weal.　It was after all a refined and more poetical version, with Italian variations, of the dish already on the menu.

'It sounds wonderful,' Mrs Martineau said.　'I'll have that.'

The manager did not smile.　'And something to drink?　Some wine?'

'Two bottles of the Dôle,' the major said.

The manager smiled very nicely and went away.

'These people are always the same,' Mrs Martineau said.　'They don't do a damn' thing until you tear the place down.'

The one thing it is not necessary to do in Switzerland in order to eat is to tear the place down.　And when the *fritto misto* arrived, fifteen minutes late and looking not very different from the escallops of veal we had eaten with so much pleasure, I thought Mrs Martineau ate them with great gusto for a woman who hated spaghetti and veal and was height-sick and not hungry.

Before the train took us back down the mountain the major drank four more glasses of Kirsch after the wine.　He drank them too fast; he also had a cognac with his coffee.　And by the time we went upstairs to the men's room he was a little stupid and unsteady from the Kirsch. the wine, the cognac and the rarefied Jungfrau air.

In the men's room he took out his false teeth. I had forgotten all about them. He was a little unsteady. And without his teeth he did not look like the spruce-proud man we had first known at the hotel on the lake below. The toothless mouth had quite an aged, unhappy, empty look of helplessness.

Swaying about, he wrapped his morning teeth in a small chamois leather bag and then took his afternoon teeth from an identical bag. Both sets were scrupulously clean and white. I had often wondered why he changed his teeth three times a day and now he told me.

'Gives me a feeling of keeping young,' he said. 'Renews me. One gets stale, you see, wearing the same teeth. One loses a feeling of freshness.'

He put his afternoon teeth into his mouth very neatly and I could understand, seeing him now with the fresh bright teeth, how much younger, fresher and more sprightly he might feel.

'You have your own teeth?' he said.

'Yes.'

'It's the one thing I'm awfully sensitive about. Really awfully sensitive. That's why I change them. I am very self-conscious about feeling a little old. You understand?'

I said it was a good idea.

He said he was glad I thought so. For a moment he swayed about in a confidential lugubrious sort of way, so that I thought he might cry. 'It would have to be something really frightfully bad to make me forget to change them,' he said.

We rumbled down the mountain in the train all afternoon. Slowly out of the dark tunnel we came down into the dazzling flowery light of the Scheidegg, and once again Mrs Martineau, altogether oblivious of the scenery and the flowers, was height-sick as we waited on the station for the lower train. All the way down through the lovely meadows of high summer grass, rosy with lucerne, the major had a much needed nap, sleeping in the corner of the carriage with his mouth open, so that I thought once or twice that his teeth would fall out. Mrs Martineau did not speak and the major woke with a start at Interlaken. He looked about him open-mouthed, like a man who had woken in another world, and then he looked at Mrs Martineau. She looked young enough to be a reprimanding daughter.

'Really,' she said.

The major worked his teeth up and down as if they were bothering him, or like a dog that has nothing left to bite on.

We parted at the hotel.

'Oh! dear,' I said to my wife, and this time she did not ask what lay behind it. She too had rather given up. It was one of those excursions on which enemies are made for life, and for some reason or other I thought that neither the major nor Mrs Martineau would ever speak to us again.


IT WAS SATURDAY IN fact, five days later, before we came near enough to them to exchange another word. Somehow we always saw them from a distance. We saw the major running back to the hotel with Mrs Martineau's bag; we saw them on the steamers, where the major no longer enjoyed the pink-eared ham sandwiches or made eye-love to the waitress; we saw them shopping in the town. Mrs Martineau wore many new dresses; she seemed to go in very particularly for short-skirted, frothy creamy things, or day-frocks with sailor stripes of scarlet and blue, so that she looked more than ever like a young bright girl and the major more than ever like a father too painfully devoted.

On Saturday came the affair of the eucalyptus tree. It was one of those trees that the Swiss are fond of for courtyards and balconies in summer; it was three or four feet high and it had soft tender blue-grey leaves that I always thought looked charming against the red pot on the major's creamy sunny balcony.

At half-past five that afternoon we heard the most awful crash on the floor below. I went to the balcony and looked down. The eucalyptus tree lay shattered in the courtyard below, and on the balcony the major, looking very unspruce and dishevelled and shattered himself, was standing in his under-vest and trousers, staring down. For a moment I could not tell whether the major had thrown the eucalyptus tree down there in a terrible fit of despair, or whether Mrs Martineau had thrown it at him in an equally terrible fit of anger.

A waiter in a white jacket and then the manager came running out of the hotel to see what had happened, and at the same moment Mrs Martineau shouted from the bedroom: 'Come inside, you decrepit old fool! Stop making an exhibition of yourself, for God's sake!'

'Please!' I heard the major say. 'People are coming.'

'Well, let them come!' she shouted. 'If you've no more sense than to take a room with a eucalyptus tree when you know I loathe eucalyptus, when you know I've a phobia about eucalyptus——'

'It isn't that sort of eucalyptus,' the major whispered.

'Any kind of eucalyptus is eucalyptus to me!' she shouted.

'Please,' the major said. He leaned over the balcony and called down to the waiter and the manager below.

'An accident! I will pay!'

'Oh! for God's sake come inside!' she shouted. 'What's it matter?'

'I will pay!' the major shouted down again.

Back in the room Mrs Martineau began throwing things. 'You're always fussing!' I heard her shout, and there was the enraged dull noise of things like books and shoes being thrown.

'Please, darling, don't do that,' the major said. 'Don't do it, please.'

'Oh! shut up!' she said. 'And these damn' things too!'

I heard the most shattering crash as if a glass tumbler had been thrown.

'Oh! not my teeth!' the major said. 'Please, darling. Not my teeth! For God's sake, not both sets, please!'

He rushed into the bedroom. I went back into my own.

'Whatever in the world?' my wife said.

'Just the eucalyptus tree,' I said. 'The major will pay.'


THE FOLLOWING AFTERNOON the major and Mrs Martineau went away. On the lake the steamers were very crowded and under the lime-trees, at the restaurant by the landing stage, the Sunday orchestra played very loudly to the crowds of visitors in the hot afternoon. It was glorious weather and on the four o'clock steamer as it came in there were crowds of happy Sunday-laughing people.

On the landing-stage neither Mrs Martineau nor the major looked very happy.  The hotel porter with his scarlet cap stood guarding their luggage, three trunks, two brown hide suit-cases, a military-looking khaki grip, a pig-skin hat box and a shooting-stick, and the major, who was no longer wearing his spruce shantung but a suit of grey tweed, did not see us on the quay.  Beside us the two Italian Swiss with their guitars were waiting to catch the steamer too.

When the boat came in there was some difficulty about getting the major's luggage aboard.  The trunks were fairly large and the porters grew hot and excited and everyone stared.  But at last it was all finished and on the landing-stage the hotel porter raised his scarlet cap in polite farewell.

As the steamer moved away the major stood by the rail, watching the shore.  I could not see Mrs Martineau.  Somewhere behind him the two Italian Swiss struck up with their guitars and began to play their little hungry-sweet gay tune.

At that moment the major saw us.  He lifted his hand in recognition and almost eagerly, I thought, in sudden good-bye.  He opened his mouth as if to say something but the steamer was already too far away and his mouth remained open and empty, without a sound.  And in that moment I remembered something.  I remembered the eucalyptus tree falling from the balcony and the crash of the major's teeth on the bedroom wall.

'How beautiful the Jungfrau is today,' my wife said.

From the steamer the major, with his wrong teeth in, gave the most painful sort of smile, and sweetly from across the lake came the gay sound of guitars.

# The Red Doe

## by RUMER GODDEN

THEY were riding down from the upper pastures to get Ibrahim, the son of Ali, the old herdsman, married. Ibrahim felt pleased and important; there was only one person whom Ibrahim knew or felt anything about, and that was Ibrahim; naturally the morning was pleasant and important to him.

It was so early as they rode that the grass in the valley far below showed in sheets of pale dew in the sun and the ice streams shone, pale too and bright, with the early reflection of the sky; later in the day it and they would be a deep August blue and the grass would unroll, mile after mile, with the belts of coloured flowers that came in spring and summer; here spring was June, July, summer lasted a month, October brought the first snow, and the rest of the year was winter; these were the high mountains of the north-west Himalayas that led into Ladakh or Little Tibet.

When they reined-in to rest their ponies, whose legs shook from the steep way down, Ibrahim could feel and smell snow in the wind; it blew

from the peaks that towered all round them on the skyline. Snow sometimes came in summer. 'But not today,' said Jassoof, Ibrahim's friend,
laughing. 'You don't want frostbite today, eh, Ibrahim?' The mountains ringed in the valley, their sides sheer of rock and slate and pumice,
snow on their peaks, their gorges filled with rubble and ice, and the great
wide brown-white glaciers crawling to the river. Ibrahim could see
eagles flying in their endless circles below the crags and he
thought, watching them, 'It is windy there.' He could hear the
waterfalls that looked, from far away, like the crystals he found in the
streams and sold in towns and villages on the way back to the
plains.

Ibrahim's people were *bakriwars*, goatherds, nomads who drove their
flocks up every year to summer on this rich alpine grazing. They moved
in clans, each with its elders. Ibrahim's clan had their encampment on
an alp, thousands of feet above the valley, in the last spruces of the forest
where a small *merg*, a meadow, spread its gentian and primulas and
anemones and geums in the grass. Ibrahim did not notice flowers, they
were part of the grass to him, grazing for his father's goats, as he did
not see the colours of the glaciers, the wicked blue of the crevasses, the
mountains or the snow-slopes of the passes; he only knew how many
marches each was, which led to fresh grazing grounds, which snow bridges
would hold. If he saw the eagles it was only to judge the wind; deer were
hunted with spears, bears were to be avoided, and the little wild marmots,
who sat up on their tails to scream at humans, were for him and his
friends to throw stones at.

Ibrahim knew goats and ponies, he did not count them as animals, but
as his life; he lived with his father, mother, uncles, cousins, friends, his
friend Jassoof; but they were themselves, he was Ibrahim, not responsible
for them, and he had nothing to bother him. Now the time had come
for him to have a wife.

'We want a good strong one,' his father had said. He had said that of
the Yarkandi pony they had bought last year. 'Not too young, not less
than fifteen, and strong.'

Ibrahim nodded and he felt a sudden curious tingling that
seemed to come in his palms and his thighs and the backs of his
knees, and his throat felt parched. 'I want her to be beautiful,' he
said.

'Beautiful!' cried his father shrilly. 'A beautiful woman is nothing
but a nuisance. No, she must be strong, not too young, and of good stock.'

'And beautiful,' said Ibrahim obstinately, and his father leant forward
and slapped him on both cheeks. Ibrahim was a young cock among the
youths of the clan but his father still slapped him when he thought it
would do him good.

AFTER THAT HE LOOKED at every woman he saw, wondering if she were beautiful. They all looked beautiful in the distance and that was the way they walked, straight from heels to head, keeping themselves to themselves. Now Ibrahim's eyes came prying among them and he saw things he had not seen before: how small their bare feet and ankles looked under the folds of their black and red pleated trousers, how their black tunics swung out in skirts below their breasts, the full hems sewn and weighted with a load of white pearl buttons, how their veils hung loose but showed under them a flash of blue from the bracelet-size cap they wore on their heads, and how their silver jewellery sounded as they passed and repassed in and out of the huts and the tents, round the fires and through the flocks. Their anklets chinked, and their necklaces and ear-rings; Ibrahim began to hear that chinking in his dreams.

On march, the men drove the flocks and rode the ponies, and carried nothing unless it were a favourite child or a newborn kid; the women carried the gear of the camp on their heads, netted bundles of the heavy iron cooking pots and platters; they carried their babies in slings, or a child on their hip; they dragged the dogs on strings and drove the slowly moving sick, hurt, animals. They were also often in childbirth; the caravans were always having to stop and wait for an hour or two, or even longer, while a woman gave birth; then the Elders were pleased; they liked to see the caps and hoods of the children running about in the clan, but the young men were impatient though they had often had to do the same thing with the herds. Ibrahim looked and wondered; some of the women seemed to him beautiful, none of them beautiful enough.

NOW THE DAY HAD COME, and he and his cavalcade rode down through the forests, which grew more and more balmy as they came lower in the valley. Here there was a noise of wild bees and of larks above the meadows, where the larch and spruce trees opened on small *mergs* of grass heavy with clover. The air smelled of resin and of honey. Ibrahim sniffed it and, sniffing, he found, suddenly, that he smelled himself.

He had been given a new turban of bright blue muslin, and he wore the wedding blanket, dark blue with fringes and a scarlet border, but his homespun coat was his own because he had no other coat, and he smelled of wool and wood-smoke and sweat and goat. To smell himself made him feel more than ever full of Ibrahim and more and more he felt that tingling excitement.

The chief thing, up to now, had been when his father bought him a saddle, but it was not a new saddle, and it was used by his uncles and cousins as well as his father and himself; it was the same when he was given his first full-size blanket, the homespun, hand-woven blanket-shawl that all the men carried like a plaid on their shoulders; the blanket was not Ibrahim's, it was family property.

The tall young man Jassoof led a small pony with an empty pad. Ibrahim, and no one else, would lead it back, and his wife, probably for the first and last time in her life, would ride beside him, back up the mountain to her new home, and she would be his own, no one else would have the right to own her or use her except Ibrahim.

They were riding faster now that the path grew more gradual as it came near the valley. They rode like Cossacks on their small thick-set ponies, that were prized if they were short below the knee, well-shouldered, with thick necks and thick manes. The mares had their foals trotting loose after them. Manes and blanket-ends flew in the wind as they crossed the wooden bridge above the noise of the river, where it burst in thunder out of the mountain; the hooves of the ponies made an equal noise on the wood. Spray blew in their faces and excited them, and Jassoof let out a cry, a whoop, that made the others whoop like demons, or wild cats, to answer him, and the ponies plunged and broke into a gallop that swept them into the valley, with the ground drumming under the galloping hooves. Then, at the far head of the valley, where a glacier spread and melted in streams across the grass, they saw a single dark speck, a hut.

Thick loud whoops came from every young man round Ibrahim, jokes cracked across him, and they all began to whip their ponies. Ibrahim's grey kicked out, though he had not touched it, and broke away from the rest into a glade where mares and foals were grazing on clover and forget-me-nots. Ibrahim knew he had seen the glade before; something else he had seen but he could not remember what; then it came into his mind that they had been riding and that it had been exciting, too, but another excitement. They were hunting. Hunting? And then he remembered. It was a doe, a red doe, who had run, startled, out of the spruce trees, in front of them into this glade.

He remembered the shout that had gone up from the men, and it seemed to him the same shout that was in his ears now, and the whips were lifted, too, the ponies lashed as they spread galloping, in a circle, to head off the doe, while the older men, who had the spears, held them ready. Ibrahim had come up with the doe as she turned, driven back, so close that he could see her red sides heaving for breath, her ears pressed down and her muzzle strained as she ran. Ibrahim swung his pony on to her and she turned again, but sideways, and the old man, his father, threw his spear, and she fell, pinned through the neck to the ground. It was Ibrahim who jumped from his saddle to cut her throat before she died.[1]

[1] Mohammedans can only eat meat if the throat of the animal is cut while it is alive.

There was something else he could remember, that he did not want to remember, and he reined-in his pony and rode slowly, step by step, through the glade. He did not want to remember, but he did remember. He remembered himself bending down with the knife in his hand and he remembered what he did not want to remember, that the doe, with blood gushing from her neck, had looked at him and then he was alone with her. No father, no Jassoof, no others were with him then; it was only Ibrahim and the doe, and he, her eyes looked, had done this to her; he, Ibrahim; and suddenly it was he who was stricken, not the doe, because he was not Ibrahim himself any more, he was Ibrahim and the doe.

'Allah! Kill it!' shouted his father, 'Owl! It will be dead before you cut!' and, dazed, Ibrahim had taken his knife and killed her.

When she was dead she was dabbled with blood to her scut, her small pale tongue hung out with blood welling still from her mouth, and her eyes slowly glazed, hiding their meaning. All day he could not forget, perhaps he had never forgotten. But now, as his pony began to trot out of the glade, went into a canter, then to a gallop to join the others, he chuckled; he had remembered that he had refused to eat venison that night, and that seemed to him, now, exceedingly funny.

THEY CAME TO THE hut. It stood by itself at the foot of the glacier on a fertile grazing plain fed by a hundred ice-springs. There were silver birch-trees and flowers and buffaloes and goats grazing. Other huts and tents stood on the edge of the forest and everywhere the smoke from cooking fires was going up. Children stood to watch these stranger men on their little horses as they splashed through the stream and rode in a circle round the hut, faster and faster with cat-calls and whoops, as the Elders and the men of the clan came out to meet them.

The feast began. Inside the hut the fires were smoking, and the men sat in a circle, dipping their hands into the iron bowls and platters of *pilaff* and roast kid and *chappattis* and apricots stuffed with mutton, and curd and honey rice. Ibrahim, feeling young and oddly light and thin, was put in the place of honour between the Elders, and he was grateful that he should be silent as became a young man. He was shy but he was also very hungry. The food was good, and he ate until he felt his stomach expanding and his legs growing warm and well-being coming up his back into his neck and face, so that he began to smile, feeling jovial again and suitably old.

All the young men knew where the women were. There was a cloth stretched tightly across the hut, nailed from wall to wall, that kept bulging and swelling as bodies pressed against it and, from behind it, came whispering and giggling and laughing, and that soft chinking of jewellery. Ibrahim looked and felt more than ever warm and jovial. The tea bowls came round, and the *hookah,* the water-pipe, with its gentle liquid bubbling sound, passed from hand to hand. Ibrahim thought that, through the cloth, he had caught a gleam of scarlet; wedding clothes were scarlet, trousers, tunic, with a dark veil and new cap and new jewellery that chinked, chinked, as Ibrahim had heard it in his dreams. She was young—he knew that because she had been born in the same year as himself, the year of the great snow—and she was sworn to be strong, but Ibrahim was thinking now of a woman's skin, and he knew that he had seen it without noticing, and he marvelled as he saw that it was fine, soft, much softer and finer than his own; he thought of a woman's hair and knew he had seen it loosed, another woman hunting in it for vermin and combing it, long and blue-black in the sun; he thought of her body, of his body and hers, hers soft where he was hard, hard where he was soft so that they matched, and he began to tingle and he had to dig his nails into the backs of his knees as he sat.

The *hookah* went round and the bowls of tea, and Ibrahim thought they would sit there for ever and that it would never end. He took his turn at the pipe politely, he drank bowl after bowl of tea, he listened politely to the jokes, barbarous jokes that made the cloth shake, and he smiled until he thought his cheeks would crack, and still it went on and on.

At last Jassoof stood up, and now the time for politeness was over and the raw thing would be done: now the Elders would lead out the girl and put her on the pony with the empty pad and Ibrahim would take its hair-rope in his hand and ride away with her.

There were no more jokes, no giggles. Silence had fallen on the hut; the men separated into two dignified groups, the chief Elder, with his aged face and sorrel-dyed beard in the centre of his, Ibrahim in the centre of the other. Presents passed and the bride's dowry, a bundle of clothes, two good iron pots, and a few coins, were given to Jassoof; Jassoof's young brother stayed behind to drive up five chosen goats.

Now the men went outside and the Elder went behind the cloth. Presently he came back, and with him, supported on two sides by women, came Ibrahim's bride. All he could see was a bundled shape in a red blanket, and the top of a bowed head. The blanket was wound to her nose, she kept her head obstinately down so that the edge of the blanket met her veil.

Ibrahim longed for her to look up until, looking round, he saw the same longing on the faces of all the men standing round. Some had wives at home, some were not yet married, but as they looked at the red bundle they had the same look, hot and thick and longing, and Ibrahim felt furiously angry and resentful and, had she looked up then, he would have beaten her when they reached home.

She did not look up. With soft slow small steps, quite unlike her ordinary woman's stride, she went with the Elder to the pony, and he lifted her on to the pad and put the rope into Ibrahim's hand. The women began to call out and laugh, a few to weep; the Elder stepped back and stood, tall and courteous, while the girl's father looked with expressionless eyes away to the mountains and Ibrahim's friends began to bit up their ponies and tighten their girths.

Jassoof had Ibrahim's grey pony. Ibrahim stood with the rope in his hand while the girl sat on the pad, motionless, her head down. As he stood there, he began to run his hand up and down the pony's neck, a cross impatient hand; he ran it up to the pad, down the neck to the head, up to the pad, and then he noticed that every time his hand moved near the pad the girl shrank back. It amused him, and he moved his hand more and brought it nearer her each time, nearer and nearer, so that first it touched her blanket, then the soft folds of her trousers and then, unexpectedly, warm and firm, her thigh. The round warmth and firmness of it astonished Ibrahim so much that at first he left his hand there through sheer surprise, and then an equally astonishing sweetness filled him, added to the warmth and thickness and longing, and then he felt her tremble. He felt her tremble and, at that, triumphant strength filled him and he pressed his hand hard against her until something warm and wet fell on the back of his hand.

It was a tear.

Ibrahim stood still. The drop lay on the back of his hand and, as he looked at it, it seemed that the Elder and the father and Jassoof and the young men and the women disappeared and Ibrahim was alone with this girl, sitting helpless on the pony, and he had made her cry. The trembling fear passed from her into him. He did not want to be married, he did not want to take her away, into his home and his hut and his bed and the days of his life, he did not want to have anything to do with such a business. He dropped the hair-rope and turned away as the pony veered round.

The Elder caught the pony and courteously returned the rope to Ibrahim, showing no surprise. Jassoof caught his shoulder.

'Owl! Can't you hold your own wife?'

'I don't want a wife,' said Ibrahim.

'You will tonight,' said Jassoof.

Ibrahim mounted his pony and Jassoof pulled up the small pony beside him so that its nose touched Ibrahim's leg. A throng pressed round them, and the calls and shouts sounded across the valley. Someone laid a whip lash across the ponies' tails and they started forward, jerking through the streams so that the riders were splashed knee-high.  Ibrahim saw the girl draw up her heels, and her hands came out of the blanket and clutched the pad.  They began to gallop over the grass, all filled, all comfortable and jovial, feeling themselves more men since the morning, pleasantly filliped and excited, and the married ones began to think of their wives, the young ones eyed Ibrahim's and wondered when their turn would come; gradually the feeling spread to Ibrahim; the girl sat hidden and inert, but under the blanket she was there, as warm and round and firm as the promise of her thigh, and presently he, Ibrahim, would undo that blanket.

He knew that, and he knew he could not be only Ibrahim again; and, as they rode back into the red doe's glade, he knew what had started in him with the doe was in him now, for ever.

All the same, he began to laugh as he led the way home.

# EDWARDIAN *album*

Most of us tend to picture the Edwardian era as one long garden party, with Edward VII himself, gruff, kind, comfort-loving, cosmopolitan, as host and universal uncle. But it wasn't much like that in reality. Of course, the Court and the wearers of coronets (those of Duke, Marquis, Earl, Viscount, and Baron are seen above) glittered splendidly, but otherwise it was a period marked by violent political struggle and social stress, with the German problem never absent.

## *Votes for Women*

The old lady on the right was one of
75 suffragettes arrested in March, 1907,
for a raid on the House of Commons.
Employment of militant tactics by
women suffragists began in 1905, and
in this early stage did not go much
farther than heckling at political meetings and window-breaking. Later came
hunger-strikes and that destruction of
property, usually by arson, which formed
one of the most sensational chapters of
public life before the first World War.

Suffragette meeting in Trafalgar Square

A demonstration outside a prison

Waiting on a Minister's doorstep

## Lords and Commons

The men outside the *Daily Graphic* offices, then in the Strand, are waiting for details of Lloyd George's 'People's Budget' of 1909, which among other things was the Chancellor's reply to the hostility of the House of Lords to Liberal bills. Accepting the challenge, the Lords defied the Constitution and rejected the Budget, thus inviting a struggle which closed with the famous Parliament Act and the humbling of the upper house.

## As they were

The boy in the boater is King George
VI at the age of thirteen. With Prince
Albert (as he was then known) are his
tutor, Mr. Hansell, and Lord Des-
borough. He was created Duke of York
in 1920, and on April 26, 1923, married
Lady Elizabeth Bowes-Lyon, youngest
daughter of the Earl and Countess of
Strathmore and Kinghorne. The Queen
is seen here at the age of nine, in 1909,
dressed in a long gown of rose-pink
and silver.

Mr. Attlee, 1910

Young Mr. Attlee became a lecturer in social science at the London School of Economics a year or two after this photograph was taken. Following Haileybury and Oxford, he had gone to live in the East End of London, studying social conditions and earning his living as a docker.

In 1908 young Mr. Churchill found a place in the Cabinet as

Mrs. Churchill, 1908

Mr. Churchill, 1908

President of the Board of Trade and married Miss Clementine Hozier at St. Margaret's, Westminster. When he carried three important social measures and threw himself with marked effect into the campaign against the House of Lords, the Liberal party were not alone in acknowledging that a star of the first magnitude had arisen in the political sky.

The cinematograph was the
infant phenomenon among Edwardian enter-
tainments, with newsreels as one of its staples. Below, two
famous stage stars perform for the well-
remembered Topical Budget.

Seymour Hicks and Ellaline Terriss

John Masefield, 1909          Max Beerbohm, 1909          James Agate, 1909

Florence Nightingale, O.M., died 1910

# *The Last of the Victorians*

Some of the great Victorians were still living legends in Edwardian times. There was, for example, the 'Lady with the Lamp', who had returned from the Crimean War a broken woman. She remained an invalid to the end, but it is strange to reflect that the end did not come until August 13, 1910, when she had reached her 91st year. The picture shows her at her house at 10 South Street, Park Lane, where, invalid or not, she worked unremittingly for nursing and other health objects. It was here that the Order of Merit was given to her in 1907.

Algernon Charles Swinburne, died 1909

A page from the original MS. of 'Dolores'

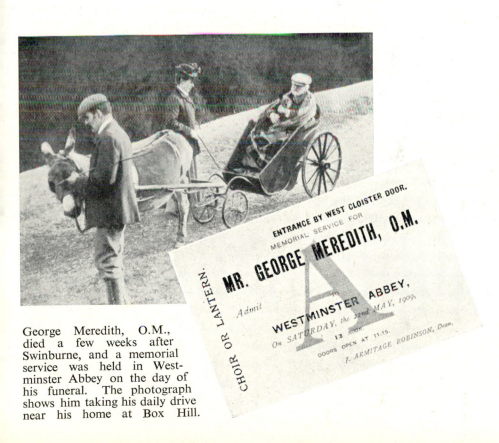

George Meredith, O.M., died a few weeks after Swinburne, and a memorial service was held in Westminster Abbey on the day of his funeral. The photograph shows him taking his daily drive near his home at Box Hill.

CHOIR OR LANTERN.

ENTRANCE BY WEST CLOISTER DOOR.

MEMORIAL SERVICE FOR

MR. GEORGE MEREDITH, O.M.

Admit

WESTMINSTER ABBEY,

On SATURDAY, the 22nd MAY, 1909,

12 noon

DOORS OPEN AT 11.15.

J. ARMITAGE ROBINSON, Dean.

Tolstoy died in 1910, Ibsen in 1906. Both were very famous in England, and their deaths evoked appreciations and explanations of a length which seems astonishing in the paper-starved present. The unhappiness of Tolstoy's later life with his family at Yasnaya Polyana was revealed to the world when, in October, 1910, he left home secretly with his youngest daughter, Alexandra, to go he knew not whither. The adventure ended tragically, for his health failed him, and he died in the following month.

Tolstoy, died 1910

Ibsen, died 1906

# *Portents*

The date was July 25, 1909. M. Louis Blériot, a young French aviator, was flying his monoplane from Calais. When he descended, under the very walls of Dover Castle, he had achieved the first crossing of the Channel in a heavier-than-air flying machine. Madame Blériot came over in a French torpedo-boat, there was an affectionate greeting between the pair at Dover, and then they faced the camera for this picture.

Three years after Blériot, a woman flew alone across the Channel in one of his monoplanes. She was an American, Miss Harriet Quimby, aged 25. The dress in which she accomplished the flight, shown here, caused a mild sensation.

Then there was Mr. Grahame-White, who in 1910 practised dropping from his aeroplane bags of flour, representing bombs, into a space marked out as a battleship. Five times in succession he hit the target from 800 feet. It was agreed that it was impossible to over-estimate the importance of the test.

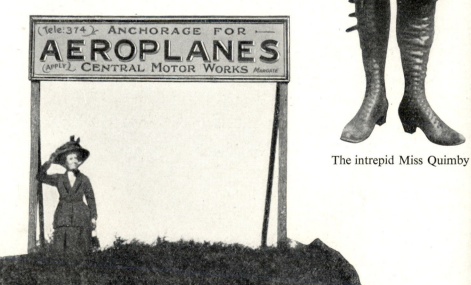

The intrepid Miss Quimby

Signs of the times, 1910

Above: Yorkshire steam wagon, 1903    Below: London steam bus, 1902

Hammersmith to Oxford Circus

The first two telephones are 1910 models. The third, invented in
1909, is an anticipation of the dialling apparatus of our own time.

The flip-flap was the great attraction of the Franco-British Exhibition at the White City in 1908, and Alvin Langdon Coburn took this photograph of it.

# The End of an Era

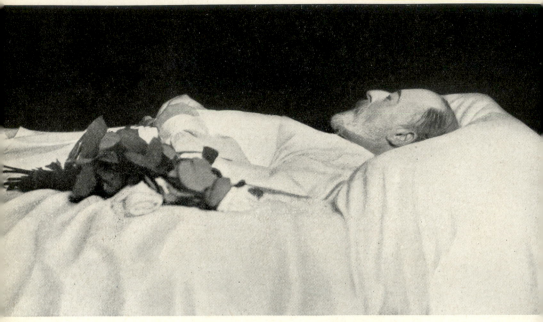

The dead King, May 7, 1910

The constitutional crisis already referred to was still in existence when King Edward VII, on returning from his usual spring holiday at Biarritz, died with startling suddenness. From May 16 to 20 the dead King lay in state in Westminster Hall. Many thousands of persons were turned away from services in Westminster Abbey and St. Paul's. The Edwardian era wrote the final words of the great chapter of 19th century English history; the next chapter, as we all know, bears the heading 'Catastrophe.'

## ACKNOWLEDGMENTS

*For assistance received the Editor's grateful thanks are tendered to the Rt. Hon. C. R. Attlee, M.P.; 'Commercial Motor'; the G.P.O.; Hulton Press; 'Motor Transport'; National Film Library; John I. Thornycroft & Co., Ltd.; and the Yorkshire Patent Steam Wagon Co.*

Mary Ashford

Abraham Thornton

William Palmer

# Unvisited Shrines

## by BERNARD DARWIN

AFTER Mr John Thurtell had cut the throat of Mr William Weare, Sir Walter Scott drove some miles out of his road to Scotland to see the genuine and only original 'green slough' into which the victim's body had been thrown.

So I was following an illustrious example last September in Glasgow. I was there to watch a golf match in Ayrshire, and after it was over a kind friend offered to drive me back, and asked if there was anything particular in Glasgow that I should like to see. Yes, I said, putting a bold face on it, there was; I should like to see Blythswood Square, Sandyford Place and West Princes Street.

I suppose I ought to add for the benefit of the less bloodthirsty that each of these places is connected with an historic case; Blythswood Square with the charming Miss Madeleine Smith; Sandyford Place with the tragedy of the two Jessies, Jessie MacLachlan and Jessie Macpherson and the unspeakable Auld Fleming, the best murder, according to H. B.

Irving, that he had ever read; West Princes Street with the murder of Miss Gilchrist, by someone as to whom the only thing quite certain is that he was not the luckless Oscar Slater.

My friend was as good as his word; we had a delightful drive; we made what Tony Lumpkin would have called a circumbendibus through Glasgow; we visited all three of these fanes.

At the end I was conscious of a duty done, and yet there was a slight feeling of disenchantment. Perhaps the sombre and uniform architecture of Glasgow made one house look too like another. It is true that Madeleine's was a corner house, and there I could picture more clearly than before the shoddy little Don Juan, l'Angelier, talking to her at her window, partly below the pavement level, and creeping in after a glance to see that the coast was clear. As to the other two—well, I am glad to have seen them, but my picture of the murderer dashing down the West Princes Street stairway 'like greased lightning,' to be lost in the shadows of a winter evening, is no more vivid now than it always had been. Perhaps even something of 'the gloom, the glamour' has departed. I have no regrets at not having inflicted on my patient guide the late Dr Pritchard's house (the number is now altered) in Sauchiehall Street.

There is much more to be said for these pious explorations in the country. In the country a house has its own distinctive and sinister character. 'Murder's crimson wand,' in a phrase of the admirable Mr Roughead, has here a more individual touch.

It was last summer, before my Glasgow jaunt, that I made a pilgrimage to the pretty, tranquil Suffolk village of Peasenhall, on which the red light had fallen some forty-five years before. A man had been charged with the murder of a girl and twice the jury had disagreed. We drove along the single street and I made a guess at the house, but I was on a sudden overcome with shyness. I was afraid to ask the vital question, since villages sometimes dislike this particular kind of celebrity; did not Rugeley, according to a well-known story, want to change its name?

Luckily I had a braver companion who went into a shop and made the necessary enquiries. Yes, was the answer, that was the house (I had guessed right) but it had changed its name. So we drove past it again and even stopped the car for a shamefaced moment or two. I thought I could identify the window in which a letter from somebody had told the poor little victim to put a light, somebody who had an odd habit of putting capital p's in the middle of a sentence. I could see the path along which somebody must subsequently have walked on that night of the great thunderstorm. As soon as I got home I read the trial right through again with an added relish and understanding. That pilgrimage had been a distinct success.

Yet on the whole I incline to regard it as an exception to prove the rule that unvisited shrines are the best. In the reader's imagination they keep for ever their pristine beauty. In reality the ruthless march of civilization and the enterprising builder combine to ruin them.

ONE OF MY OLD favourites is the trial of Abraham Thornton for the murder of Mary Ashford in 1817. It is now only to be found recorded in the books on a point of mere law, as the last example of 'wager of battle.'

After Thornton had been acquitted, an 'appeal of murder' was brought against him under an ancient and recondite procedure by Mary Ashford's brother. Thornton's advisers produced an equally ancient answer to it. When bidden to plead, he threw down a gauntlet on the floor of Westminster Hall and replied, 'Not guilty, and I am ready to defend the same with my body.' William Ashford, whom his friends called 'our poor little knight,' was not prepared for single combat in the lists; there was no 'battel'; Abraham Thornton disappeared into the mists of America and wager of battle and appeals of murder disappeared through an Act of Parliament hastily introduced by the Attorney General.

As to these legal niceties, though quaint and seductive in their way, I feel rather as did Sherlock Holmes when he heard the legend of the Hound of the Baskervilles. 'Do you not find it interesting?' he was asked, and he answered, 'To a collector of fairy tales.' It is the case itself, still palpitating with life after a hundred and thirty years, which attracts me, and would have attracted Mr Weller senior, for it depended on an alibi, and a cast-iron alibi at that, unless indeed there was a conspiracy among all the clocks of the neighbourhood. Abraham Thornton was a thoroughly unpleasing creature but he was not a murderer and indeed there was no murder at all.

Having never visited the scene, which is not far from Birmingham, I can roam in happy fancy through lonely green fields, and cross rustic stiles on which the lovers sat in the dews of a summer morning. I can see, in my mind's eye, the harrowed field with its two sets of footsteps, the one set dodging the other, a 'gravel page' in which Holmes would have revelled. But suppose I were to go there in the flesh, all my visions would dissolve on the instant. There was a solitary lane called Bell's Lane; it is now, I read, called Orphanage Road and is bordered by suburban villas. There was the old Tyburn House where Thornton and Mary danced. It has been pulled down and a red brick building stares in its stead. In 'the fatal field' was once a pit full of water, as it were the green slough; it has been filled up 'on account of building developments.'    Almost worst of all, another important lane in the story now skirts a golf course.   I do not object to golf courses in general; I should be ungrateful if I did; but is there not something indecent in this hooking and slicing on historic meadows?    Were I to go there today I must needs say to my brother golfers, 'Procul, O procul este profani.'

As long as I stay away, the harrowed field and the fatal field, the two lanes and the stile are all there, and I must take care lest they fade as a dream.    Nevertheless, I am often tempted to make a pilgrimage in the same romantic Midland country to Rugeley.    When my train for Shrewsbury, bound for Aberdovey, went from Euston I used constantly to pass through Rugeley station and looked out of the window with yearning eyes.    Now that my train goes from Paddington, the temptation does not so often recur, but some day in a slow train it may yet be too much for me.

I hope I need not say that Rugeley was the home of the greatest of poisoners, William Palmer, who unquestionably murdered his wife, his brother, and his best friend, and according to rumour a number of other inconsiderable people into the bargain.    I have pored so often over the shorthand note of his trial for the murder of John Parsons Cook, and feel that if a magician were to drop me in front of the Talbot Arms I could find my way about Rugeley blindfold.    That is doubtless an amiable delusion, if only for one important reason that Palmer's house over the

way is there no more. My precious volume can help me to imagine it. It has a picture of the house seen from the garden, full of flower beds in fantastic shapes, which doubtless poor Mrs Palmer used to water.

That is only one of its many enchanting woodcuts. There is Rugeley High Street on a busy day with tall-hatted gentlemen on horseback in front of the Talbot Arms. There is the maypole (is that still there, I wonder?) and the chemist's shop which the great man patronized for his strychnine; there is the house of his mother, a rich old lady whose name he had forged, so that he was compelled to obtain money in regrettable ways.

Then there are many of the witnesses, and in particular one whom I love very much, Mrs Ann Brooks, who 'was in the habit of attending races.' She is rather a handsome lady in a black pelisse, with a firm set of the mouth, eyes like slits and a sinister droop of one eyelid. She affects me with an agreeably cold shiver.

Mrs Brooks was, I take it, rather a fortunate lady. Being at Shrewsbury races she called at the Raven (I *have* been there) to talk to Mr Palmer, and she saw him in a passage, with a glass in his hand; there was something in the glass that looked like water, and he held it up to the light once or twice and shook it. Mrs Brooks 'made an observation about the fineness of the weather,' whereupon Palmer disappeared through a door and came out again in a moment with a hospitable glass of brandy and water for his visitor. She drank some of it and it 'produced no unpleasant consequences.'

Considering what she had seen, though she did not fully appreciate it at the time, and considering what unpleasant things happened to some of Palmer's acquaintances, I really do think Mrs Brooks was lucky. She had seen him juggling with antimony and she was still alive.

There is, rather mysteriously, no portrait of Jerry Smith; Mr Jeremiah Smith, attorney at law, who was up to the neck in some of Palmer's insurance transactions, and of whom Sir Fitzjames Stephen has given a vivid picture under Cockburn's cross-examination, with the sweat pouring from his face and the papers rustling in his hand. 'Don't "Mr Attorney" me, sir,' says Cockburn. 'Answer my question,' and the mean little creature cringes with a wretched assumption of dignity. I can almost find it in my heart to be sorry for him.

There is a picture of Mr William Stevens, kindly but determined, looking over his spectacles. He was Cook's stepfather, and he played an important part in having the poisoner arrested. Other people had died suddenly and mysteriously, and Rugeley had clearly been buzzing with suspicions for a long time, but everyone had been afraid, or had been hypnotized into silence, until Mr Stevens came on the scenes, a stranger from London.

There is one most dramatic little moment in his evidence, which I have quoted before elsewhere but must quote again, for the mere selfish and sensual pleasure of writing down the words. Mr Stevens and Palmer have travelled in the same train from London and in the course of the journey Mr Stevens has asked one or two apparently innocent questions as to a post mortem.

Then, when they get out at Rugeley, he thinks it time to unmask some of his batteries. 'Altering my tone and manner, I said "Mr Palmer, if I should call in a solicitor to give me advice, I suppose you will have no objection to answer any questions he may put to you?" I altered my tone purposely; I looked steadily at him, but although the moon was shining, I could not see his features distinctly. He said, with a spasmodic convulsion of the throat, which was perfectly apparent, "Oh, no, certainly not." After I asked him that question there was a pause of three or four minutes.'

In the course of those minutes I think Palmer must have seen, perhaps for the first time, the shadow of the gallows black in the moonlight. He came to see Mr Stevens at the inn later that evening, but did not apparently propose brandy and water. If he had I am sure Mr Stevens would have known better than to accept it.

Oh, there is no one like Palmer! 'No more horrible villain,' in Sir Fitzjames Stephen's words, 'ever stood in the dock,' and apart from his own murderous attractions he has a point of contact with a rather squalid world which has its fascinations for me, the racing world of early Victorian days.

One of the creditors who were pressing him for money, and held some of the forged bills, was Mr Henry Padwick, a most polite and gentlemanly person who was the king of the moneylenders of his day. In 1854 he was the partner and confederate, as it was then called, of the famous John Gully in the ownership of Andover, the horse that won the last of his three Derbys for Mr Gully's lilac jacket. That was just two years before Palmer stood in the dock at the Old Bailey. I wonder whether he backed Andover.

THERE IS ANOTHER unseen shrine that I often visit in imagination. I have to cross the Atlantic to get there; it is in the town of Fall River in the State of Massachusetts. The story that belongs to it is comparatively modern. It was on a sweltering August day in 1892 that a fierce light unexpectedly beat on Fall River, where Mr Andrew Borden, one of its leading citizens, and his wife were both killed with an axe, the wife first, the husband perhaps an hour and a half later.

The house was a small one, in a street with neighbouring houses clustering close to it; the maid, Bridget Sullivan, was cleaning the windows; the elder daughter was away, but there was—somewhere—the younger daughter, Lizzie. 'Where was you, Miss Lizzie, when it happenned?' asked Bridget, and it was a highly pertinent question. Miss Lizzie, by her own account, was first ironing handkerchiefs. After that she went out into the barn to get a piece of lead to make sinkers for a fishing line that she had not used for five years. After that again she went up into the loft, the most stifling place she could find on that stifling day, and meditatively ate pears. It was very fortunate she did, so her friends said, as otherwise she would herself have been murdered by the unseen, unknown assassin who had crept into the house (always kept doubly locked) and had lain hidden there for an hour and a half.

The rustic jury thought that this crude work with an axe was one of the things that a woman could not do, still less one who was a member of a respected family and the Secretary and Treasurer of a Christian Endeavour Society. To make it more incredible and indelicate scandalous persons had suggested that she had taken off all her clothes to do it. They joyfully acquitted Miss Lizzie and she lived in Fall River, an undaunted outcast for the rest of her days.

If she has any secret it is buried with her, where she lies with her murdered father and stepmother, her own mother, and her sister in Oak Grove Cemetery. It is said that the custodian does not like being asked the way to the grave.

THIS IS BUT THE barest outline of a wonderful story, and I beg and beseech anyone who likes such things to read the trial, the more so as Miss Lizzie had as her *Vates Sacer* a distinguished American writer, the late Edmund Pearson. The taste for murder trials is not by any manner of means only a taste for horrors. So much of the interest is to be found in the sidelights thrown on the way in which other people live, and the case of Lizzie Borden is rich in such illuminating details.

Here, in a photograph before me, is No. 92, now renumbered No. 230, South Street. It is quite a humble house with a single tree to shade it, just such a wooden house, though on a slightly larger scale, as I could find by walking a few steps in my own Kentish village. It does not look as if its owner had more than a quarter of a million dollars; but the family lived quietly, and Mr Borden was a careful man; on his walk from his office that morning, when he was coming home to his death, he had picked up an old lock thrown away in the street and methodically wrapped it in paper.

There was but the single maid, Bridget, who had inherited the name of Maggie from her predecessor: Mr and Mrs Borden 'did' their own rooms, and the food seems to have consisted almost wholly of mutton soup, which appears and reappears, for breakfast, for dinner, and for breakfast again. Cunning old Governor Robinson, who defended Miss Lizzie and adopted a rustic accent for the purpose, made great play with the mutton soup, as evidence of a simple, decent, family life, such as the jurymen led themselves. How different from the 'fixed-up notions' of the hotels in great cities, for which they would have a proper contempt!

It was on the face of it a homely, respectable, humdrum life, such as was being led in thousands of country towns all over the world, not merely in New England where a puritan simplicity is supposed to flourish. The house looks the very last house in which anything exciting could happen, a haunt of peaceful, middle-class dullness. Yet, as I gaze at my photograph, I fancy I can sense something of the fires of hatred and jealousy that smouldered unsuspected within. That sultry August day seems to foreshadow the storm brewing. The crimson wand has most palpably touched and transformed No. 92, South Street.


I AM COMING TO THE END of my space, if not of my subject, but there is yet one more shrine. It is worthy of the name, for it is in a churchyard, and I hope soon to see it again, when I go to bathe once more in the healing waters of Droitwich.

The kindest of friends and physicians, knowing my outrageous tastes, once took me a walk across the fields to a pretty little church, where he said there was a unique inscription. I have since regularly made pilgrimage there and can find my way on the instant through the forest of tombstones. After the name and rank of the dead, there is added (I hope I have the words aright) 'whose name was mentioned in connection with the murders at' a certain neighbouring village. By all accounts the deceased gentleman entirely deserved his epitaph. He first employed a bravo to murder a clergyman who insisted on his pound of flesh in the matter of tithes. Then, in order to 'mak siccer,' he had the bravo murdered too. And he died in an odour of at least moderate sanctity.

What I do not know is who put that inscription on his tombstone. Was it the then clergyman of the parish, who thought to discourage such deeds against the cloth, or was it some admiring friend? I am afraid I shall never know, but, even as Sir Walter saw the green slough, I have seen the field where the deed was done.

# Hillesden

## by  A.  L.  ROWSE

F you take a map of Buckinghamshire and look a few miles south of
the old county town, between it and the Claydons—that have their
memories now for all lovers of English letters— you will find a name
that means nothing to you: Hillesden.  It is indeed a forgotten place :
hipped up there on its little hill, the fat pastures and flat water-
meadows all round it, isolated from any main roads, with only one little
road winding up to it: a dead end.

And yet it was far from being that in its heyday; only its heyday was
three centuries ago, the time of the Civil War, which left such a mark
upon it and on the lives of all that lived there.  Now, hardly anyone;
just a cottage or two, a church, a farm, where once was all the bustle,
the coming to and fro of a great house, with the family, important,
numerous, ramifying in every direction, affecting the life of all this
countryside.  Now all vanished and gone; where the house stood but an
open space in the fields, the fields revealing under the grass the slopes of
the former terraces.

It was on a November day, the first of the month, that my friend and
I set out in pursuit of this place.  We were walking from Steeple Claydon,
the way that so many generations of Verneys had gone to visit so many
generations of Dentons.  There in the village was the big Camp Barn
around which Cromwell's small army, some two thousand men, was
encamped and from which they advanced to the attack on Hillesden
House: March, 1644, three hundred years ago.  Over the Planks we
went, directed by a superb young soldier newly returned from the wars :
duly we negotiated the duck-boards laid across the low-lying water
meadows and out into the open, lonely country beyond.

Sitting on a gate at the foot of the slope we ate our sandwiches, looking
up to the corn-yellow haystacks moulded firm and clear by the November
sun.  There was a mellowness in the colouring, a water-clear purity in
the air; the autumn fruits in the hedges glowed red and gold.

So we approached the place, the same way that Cromwell came.
Drawing near we observed the remains of the park, a few oaks, the great
ruined trunks of elms, the rich red-brick wall that bounded what had
been the enclosure.  Inside, nothing but space, every vestige of the house
gone, except for the falling terraces under the grass, going down to the

ornamental water that had now—saddest touch of all—become a cow-
pond; to the east, the great avenue running down the slope and away
into the blue Buckinghamshire distance; on the horizon, the spire of
Steeple Claydon whence the attack came; the dominant colour here the
lemon-yellow of elm leaves lying everywhere.

We entered the church, dedicated (I noticed) to All Saints—and this
was All Saints' day on which we had come. I took it as a good omen,
that was at once in part fulfilled, for on throwing open the door a splendid
interior was revealed: a late Perpendicular masterpiece in this sequestered
spot, a jewel of a church, with its high graceful arcade, the nave so light
and airy, with a continuous clerestory admitting the white November light.
It was like being in a glass-house, but all the same with what richness!

One was transported with its loveliness—one held one's breath—and at
the same time there was the unspeakable poignancy of a place that had
kept its witness through all the ages and that was now left high and dry
like some shell cast up by the retreating ocean, now unregarded, unvisited,
empty and alone.

Something was listening in the silence; perhaps the silence itself was
listening: something that could not get through, that could not be said in
words. The spell was not broken, only deepened, by the comfortable
noises of the afternoon outside; the clatter of the hens in the farmyard,
a cock-crow further away, the lonely sing-song voices of children calling
to each other across the fields.

I WENT UP INTO THE CHANCEL and there were all my friends: all the
people that had lived here and loved this place in centuries gone by,
to me so many living individuals with their troubles and their memories,
the things that had happened to them thronging in my mind. For a
moment it was too much: to find them all here just like that. I sat there
a moment, reflecting on an easier plane how odd it was that I, a stranger,
should come into this place, knowing so much about the men and women
buried there, when I suppose they mean little or nothing to the living
whose place it is.

There on his altar-tomb in the chapel lies Thomas Denton with his wife,
the founder of the family, a lawyer who did well out of the Reformation
and got this manor from the Crown on the crash of the Courtenays. There
they are, two fine alabaster effigies, he in armour, she in close-fitting head-
dress and costume of the mid-sixteenth century, the impulse of the
Renaissance in the motifs on the pilasters on the sides of the tomb.

But the figures have been deliberately slashed, evidently by Cromwell's common soldiery, the sort of people that in all ages hate what is

beautiful because it is beyond them.   The hands of both figures joined in prayer have been cut off at the wrists, one leg of the man and the cushion on which his head rests, so decapitating a pretty little lion creeping up to him.    (I remembered the similar lion on the tomb in Hereford cathedral, that splendid Elizabethan affair on which Thomas Denton's son lies with his first wife, though his body is here with his second.) There are dents on the cheek and on the chin, evidently slashed with a sword or a pike; yet traces of colouring remain on coat and cushion. How brave and fine—and annoying to Puritan Philistines—it must have looked three hundred years ago, when they descended on the place.

Not far away is the Elizabethan limestone monument, with its sarcophagus, to his eldest son Alexander Denton and his second wife : very different from the magnificent altar-tomb on which he is depicted at Hereford, wearing a double chain round his neck and holding a cross in his hands.   He evidently thought to lie there by his young wife, who died in childbirth at the age of eighteen.   But life gained renewed hope for him, and here he is at last, gathered to his father and his descendants. These are many : they lie all around one under the flags, or under their slabs, their monuments upon the walls.   One cannot hope to go into them all : sufficient to note two : the plain white and dove-grey monument to Dr. William Denton, with coloured coat of arms and flowers and fruit at the top—the most appealing member of his family and the one of whom by far the most has come down to us.

The second is a splendid work, a masterpiece by that admirable eighteenth-century sculptor Sir Henry Cheere, of whom Roubiliac was a pupil, and who executed the statue of Christopher Codrington at All Souls and the series of busts that decorate the bookcases in the library there.

Here he has a fine bold composition : a sarcophagus of a rare dark-grey veined marble, slotted or grooved, with beautifully carved great lions' feet supporting; above, an urn in white marble; on either side a portrait-bust, of Judge Denton and his wife; the whole built up on a base and backed by a tall diminishing shaft of dull grey.   The portrait of the Judge is of a speaking character : in cap, ermine, and bands, a full heavy face, of an amiable, kindly man, well-liking and pursy, a face troubled with grief; his young wife, a small well-shaped head poised on an elegant slender neck with one curl coiled round.   The whole thing is a splendid piece of work with its gradations of colouring from dark green-grey to dove-grey and white, and of texture from plain stone to highly polished marble.

He was the last male of his line : Justice of the Common Please and Chancellor to Frederick Prince of Wales, of an excellent reputation for bounty and hospitality.   His youngish wife died before him : *Siste et defle*, etc. After them came heiresses who in two generations carried the place away to the family of Coke of Holkham, who pulled the house down and sold the land.

But before that the house had had its vicissitudes, above all during the period of the Civil War. We derive a fairly full account of events there, and of happenings to its inmates from the *Memoirs of the Verney Family*.

THESE NEIGHBOURING BUCKINGHAMSHIRE families formed as in every county a close-knit, well-defined cousinage, with their own friendships and feuds, their quarrels and joys. Verneys of Claydon, Dentons of Hillesden, Hampdens of Great Hampden, Temples of Stowe, Grenvilles of Wooton: one sees the picture moving through the conflicts, the Civil War, of the seventeenth century into the serene calm, well established and secure, of the Whig oligarchy of the eighteenth.

It is the connection between the Verneys and the Dentons that is closest and to that we owe so much of our knowledge of their common family life. Though they are all gone now, the fields remember them. The tradition is that two black trumpeters in red used to sound a reveille from the hill at Hillesden to be answered by two trumpeters from the other hill. In the intervals left by passing planes one could hear those echoes still.

The foundation of the close relations that subsisted for a century between the two families was the marriage between Margaret Denton, eldest daughter of the house, and Sir Edmund Verney, the King's standard-bearer, who fell at Edgehill, torn between loyalty to his master and his inner conviction that Parliament was in the right.

Margaret's mother, Lady Denton, was a Temple of Stowe: a formidable, dominating old dowager with all the cross-grained character of her family. But like such women she was an excellent manager, a tower of strength to her numerous family and she had a way with children down to the third generation: in her time Hillesden was a matriarchy. Her daughter always came back to her mother for her confinements and almost always one or other of the Verney children was with grandmother for the benefit of 'Hillesden's sweet air.'

Stern with everybody else, the old lady was gentle with her great-grand-children, and we find her pleading with Ralph Verney that his little Mun should not be whipped for being rustic and shy. 'i heare he is disliked, he is so strange. Sonn, you did see he was not soe, nor is not soe, to any where he is a quanted, and he must be wone with fair menes. . . . i pray tell him [Ralph's father] from me, I thought he had more witt then to thinck a childe of his adge woulde be a quanted presently. He knowes the childe was feloe good a nofe in my house. i preye shewe him what I have written abought him, and be shore that he be not frited by no menes; he is of a gentel swet nature, sone corrected.'

'Spare the rod, spoil the child': the horrible adage throws light on the ways of our forefathers: life was apt to be a strenuous struggle for survival for the children.

TROUBLES OF ANOTHER SORT came over the marriage of a younger daughter, another Margaret, who, having been left a rich widow, was much sought after. Her mother objected to one well-qualified suitor because he did not live in Bucks; the daughter observes tartly, 'it was knowne before ever he came to the howes where his estate laye.' It was quite a good one: £2,500 a year in demesne, £800 per annum parsonage land held of the Church, subject only to £300 old rent and his mother's jointure of £100 per annum.

Old Lady Denton could hardly gainsay that: 'for the man, my mother sayes she canot as far as she sees Dislike him, & for my owne part god send me a good hus:, & I care not wher his land lies.' The truth was that her mother favoured a nephew of Lord Falkland's, with a still larger estate, 'but i am soe much against it that I will for no conditiones in the world here of it. . . . Suer I am not so fond as to be in love with any at tow days sight.' Fortunate for her that, being left well-off, she could choose for herself.

These two suitors, cancelling each other out, were followed by Lord Howard of Escrick, a widower with five children. This was no recommendation to Lady Denton, for though she recognized that 'he is honorablye desendede, & upon report is onest & worthye' still 'i will speake it to you I should nevar ventar upon so many children as 5, althoughe the ware wel provided for, for you know it is a grate family.' However, she did not dare to oppose the match, pressed as it was by Lord Pembroke and other great personages at Court.

Her daughter took the matter in her own hands and married some-body off her own bat: the son of Lord Eure, a North Country Catholic peer of no particular fortune. She had evidently been looking out for someone she fancied. Having been married once before, she knew.

At once alarm and despondency spread throughout the family. Ralph Verney wrote to his father, the Standard-bearer, now on the Scottish expedition with the King: 'Oh Sr shee is married, shee is married! and therefore now tis past recall. this unlucky deed was don before I mistrusted ever twas.' His father replied from the campaign: 'This woman laye soe neare my heart that I shall find her folly ther whilst I have an hower to live.' She must have been an attractive girl for them to feel like that about her; but no doubt the thought of a fortune slipping out of the family had something to do with their grief.

Old Lady Denton was furious and in her anger blamed her grandson, Ralph Verney: 'Your mother writes me word about a samite gowne, i remembar i did here before of such a thinge, but no i pray tell her if she would provide sack cloth and line with asshis, then I mought morne for the folie of my wise disobedient children.' Only Ralph's father, Sir Edmund, was spared from this general commination: 'for she often saith you have dealt wisely and honestly and lovingly in this businesse, but all the rest of her children are fooles, and the night before I came from Hillesdon she told me that (except you) wee had all dealt unfaithfully with her.'

There was in fact nothing against the young man, who was a gallant, handsome fellow, save his religion. It was his Catholicism that the old lady had taken so much against—and the disappointment of her own projects. But a visit from the repentant, but safely married couple, did a world of good; and Mrs Eure's sister writes: 'the party (i.e. the old lady) is beter contented a great dell and showes him more respecke then I thought she would a done.' She even went so far as to be willing for the young couple to live with her at Hillesden; but her daughter was not inclined to risk that. 'I must confes to you I like it not by aney meanes, nayther do I thinke as he will.'

Her intention was, 'to youse all the meanes I can to convert hime, for if I live neere London I can have the best devines to my own house, and besides I intend to keepe on myselfe.' Actually it was she that was converted: not surprising considering that she was much in love with the husband she had found for herself. When he was killed, in the autumn of the year 1644, that brought such disasters upon the house at Hillesden, one of the women wrote of him: 'a gallant man, the whole nasion has a lose in him; he had but one fault.' That was his religion, for both the Dentons and the Verneys were strong Protestants.

Lady Sussex wrote to Ralph: 'Your ante is i believe a very sad woman for the lose of her fine husbande—I belive he hath not left her so good a wido as he founde her.' The young Royalist Colonel evidently had the suffrage of all the women; his inconsolable widow wrote of him as 'the galentest man that ever I knew in my Life.'

But within the year she consoled herself with another husband. Her brother, the delightful Doctor, writes to Ralph: 'I hope for the best, for I have great reason to believe she will quickly marry & (which is my comfort) to a Protestant this time.' Her third husband was the second son of Lord Sherard, another soldier, captain in the army of the Dutch States. Within a year he too was dead. She certainly had an improvident way with husbands. But by this time her mother was no longer there to impede or advance her marrying again. Old Lady Denton died before the Civil War brought ruin upon the house.

Her figure loomed so large in the family that we hear little of her husband; but that Ralph Verney was much attached to him we learn from a passionate letter of regret: 'The greate God in whose hand is the soull of every livinge thinge hath by death taken my grandfather into an endlesse life.' His friend advises him to console himself and divert his thoughts with 'Breerwood's Logicke' and 'The Figures and the Tropes Rhetoricall.' Shortly after his mother died: 'Let me be buried in leade att Claydon next where yr ffather porposes to ly himselfe, and lett no strandger winde me, nor doe nott lett me bee striptte, but put a cleane smoke over me . . . and lett my fase be hid and doe you stay in the roome and see me wounde and layed in the firste coffin. . . .' (It is just like the last instructions that Elizabeth Henchard, in *The Mayor of Casterbridge*, left after her death: evidence of the absolute fidelity of Hardy to the old country life.)

After the death of Lady Denton—much concerned to the last about the disposition of her large fortune—her son Alexander reigned in her stead. He married Mary Hampden, a cousin of the great John Hampden; and we hear of a family gathering at Claydon for the christening of their son. At Hillesden a large family were gathered in the house in the first years of the Civil War: not only Alexander and his wife and children, but his sister Mrs Isham and hers, and his unmarried sister Susan.


SUCH WAS THE HOUSEHOLD upon which disaster descended in the year 1644.

The Dentons were Royalists; the convictions of Ralph Verney and his father, as we have seen, on the side of Parliament. But this did not break the good feeling that subsisted between the two houses. At the beginning of 1644 Mrs Isham complains of having soldiers quartered upon them: 'one hundred men in our one house, which my thinkes is very harde to be put in one house, and we being allmost 50 in family.' Hillesden lay in an awkward strategic position out there in the no-man's-land between the King's headquarters at Oxford and the Parliament's forces at Aylesbury, covering the north road to London.

Early in 1644 the Royalists decided to fortify the place. Colonel Smith took command, dug a trench half a mile in circumference, enclosing the house and church. Forage parties from both sides swept the country round; and one day Royalist troopers drove off cattle belonging to a tenant of Mr Hampden's. There was a characteristic dispute as to the rights and wrongs of it—in the middle of a Civil War—and the injured tenant carried his complaint from the Royalists at Hillesden to the Parliamentary commanders at Aylesbury. This woke them up to the danger of allowing the place to be turned into a strong-point; and a surprise was attempted by a force of three hundred horse and foot. It was driven off and the Parliamentary commanders prepared for a regular attack in strength. Half the forces were under the command of Colonel Oliver Cromwell—ominous name, if the Royalist defenders had known.

For with his usual dynamic drive he caught them in the midst of their preparations to stand a siege. Colonel Smith was still engaged on his trenches and throwing up a mound on which to mount the small ordnance he had obtained from Oxford, when out of the March morning, from over the hill at Claydon, Cromwell appeared with overwhelmingly superior forces. A parley was sounded and unconditional surrender demanded. When this was refused the place was carried by assault.

From the first the defenders were overpowered, and driven into the house and church. A second assault followed and the church taken: you may still see the bullet-holes in the old oak door. Seeing the hopelessness of any further defence, Colonel Smith surrendered the house on promise of quarter.

THE PARLIAMENTARY FORCES had certainly made a good haul at Hillesden: a store of ammunition in the church—to think what a narrow escape it had from destruction!—the cellars of the house full of beer, the stables full of horses, the yards of oxen and beasts. In the house a large sum of money was discovered behind the wainscot and in the roof. There were some forty casualties among the defenders. Sir Alexander Denton and his brother were marched off into captivity, the former protesting that he had only come to the house two days before to remove his family thence on the King's placing a garrison there. It was of no avail: off he was marched into the imprisonment from which he did not emerge. Next day, on the rumour of large forces approaching from Oxford—as usual, too late—the house was fired and burnt down: a Cromwellian touch. Having accomplished his purpose, he retired on Buckingham.

It was a melancholy procession of women, with such belongings as they could collect together, that made across the fields to take refuge at Claydon with their relations. Penelope Verney was among them and wrote: 'We were not shamefully used in any way by the souldiers, but they took everything and I was not left scarce the clothes of my back.' Mrs Isham described how 'Hillesden park pales be every one up and burned or else carried away, and the Denton children like to beg.'

On his way to the Tower, Sir Alexander wrote to his Steward to 'take a viewe of the house that was burnt upon Tuesday, that I may have some certayne information of what destruction is fallen upon mee, and whether it bee possible to rebuild those walls that are standing if the distractions of the times should settle.'    Ralph Verney wrote to his brother : 'Suffer me to tell you how much I am afflicted for the ruine of sweet Hillesden and the distresses that happened to my aunt and sisters. God knowes what has become of my unhappie brother that was there taken.'

The taking of Hillesden had its consequences in two romantic episodes to which the stress—and the excitement—of war gave opportunity.   One of the Parliamentary assaulters, Captain Jaconiah Abercrombie, fell for one of the distressed Royalist ladies, Sir Alexander's unmarried sister, Susan, already well on the way to becoming an old maid.   Like his commander, the Captain must have been very prompt in action.   Three days after, John Denton writes: 'My sister Susan, her new husband Captain Abercromy is quartered at Addington.'    But in June we hear from gossipy Mrs Isham—now silent enough under her slab in the chapel— 'My sis: Susans marage is to be accomplished very suddnly if her captive be not killed, it tis him as did first plunder Hilsdon. . . . The Capt. his land is in Irerland, he is half Skotts, half Irish.  I think fue of her frinds lik it, but if she hath not him she will never have any, it is gone so far.'

What is the explanation?   Are we to conclude that the impetuous Ulsterman carried his woman off with him as part of the spoils?   Anyway their brief happiness, snatched out of the chances of war, was soon at an end : next year he was killed by a party of Cavaliers from Boarstall and was buried at Hillesden among the family whose house he had plundered and whose daughter he had married.

A SECOND MATCH was not much longer in train.   The Royalist Commander, Colonel Smith, had in the course of the operations fallen in love with Sir Alexander's young daughter, Margaret.   His imprisonment in the Tower along with Sir Alexander advanced his suit.   In August we hear from Mrs. Isham, who was sharing imprisonment with her men-folk, her brother and her husband, in order to look after them: 'I thinke it will be a happy mach if these ill times doth not hindre it, but he is still a Prisenor.  So you may thinke itt a bolde venter, but if these times hold, I thinke thay will be non men lefte for woman.'

She at any rate was determined to do her best, and with the aid of Susan Verney procured the Colonel's escape—for which they earned a spell of

P

incarceration on their own account.  Truly did Dr Denton declare that 'women were never soe usefull as now.'  As for Colonel Smith, he died in his bed, a baronet.

Sir Alexander's troubles were not yet at an end.  There was his eldest son, John, a gallant fighting fellow who was shot through the thigh 'endeavouring to gett my house then in the parliaments possession.'  In August he was killed in leading the assault on a Parliamentary outwork at Abingdon.  He seems to have been a well-loved young man—'that good young man whose very enemies lament him,' one account says.  'I must ever account it as on of my greatest and particular afflictions to loose the man that you and I did love soe well,' wrote Ralph Verney to Sir Alexander, 'but this is our comfort, hee lived and died most gallantly, and questionlesse is now most happy.'  What a consolation—that is not for us—it was to them in their day to be so sure of a better world!  Not long after, Sir Alexander received his quietus: he was not yet fifty, but the succession of blows had worn out his resistance.  He died in captivity on New Year's day, 1645, and was brought home at last to Hillesden.

He had borne his troubles with all submission, in the spirit of his contemporary, Herrick:

> Rapine has yet took nought from me :
> But if it please my God I be
> Brought at the last to th' utmost bit,
> God make me thankful still for it.
> I have been grateful for my store,
> Let me say grace when there's no more.

This was far from being the spirit of Aunt Isham—as she was known to all the family: she did not cease to complain of her misfortunes to all her relations: 'For our clothes we must sew fig leaves together, we lost all by fier, and since I have had but one gown.  I could wish as it would last me forty yeres as the childrenes of Iserells did, but, however, now I am come to town, I have not where withal to buye another.'  She had not lost all interest in the world's affairs, however, when she adds: 'Ye fust of May but never so dull an one, and so fue chases [chaises] in hide Parke as I heare.'

WITH THE END OF THE CIVIL WAR, things became more settled and people began to make the best of things, whether they liked them or no.  They began to reconstruct their lives on the old foundations in the old places.  Already in 1648 we hear of Hillesden 'they are building there againe and

intend to sett upp a little house where the old one stood.' In spite of
Ralph Verney's lament, under the rule of Cromwell's Major-Generals,
'I confess I love Old England very well, but as things are carried heere the
gentry cannot joy much to bee in it'—or perhaps rather because of it—
there was a tendency for the gentry to draw together, whether Royalist
or Parliamentarian, in self-defence against the new order. It was the
foundation upon which the Restoration came about.

We find one of the Isham correspondents writing: 'In these degenera-
ting times, the gentry had need to close neerer together, and make a banke
and bulwarke against that sea of Democracy which is over running them :
and to keep their descents pure and untainted from that Mungrill breed,
which would faigne mixe with them.'

In reaction to their exclusion from politics and power, and to the social
dullness of Puritan rule, the gentry went in more and more for horse-racing
and gambling: already the gracious wind of the Restoration is blowing.
Life has returned to the house of Hillesden, and Aunt Isham, who dearly
loves a little gambling, complains that she is quite worn out by the late
hours her rakish soldier-nephew, Harry Verney, keeps: 'he will never give
one over as Longe as one is able to sit up.' Visits are resumed; the connection between the families is as close and affectionate as ever. The
chief bond is between Ralph Verney and dear Uncle Doctor away in
London. But now the Ishams are staying at Claydon; now Ralph is with
his cousins at Hillesden.

His sister Penelope married another Denton, John Denton of Fawley
in Oxfordshire. They were always in trouble. Now her husband is in
prison at Oxford Castle for debt, and Pen is 'almost brought to deth's
dore . . . this 3 days I have not eate more then a mess of milk and a
negg. I must sell myself to my sking, goods & all to defray this great
chargis.' Their three children died young. And then it turned out that
her husband was cracked: 'Mr Denton has bin so outragious with me,
that he has run after me with his knif in his hand and vowed to stob me.'

It throws an odd light on the attitude of earlier centuries towards
insanity that at a wedding feast at Claydon an elaborate practical joke
was played on him: a letter was composed telling him that his mother
was labouring to have his younger brother made a lord, but that if he
would part with £500 he should have the honour himself; that his kins-
woman, Lady Studdall, was working so successfully for his interests at
Court that it was thought he was to be made a Lord of the Privy Council,
and so on. There this cruel jest remains among the Verney papers,
carefully endorsed 'A Sham Letter to John Denton that is crackt.'

But a year or two and he was dead. He had not been an unlovable
man: he had had something of that quality of the Dentons. Sir Ralph
wrote to his sister: 'though you have been unhappy in him, yet hee was

a Gentleman & your Husband, & twill be your Honour to conceale his faults.' Pen put on handsome mourning for him, but she was not inconsolable. She set up house in London with her gallant racing brother, Harry, whom she adored; there was not much love lost between her and the Dentons.

Before the Restoration the young squire at Hillesden died. He had never been able to get upsides with the devastated inheritance he took over from his father: the losses had not been made good, debts accumulated, he ran through his wife's fortune: he was no manager, things were too much for him. Shortly after, the bells of Claydon and Hillesden rang out and bonfires burned on the hills for the return of the King. Pen Denton expressed everybody's thoughts in her woman's way: 'I pray God send we may live to see peace in our times, and that friends may live to injoye each other.'

Aunt Isham, who had for so long been a feature of the landscape, was next to go, scattering little bequests to all her female relations: to one 'my little silver grater and my silver measure,' to another 'my diamond Bodkin but first put a stone in it,' to a third 'my little gold ring with a posie Ever Constant.' Except for her brother, the Doctor, she seems to have had most personality of all her family; 'she lived & dyed a good Xstian,' he wrote of her, 'and the best of us can doe no more.'

There is a genuine tribute to her personality behind the formal phrases of her Latin epitaph in the church where she worshipped from her girl-hood and where she had witnessed such vicissitudes: 'Pia Mater! Certa Amica! Optima Conjux! Hic jacet quae virtute sua praelucet vivis sibique fit superstes matrona tam tenax, amicitiae tam jurata cultrix. . . .'

SO LONG AS SIR RALPH VERNEY and the Doctor lived—and they both lived well into their ninth decade— relations between the two families continued close. But there was a new generation at Hillesden, where another Alexander, grandson of him of the Civil War, was growing up in the reign of Charles II. On the King's death we find him consulting his great-uncle, Sir Ralph, 'whether it be my duty for to goe into mourning . . . being in the Country, or if it be necessary for me, then whether my wife must doe the like, & whether it must be black cloth or Crape. I would not be singular.'

His wife was Hester Harman, only daughter of Nicholas Harman of Middleton Stony in Oxfordshire: beautiful and an heiress. Her pathetic story is told by John Verney: 'After she had had 7 children, on Thursday 29 March 1688, she left his house and him, & Monday 17 September 1688, she was delivered of a girle, which he would not own, named Eliz.

who soon died. This his wife Hester died in Aug. 1691 about Spittlefields & was buryed in Stepney Ch. meanely.' The poor woman's fortune he had apparently already squandered. Sir Ralph wrote once to let Alexander know that he had heard of Hester in London; he only replied that he wished her at Jamaica. Within a few years he too was dead: like her, still young.

WITH THESE LATER generations it seems the Denton stock was failing; they had never been long lived. And with the deaths at length of Sir Ralph and the Doctor the intimacy goes out of the relations between Verneys and Dentons, that had subsisted so long, and with such fortunate results for posterity. A slightly hostile note creeps into the references of one to the other, exacerbated by politics. For after the Revolution of 1688, young Sir Edmund Denton came under the influence of the Whig Lord Wharton and marched along with the Temples in Buckinghamshire politics; while the Verneys adhered to the Church and Tory interest: a curious transposition of rôles from earlier days.

We hear of Sir Edmund become 'rich and great'; perhaps by marriage, for he married the daughter of a Court official, who was Clerk of the Board of Green Cloth. He held some office himself, which he lost on Queen Anne's accession and promptly quarrelled with his wife. He too died young, and is buried under a finely cut slate slab in the chancel of the church.

It is pleasant to record that in later years relations improved and neighbourly visits were paid between the two houses. In October, 1709, we read of all the Verneys being invited to Lady Denton's, 'and a fine entertainment we had; it was a Leaven dishes the first course, and a Doe killed on purpose on this occasion.' Alas, that we cannot keep up the standards of our forefathers! There was a large company to enjoy the Michaelmas venison.

Judge Denton succeeded his brother: the last of the male line at Hillesden. He was evidently a hospitable, agreeable, easy kind of man, a very worthy representative for the family to end with. He had scholarly inclinations and was a friend of Browne Willis and Parson Cole of Bletchley, who describes a visit to Hillesden in the autumn of 1735. He calls the house a good old one, on a beautiful hill, commanding a delightful prospect; before it a large parterre; below, a canal; below that, a very bold terrace; and through the gardens, charming vistas terminated by groups of trees and windmills. It must have been delightful. But 'the best thing belonging to this place is its master; to speak of whose humanity, probity and bounty, would be like telling the world that the warmth of

the sun produces the fruits of the earth.' The Judge was—have we not
guessed it already?—a martyr to the gout. 'I cannot say that I am much
better for the country,' he writes to his neighbour at Claydon, 'though
my spirits and appetite are better but my pains are very violent.' His
neighbour replies wishing he may find benefit from 'Hillesden's sweet air'
—the long correspondence between Verneys and Dentons ends on that
appropriate note—and with the hope that 'your pains will cease quite.'
With the spring, they ceased for ever.


SO MUCH FOR THE DENTONS at Hillesden.

But half the richness of English history lies in the way layer upon layer
is to be descried under the surface by the discerning eye. Before the
Dentons there were the Courtenays. And there lies a very nice point
about the nature of the Reformation changes in this country. As the
result of them, eligible estates like Hillesden were apt all over the country
to fall away from the great absentee nobles consuming their substance
away at the Court or in some great house, and to come into the hands of
smaller families who made their homes on the spot, cultivated them for
all they were worth, identified themselves with them, prospered or
declined with the place itself.

In fact we may say that the heart of those changes, the permanent
upshot of them, was the rise of the gentry; the symbol, some such thing
as here at Hillesden—the arms of the Dentons painted on the east wall
where once stood the statue of the Saint.

The fabric of the church, save for their monuments, knows nothing of
the Dentons—except that it holds their dust. It belongs to the century
before they came, itself a moving memorial to the sense of beauty and the
art of the late medieval craftsmen. The parishioners of Hillesden, all
those coloured medieval tillers of the soil, those ploughmen and peasants
in from the fields, and the distant Black Canons of Notley who owned
the rectory and so were responsible for the chancel, must have been
determined to do themselves proud. Look at the magnificence of the
chancel: high up under the roof a choir of angel-figures, elaborately
carved in stone with traces of their colouring still remaining, red and
blue, ending up with the angel musicians playing upon their organs, their
viols, lutes, and pipes. How it speaks of the certainty of the world of
faith, the unity of all things visible and invisible!

What must this chancel have been like in the first flourish of its beauty
with all the glass in its windows—that forgotten art—red and blue and
green and gold! There are lights remaining in only one window to tell
us something of what we have lost—wonderfully vivid scenes in the life of
St Nicholas, patron of sailors and all in peril on the sea.

Here is the boy in red falling into the sea, the sailors hoisting sail:
the inscription, *Cadit puerulus quem mox salvat Nicholaus*. Here again
is a three-masted ship, with rigging and sails furled, at the quay-side with
men unloading corn and tying it up in sacks: the whole full of life and
action and that *naïveté* of spirit which enabled the medievals to transmit
their vision so powerfully to the world. (Our dreams have no permanence,
no lasting quality, in comparison.)

I wonder if we owe the theme of this window to that John Courtenay,
an earlier owner of Hillesden in the thirteenth century, who was once in
great peril on the sea by reason of a tempest rising at night. The mariners
expected shipwreck; but he bade them have courage and labour one hour
more, for that would be the time when his monks of Ford rose for matins
and they would be praying for him, and by their prayers they would be
preserved from danger. One of the company said that there was then no
hope for they were all still asleep. Courtenay answered that they inter-
ceded day and night, and 'because I love them, and they love me, I know
and verily believe that already they are interceding to God for me and
mine, in safety and in calamity. And immediately the tempest ceasing,
they all came safe to land.'

SO, OUR MINDS TEEMING with memories, half in a trance so strong was
the impression that forgotten place had made upon us, we went down
the little winding road to where the pastures opened at the foot, on
either side.

Looking at the velvety emerald-green of shadow resting on the
ploughed land—suddenly the All Clear sounded across the countryside.
Astonished, we could not believe our ears—the war now sometime over
and behind us. For a moment we stood there incredulous, struck-still,
in the road, the familiar nightmare once more returned. Then a few steps
forward around the bend and a David Cox scene presented itself: the
corner of a plaster cottage, a little girl pushing a wheelbarrow, with a red
hat to punctuate. The siren went again across the fields of Hillesden now
behind us.

We went on our way to Buckingham, the road trodden by so many
Dentons in the past—one disquieted, troubled mind turning backwards
from the nightmare of our time to the troubles of theirs, and before them
to the troubles and the bloodshed of the Courtenays, and before them the
de Veres and the Boelbecs, who held Hillesden from the Giffards, who
got it from the Conqueror; and before that, to Alric the thegn who held
it of the Confessor, and so back to the original Saxon settler who gave
his name to this place on the hill, standing above the swirl and conflict of
peoples out of which we came.

# 1848: The Year of Revolution

## by *ROHAN BUTLER*

NEXT year, 1948, will be the centenary of the Year of Revolution in France, Italy, Germany, Austria, Hungary and Czechoslovakia. Since in 1848 revolution was international. That was what made it so startling, and makes it still significant. In this revolutionary spread the two big exceptions—for history is the home of exceptions—were the two great outlying powers on either flank of the Continent: England, in relation to which Ireland was only moderately disturbed that year, while Chartism fizzled out in a rainstorm; and Russia, in relation to which Poland achieved no national-liberal uprising comparable to that of the earlier wave of insurrection in 1830. And so the Czar Nicholas I could write to Queen Victoria on April 3, 1848: 'What remains standing in Europe? Great Britain and Russia.'

By April 3 much had happened, so much that it may be best, instead of trying to survey straight off the whole panorama of revolution, to begin more modestly with a single close-up.

At about half-past nine on the night of February 23, 1848, young Gustave Flaubert, up in Paris from Rouen to see the fun, was walking back with a couple of friends from dinner at the *Trois Frères Provençaux* to the flat of one of his companions at No. 30 Place de la Madeleine. The three were hurrying in order to get past a disorderly column of unarmed national guards waving torches and coloured lanterns in the same way that the crowds had been doing for most of the evening. This was in celebration of the fall, announced that afternoon, of the ministry of the sagacious Guizot who for eight years had directed an unlovely rule of the rich until he became 'puffed up by his unpopularity.' To add to the festivity, more lanterns, together with candles and spluttering gas-jets, illuminated the housefronts and were caught up in dancing reflections upon the helmets of the dragoons massed on the Boulevard des Capucines. The trio made a detour and had just reached the door of No. 30 when a loud report rang out. 'It's a volley. Let's go and see,' said Flaubert. The owner of the flat answered: 'A volley! Are you mad? That's children letting off fire-crackers in celebration. Let's go up to my place.' They did so, and spent an intellectual evening listening to the third member of the party, a minor poet named Bouilhet, reading a long and dreary poem of his called *Melaenis*.

But Flaubert had been right. What he heard was the shooting on the Boulevard des Capucines which suddenly, before people quite realized what was happening, brought the makeshift July Monarchy toppling down and substituted the Second Republic. And the repercussions were wider still. The shots of February 23 rang out eastwards across Europe and were repeated in the affray of March 13 in the Herrengasse at Vienna which ended the reactionary age of Metternich and prompted that prudent statesman to fly the city next day in a laundry cart. On March 18 the 'two shots' at Berlin began the battle which raged round the barricades despite the display from the palace of Frederick-William IV of a characteristically pathetic banner inscribed 'Misunderstanding!'; three days later the King of Prussia rode through Berlin under the black-red-gold banner of the revolution and issued his famous proclamation that 'Prussia is merging into Germany.' On the same day as the uprising in Berlin the citizens of Milan likewise took to the barricades and after five days of furious fighting compelled the withdrawal of the Austrian whitecoats whose morale had been reduced not only by hunger and insurgent assault, but also by the constant clanging of the city's many bells. On the same day that Milan was freed, March 22, Austrian power collapsed at Venice where a republic was proclaimed by the Jewish insurrectionist Manin. Next day Charles Albert, the 'wobbling king' of Sardinia, declared war on Austria. Simultaneously the cohesion of the Habsburg Empire was threatened from the other side by the nationalist ferment of reform in Kossuth's Hungary. All across Europe, in small states as in big, revolutions came frothing to the surface in sympathetic impulse, so that the anarchist Bakunin later wrote of those heady days: 'We were in such a state of mind that if somebody had come and told us "God has been turned out of heaven and a republic proclaimed there," everyone would have believed it and nobody would have been surprised.'

After only four months, from February–March to June–July, 1848, this froth had largely subsided. By mid-June Bakunin himself was in flight from Prague where the Austrians under the methodical Prince Alfred Windischgrätz knocked the stuffing out of the Czech insurgents by bombarding the city, thus, incidentally, avenging the shooting of the Princess Windischgrätz. (Bakunin found refuge in Anhalt where he apparently consoled himself by writing a fragment of an erotic novelette.) This was the first notable victory of reaction. Thereafter the tide turned rapidly. In Paris the balance of political power had shifted more to the right and the disbanding of the national workshops provoked a proletarian rising which was crushed by the waddling General Cavaignac, with his new technique of house-to-house clearance of barricades, after four days of most ferocious fighting—it is said that they cost the French Army more officers killed than any one of the great Napoleonic victories. A few days later the German parliament at Frankfurt, which had been busy steering the revolution into safe channels, elected the learned Austrian Archduke John to be Imperial Vicar at the head of a provisional government for federal Germany.   The Habsburg interest was further strengthened by the octogenarian Marshal Radetzsky's victory over the Piedmontese at Custozza on July 25.   Next day the parliament at Vienna unanimously carried a most important resolution for the emancipation of the peasantry of the Austrian Empire, thereby strengthening it still further, since after the entry into force in September of this judicious measure the Austrian peasants mostly lost interest in revolution.

Thus, by one means or another, were the revolutionary forces in Europe tamed.   They were not extinguished yet, as was demonstrated by later episodes such as the October rising in Vienna and scattered outbreaks in Germany, while the revolutionary movements in Hungary and Italy were not broken until 1849.   But henceforth the counter-revolutionary tide came flowing in.   Already by the end of 1848 Bonapartism was at the head in France, and Austria was under the domination of the masterful reactionary Prince Felix Schwarzenberg, brother-in-law to Prince Alfred Windischgrätz.   Schwarzenberg further made his overbearing influence felt in Germany during the liquidation of the Frankfurt parliament and the federal régime in 1849; and next year he inflicted on Prussia the diplomatic Humiliation of Olmütz which was only to be wiped out upon the field of Sadowa, the first landmark in the Bismarckian unification of Germany by blood and iron.   That, rather than parliamentary liberalism, was in future to be the German way of development.

Such, most briefly, was the course of the revolutionary movement of 1848.   One may well ask how it was that this movement should so quickly have gathered international impetus, sweeping all before it; and how it was that such a surge of revolution should have been so quickly and relatively easily overcome.   The answers to these two questions are closely interrelated.

The revolution of 1848 was international because, fundamentally, it was the joint outcome of the two great earlier revolutions which, though national in origin, were international in significance.   These two were the Industrial Revolution in England and the French Revolution of 1789.

By comparison with the dynamic pace of the English industrial revolution the corresponding trends in France and, still more, Germany during the first half of the nineteenth century were evolutionary rather than revolutionary.   In 1848 both countries were still predominantly agricultural.   But within this traditional setting great changes had none the less been under way, especially in the two fields of railway transport and the mechanization of industry.

In France as in England the 'forties were the great age of railways, and by 1848 there were between thirty and forty French railway companies. This newly imposed network produced corresponding social changes, as for instance in the organization of mobile labour where it disrupted the very old French system of *Compagnonnage* based on craft practice. (The *compagnons* were still grouped in sections bearing such mediaeval titles as the Children of Solomon and the rival Children of Master James.) Similarly in Germany, where the vigorous economist List constituted himself a kind of railway-promoter-general. To take but one example, when the railway between Berlin and Frankfurt was at last completed, despite Hessian obstruction, it put an end to the easy prosperity which the old Thuringian coaching villages had derived from their central position. Throughout Germany, and indeed Europe, independent transport workers such as carriers and bargees were fighting a losing battle against the competition of railways and steamboats.

This economic shift of stress, with its accompanying dislocations, was sharply intensified by the mechanization of industry even in its early stages. According to admittedly defective figures the number of French establishments of all kinds possessing steam-engines rose from about 15 in 1815 to 625 in 1830, to 5,200 in 1848. It was during the same period in Germany that effective exploitation of the great Ruhr, Roer and Silesian coalfields began, while in the 'forties such names as Borsig and Krupp begin to crop up. In 1844 the small Silesian spinners, who could no longer compete with the big manufacturers, rose in revolt and were suppressed with bloodshed.

The human background to this bare recital is the rapid growth of urban agglomerations of sweated labour which were a prey, as never before, to the boom and slump of an industrial economy, that is, to the twin enemies, hunger and unemployment. In 1840 nine out of every ten young men called up for military service from ten predominantly industrial French Departments were rejected as physically unfit. In Vienna the starving and homeless slept in the sewers, and there grew up bands of youthful unemployed known as the Lads in Caps (*Kappelbuben*). The Hungry Forties reigned upon the Continent no less than in England, especially after the successive harvest failures in 1845 and 1846. On top of this came the financial panic of 1847–8 with many business crashes, many thrown out of a job. Economic incentives to the urban revolutions of 1848, symbolized by the street barricades, were certainly not wanting.

Against such a background it is not difficult to understand the growth of socialist thought and its international tinge in the years preceding the Year of Revolution. The widespread uprisings of February and March, 1848, seemed to come almost as a spontaneous response to the ringing call of the Communist Manifesto, issued a few weeks earlier: 'Workers of all lands, unite!' And if Germany was having its first taste of the dialectical materialism of Feuerbach and Marx, France was stirred by the socialist teaching of the combative Proudhon with his ominous war-cry, 'Property is theft,' and by Louis Blanc's programmatic best-seller

*L'Organisation du Travail* which set up the ideal of state-controlled socialist *savoir-faire* against the prevalent liberal doctrine of *laissez-faire*.

The socialist growth could trace its pedigree back to 1789, and Heine, for instance, noticed that Parisian workers in the Faubourg Saint Marceau were in 1842 reading 'new editions of speeches by old Robespierre, Marat's pamphlets at two sous a copy, Cabet's *History of the Revolution,* Cormenin's poisonous little works, and Buonarotti's *Babœuf's Doctrine and Conspiracy*—all writings which smell of blood.'  The after-influence of the great French Revolution was, however, so comprehensive that it embraced the liberal outlook no less than the socialist, indeed rather more so.  When after 1815 the Holy Alliance under the inspiration of Metternich tried to clamp down international reaction, the international answer was the growth of a liberal demand for responsible government which, whether consciously or no, derived in large measure from the principles of 1789.  Here, then, was another international current making for 1848.

Thus liberal and socialist currents of opinion flowed largely from a single source, but in different directions, so that when they converged again in 1848 they ran foul of each other.  This inner contradiction between middle-class liberalism and working-class socialism was one of the main causes of the quick disintegration of the revolution, especially in France, where, as Marx pointed out at the time, the social structure was in a more advanced stage of development than elsewhere so that the revolution there was, so to speak, one lap ahead of those in other countries. In Paris the moderate elements managed to take over the revolution in the early days, as was symbolized by the success on February 25 of the poet Lamartine (who became Foreign Minister) in persuading the revolutionaries to adopt the old tricolour flag with a red rosette on the staff instead of the uncompromising red flag which they had wanted.  After four months of growing tension the clash came in those June days which saw the first socialist revolution in Europe.  It came as a naked and sanguinary class-conflict, a new phenomenon which struck sudden horror into contemporaries who did not know how properly to describe it—they sometimes called it a new 'servile war.'  This social revolution was, as has been seen, suppressed until its next outbreak in the Commune of 1871.

If the success of the revolution in France was compromised by the cross-currents of liberalism and socialism, the revolution elsewhere was compromised by the cross-currents of liberalism and nationalism.

Nowadays it is not very easy to appreciate the great significance at that time of the nationalist legacy of 1789, the novel ideal of *la patrie* of free and equal citizens.  But so great was it in fact that liberal and national tended to become almost coefficient terms, especially in those countries which were not nations yet, especially in Germany and Italy.  This explains why the German revolution so quickly became bogged down in intricate disputes between the Great German and Little German parties about the desirable composition of the new Germany and, more particularly, the question of an *Anschluss* with Austria (the word first appeared then in this connection). It likewise explains why in Italy the revolution had, in the ultimate calculation, to take second place to the prime necessity of a national struggle against the Austrian overlords.

One notices that in the case of both Italy and Germany a cardinal position was occupied by Austria. It has been truly said of that time that if Germany was lurking in Prussia, Europe was lurking in Austria. East of the Rhine Austria was the main pivot of revolution and counter-revolution. For the brutal fact was that the only way of achieving the national-liberal programme was by tearing the Austrian Empire to pieces, as was in fact done just seventy years later. But in 1848 the time for that was not come by a long way. It is remarkable, for instance, how many of the staunchest supports of the Habsburg régime at that time were Slavs like the Czech savant Palacky or the Croat general Jellacic; they supported it because they knew that they could not then cope alone with the master-races, the Germans and the Magyars. Thus did the real fortunes of the revolution in Central Europe come to depend much less upon the high ideals of the revolutionaries than upon the hard power-politics of the chancelleries of Europe. That was how the revolution was stifled beyond the Rhine.

If, then, one seeks a verdict upon the revolutionary phenomenon of 1848 it must be something of this kind. It was, despite the socialist spearhead, above all a liberal revolution. And a liberal revolution is a very difficult revolution to pull off successfully, as Marx and Lenin drummed home in later years. Yet 1848 did demonstrate some of the strength of liberalism, even as a revolutionary creed, as well as its obvious weaknesses. If the events of that remarkable year constituted an immediate defeat for the people militant, they were an ultimate victory for the people appellant. Despite the reaction, things after 1848 were not as before. Even the most reactionary régimes had to realize that serious demands for reform could not just be dismissed as 'Jacobinism.' The Year of Revolution distinguished liberalism from socialism in people's minds, and largely imparted a liberal flavour to the nineteenth century upon the Continent of Europe.

Thus the lesson of 1848 is, like most of the lessons of history, double-edged. It suggests that in the processes of state and society the harsh realities of power-politics, of money, of organization, of armaments are very heavy and, one might think, decisive factors. But it also teaches that even power-politics are subject to the influence of other forces of idealism and belief: that convictions still count in the ordering of the affairs of this imperfect world.

# A Portrait of a Port

*by ROBERT HARLING*

*drawings by John Nash*

'A LARGE and respectable village, seated on a picturesque acclivity at the point where the navigable river begins to expand into a broad estuary,' records the *History, Gazetteer and Directory* of the County, published a century ago. 'Colliers and other large vessels here receive and discharge their cargoes by means of lighters,' added Mr. William White, the compiler of the *Directory*, and then, not unmindful perhaps of the real pride of the village, he wrote, 'it may be termed the shipping port of the town.'

Yesterday, Saturday, we left the quayside house of friends and crossed the river in the small rowboat, sculled by the sturdy, sunfaced ferryman. From midstream we looked back to see the 'large and respectable village' almost as it was in Mr White's day. The other, later part of the port is shut away behind the simple elevations of the houses which stand along the quay. The illusion is beguiling, almost complete.

The ferry grounded gently on the causeway that rises towards the other bank. Nash climbed out and began to walk along the uneven marshland. I sat in the boat and watched him fumble for the odd stubs of pencil he carries in his waistcoat, for those ancient envelopes he carries in his jacket and on which he notes, in draughtsman's shorthand, first impressions of anything that takes his eye. The boat began to stand away from the causeway, but the ferryman waited for travellers to the northern bank. He, too, watched Nash.

'Quiet today,' I said. The dullest opening is, after all, the safest and often the most rewarding.

'Aye, quiet enough. No sailing. Tide's making though.' He let his oars rest inboard for a minute, rolled and lit a cigarette, cupping his hand around the flame, wary of the rising wind that soon would bring the rain.

'Much shipbuilding here these days?' I asked, watching Nash take an uneasy stance against the breeze, begin to make his notes.

The ferryman sent out an appreciative puff upon the breeze. 'No, no building gown on 'ere now. Just finished the last job. Only conversions now. That owd wooden minesweeper down river there'll soon be a frozen fish ship. As soon as they c'n git the timber, that is, but seems they can't get it yet awhiles.' He spoke slowly in the flat voice of that part of the coast, the 'ow' sounds emphatic and displeasing to the ear.

I said it was the same everywhere.

'Aye, mebbe, but not for them. The Norwegians had 'er first and now they sold 'er to the Icelanders. Now they're getting priority. The Icelanders'll git their timber from the Norwegians, then they'll all be happy. And we can't git a standard o' timber for oursels.'

He began to talk about another vessel that the yard had just built. 'Launching next Monday,' he said gloomily. 'Then there's no more shipbuilding 'ere. Gov'ment's stopped it. Not economic they say. S'pose we're s'posed to keep alive on repairs.'

Nash was now at work. He seemed stubbornly to draw, to smoke, to clutch his hat. I wondered what he would be noting, and looked again to the port.

To the left, downriver, is the eastern shipyard; then, nearer, the fish-cannng factory, a great weatherboarded structure that dominates the lower part of the village.

'Do they can only fish?' I asked.

'No, anything they c'n git 'old of. They canned shrimps before the war, but now it's fish or anything. Meat if they c'n git any these days.'

'I've never seen a local label on a tin of fish paste.'

'An' not likely to. This stuff's sold in bulk to the big manifacters. In the old days they'd buy up all we ever cetch. They liked shrimps mostly.'

Nearer, standing back from the quay, is a group of small houses, built originally in Tudor times, but bowed windows and trellised porticos were added during those years we loosely term the Regency. Their prim uniformity is now lessened by architectural oddities and subfusc paints added by the individualists of our own time. The houses must have been pleasurable to many eyes a century or more ago, stucco translations from the heights of Hampstead or St. John's Wood.

Next, huddled above the river, is the sailing club: a small hut within a rickety stockade, rather like a set in a wild western film. The club-house is built partly on piles, partly on the old oyster beds which two brothers built here long ago. Then the brothers quarrelled and divided the beds. The foundations of the beds and their wall of division are still to be seen. Now there is talk along the waterfront that part of these old foundations should be made into a paddling pool for children, but so far there is but talk, and children test the temperature of the river farther upstream, where the ferryman awaits his passengers.

Most of the boats that are sailed from this small club are half-decked, twelve- or fifteen-footers, craft for amateurs and enthusiasts. Here are no fashionable folk or upstage pennants, few peaked yachting caps and no attendant cars and launches. The river is too narrow and too muddy, and the sailor must always wait upon the dictate of the tide. Only the local Liptons know the joys of the beat down to the estuary: only they would defend the vagaries of this river against the splendours of the Solent. A few larger yachts and a two-masted schooner of impressive tonnage are hauled out near the ferry, but they are more like pathetic visitors, left high and dry and now forgotten.

The main part of the port is built along the quay: a row of grey, stock-brick buildings: two or three dwelling-houses, an old storehouse where our friends now live, and the sailmaker's shop with its large window and loft above—at least, it *was* the sailmaker's house, but last year he sold out, and the house has now become an institute for training local youngsters in the disciplines of seamanship. The institute has been repainted. Where bales of sailcloth were once unrolled, to be measured and stitched into the cunning shapes of mainsails, jibs, and spinnakers, there is now the hull of a small sailing craft set upon trestles so that novitiates may walk around to point their hesitant queries.

Another house abuts the sailmaker's house, then a pub, with large

Q

overhanging, weatherboarded bays above the quay, then an alleyway leading into the town.

Across the alley is the house of a merchant of Georgian times, a careful man without a doubt, for he built himself this pleasant home with its simple, sixteen-pane windows and large walled garden, carefully shielded from chiding east winds by his adjoining warehouse.

The four-story warehouse, with its outside staircase, rises high above the old boathouses which are built above the sloping hard. Here, too, is what is left of the old Excise House, but if you are inclined to anger when you see architectural desecration this part of the port will make you mad and sad, for here, not long ago, was the tower from which the customs man once scanned the river. The tower dated from the seventeenth century: to reach its platform you climbed an earlier Jacobean staircase, substantial and unspoiled; but in this country there is always someone strong enough to spoil such things, however substantial, and now the tower has gone and the remains of the staircase are broken and irreparable.

Across another alleyway is a row of red-brick Georgian cottages, cramped and orderly, with white doors, white window-bars and a white communal fence.

These houses, warehouses, and cottages were built between the ship-yards which make the limits of the port. The skeletal shapes of these small yards have not greatly changed since Nelson's time, when ships were built here for that great sailor's fleet. Local legend says, indeed, that England's last wooden man-o'-war was built in this small river port just over a century ago.

That is the port I saw. I wondered what Nash would see. The quay, under the vast skies that lie always above this low landscape, seemed as unpretentious and precise as an engraved vignette in an early guide-book. From here, seated in the bows of the ferry, the rows of Victorian villas built along the straight streets of the new town, spaced mathematically apart like a regiment of little pillboxes, are hidden. Here are no shops with tins of pilchards and baked beans. Such things are shut away. Here is only Mr White's large and respectable village.


OVERBLOWN BLOBS from thundery clouds began to fall upon the thwarts of the boat. Nash came back along the bank, unhurried, looking back across the marsh. He stepped into the boat.

'Any luck?' I asked as we shoved off.

'Interesting,' he said, turning up his collar. 'I've rather neglected this sort of thing lately. Too many pastoral studies. Makes one want to start painting ships and quays again. Look at that!' He pointed inland.

'There! That clump of trees, then the river and then the estuary under this sky. Superb.'

Three unwise, fretful travellers called from the bank, but we were now in midstream.

'Aye, I c'n see you,' said the ferryman. 'Y'can wait there awhiles. I'm gittin' me coat. I ain't sittin' 'ere gittin' soaked through for anybody. Aye, y'can shout.'

We reached our shelter. For exact reporting, I should perhaps say that I ran and Nash followed, still unhurried, perhaps still speculative upon the prospect of many paintings before him.

During the storm we sat talking within the large white room, once a store-room and a shop. Now the room is filled with books, paintings, old canvases, prints, pottery, desks, a large table, and settees; it is a medley of work in progress and prizes gained from travels and wily collecting. A staircase rises straight from the middle of the room to the living-room above. From there the river is seen as a narrow runnel scarcely worth the name of river. Over on the southern bank are the gravel pits, their great scoops gaunt against the sky. Along the desolate marshland the lightning plays. To the east are the old flour mills, now giant storehouses for pig and cattle meal. Below the window is the port, forsaken and declining. Yet, says our host, there are eleven pubs here, sign surely of some vitality, and one of the pubs has just applied for a catering licence. 'Soon you'll be able to sit by the window, eat a meal and watch the barges going downriver,' he says, and answering my further questions tells me that the port is far from decay. 'There are fifteen hundred voters on the lists here and they're certainly alive!' but politics is not my subject and I do not fall easily into disputation. Instead we began to talk about his paintings. Sometimes he paints ships and yachts, but they are patterns of mathematical exactitude. 'I know a ship is exactly made,' I said, 'but not in quite such over-simplified patterns.' Nash stood aside and smiled. He worked out his ideas about drawing and painting ships and yachts long ago, and is not easily to be drawn. We began to talk about other things. The idea of the children's bathing pool seemed sound, I ventured.

'Does it?' said our host. He smiled wryly and seemed sceptical: I looked again: the pool would be ten yards in front of his house. I could see his point. Would I like a children's paddling pool ten yards away from my house? A testing question for Mass-Observation or Mr Gallup to try upon the democratic masses.

The tide was rising. Many yachts and dinghies now lay berthed in mud. By the early evening they would be afloat, lifting once more to the rush of water from the sea. If the storm passed and the day were claimed again by the sun, a few yachtsmen would pole or scull pram dinghies

out to their craft, board and dust down towards the estuary. The local
doctor will be there if he can fit in his excursion between surgery hours,
for he is keen. The artist from this house will go. Others will follow.
The professional hands about the port will watch from windows of quay-
side pubs or look up from their chores on board the three large yachts
hauled out on a lower hard. Their remarks will be quick and pungent,
for professionals must profess; they have not taken their yachts from
their berths in all this summer, and pride must have its say if not its
show.

Between the wars, the skippers and paid hands from this small port
made names as helmsmen in all the yachting world, and some were

members of *Endeavour* crews that essayed the impossible task to bring the America's Cup back from the seas that run off Brenton Reef. Now millionaires are in short supply; there are no more J Class craft, few 12-metres, and paid hands must move to more rewarding berths than unfashionable East Coast river ports.

This evening, if the breeze should hold, yachts will tack downriver, coming about under the black hull of that famed ship a young man sailed around the world before the war. Now the barquentine lies at anchor, rotting, for the sea has no kindliness towards a ship that does no work, and will rot her to her water-line. Last winter I sailed down this river in a spritsail barge bound for London River. We went close to the sailing ship. She was a sorry sight after her perilous, foolhardy and triumphant voyaging, and then the years of war. The gulls had left their droppings through all the craft. She looked unkempt, forsaken, and as melancholy as only a dying ship can look. She would be a sound training ship for youngsters, much sounder than the institute in the sailmaker's shop, but quickly; although a ship's timbers are strong, they are strongest when under way.

THE FERRYMAN WAS right. Two days later, Monday, a pilot boat, built for Trinity House, was launched from the shipyard. She was a splendid craft, nearly one hundred feet long, powered with a 240 horse-power Diesel engine. She went assuredly down the slipway with a flurry of foam at the river's edge.

In the town there was a ceremony, with speeches. An Elder Brother of Trinity House said that it seemed very sad that his pilot boat would be the last ship to be built in the port. A director of the yard said that ships had been built there since the days of the Armada. The Secretary of Trinity House, proposing the toast of 'The Builders,' said that it was a matter for regret that the first ship which the yard had built for Trinity House should be the last from those slipways, but it was to be hoped that the yard would still take Trinity House ships in for repair. Another director of the yards spoke of the many ups and downs of shipbuilding, but despite the downs, the work of the yard was known throughout the shipyards of the world; such work could never be forgotten; had it not been responsible for building part of Mulberry Harbour, the greatest of all nautical enterprises? It was sad that the yard would build no more ships, but certain yards must close to enable others to live; to recondition the yard would cost at least one hundred thousand pounds. The mayor said that although the days of the big class yachts were over, surely the yard would live again in better times to come.

The wife of the Elder Brother was presented with a silver salver.

The celebrations continued in sadness and solemnity.

The local newspaper reported the ceremony and an editorial writer lamented the passing of the yard, 'with its great tradition, and the only dry dock between London and Lowestoft,' thus placing nobility and practicality of outlook in dangerous proximity, almost in anti-climax.

During the war this small yard built over fifty ships and docked another

two hundred for repairs. Planning, one supposes, plans some things into limbo, others into life abounding, but some men, more cynical than others, will wait to see these brave new shipyards where everything will be so well planned that these small yards will be unwanted.

LIGHTNING STILL SEARED the dark sky, but the storm was passing. We went out to the car and said farewell, and drove warily along the quay.

Take any of the alleyways away from the quayside and the character of the port changes within a hundred yards. No longer are the houses the small, serene dwellings of the waterfront: they become the rows of terrace houses the Victorians built in imitation of the Georgians and, in imitating, failed. The houses are of red brick, yet even the red they chose was a colour without charm, harsh upon the eyes, unrestful. The roof slates, too, are not grey as they were at the turn of the century, but almost black. There is no gaiety or warmth about these houses: they were built for a race of workers who were regimented into these small towns for the working convenience of owners, overseers and shareholders. Perhaps there were not many who consciously crowded those workers close upon the new shipyards, factories, and railways, but now the pattern is as obvious as if we were looking at a plan for evil concentration.

The terraces make a maze between the quay and the main road leading towards the larger town. Soon there is the level crossing beyond the railway station. The station is set above the main road, built upon the summit of a modest gradient. The station building, with its fretworked wooden canopy above the platform, is also in red brick and blackened slates. Here, in the centre of 'the large and respectable village,' are more pubs; larger, lacking the friendliness of the quayside inns. Here the pubs have closed doors with frosted glass panels and plate-glass windows; the name of the brewer is far larger than the name of the inn, always an intimidating sign.

The road widens, macadam and 'thirty' signs appear, also the bungalows, some built in red brick, others in white-tile-faced bricks, suitable perhaps for the public convenience, ill-placed in the English countryside.

Soon even the bungalows are forgotten and we are back to the small red-brick cottages, some with Dutch roofs of old red tiles, set at roadside frontages to far fields of barley, wheat and sugar beet.

Then the outworks of a wartime aerodrome, now an overgrown, forgotten, monstrous scar.

Now we know that we have left the port: we are back in modern England.

# Notes on Writing

## by ARCHIE HARRADINE

*Acting is one of the most dangerous of trades. It is the rarest thing to find a player who has not had his character affected for the worse by the practice of his profession. Nobody can make a habit of self-exhibition, nobody can exploit his personality . . . and remain untouched by the process. . . . Acting inflames the ego in a way which few other professions do.*

**A**ND so on. I keep this warning from Mr Aldous Huxley's *Ends and Means* above my desk, hoping thereby to lessen the inflammation. I quote it here to help you realize that if this article contains too many 'I's' it is not the fault of my nature but of this acting business. Indeed I had thought of trying to profit further by using, like a character in Mr Huxley's play, *The World of Light,* 'one' instead of the first person singular throughout.

To help the chastening process I recall two phrases about my last pantomime performance. A friend wrote: 'I am pretty sure you were a howling success. . . .' Just careless phrasing, I hope; only I was already rather sensitive on the subject, as one dramatic critic had written, with some subtlety: 'Archie Harradine played Widow Twankey in a style peculiarly his own.' It was that same pantomime which has led to this my nervous proud appearance in THE SATURDAY BOOK, as it was the occasion of a letter of mine to the Editor, who noted my handwriting.

Well here it is— I don't think it specially notable or even peculiarly my own— in fact another dear friend dubs it characterless. At least, like Duncan's murder, 'tis done quickly — that is at average writing speed. And as to lack of character, wouldn't Mr. Huxley approve such an unusual and welcome vacuum? After all, how often does the egocentric personality of the actor interpose between dramatist and audience!

Anyway I gather that it linked up in Mr Russell's mind with the piece on 'The Art of Writing' in last year's SATURDAY BOOK, and he's told me to say something about it.

I don't know how much handwriting depends on heredity and environment. My father, who was a lawyer's clerk for fifty years, filled many leather-bound ledgers with his meticulous entries. He used 'Church' lettering for the inscriptions in his pocket-books and gift-books, writing his name or the recipient's with a double nib which produced impressive parallel lines, one thick, one thin.

I have by me one such, a small account book which he kept as Honorary Secretary of the Temperance Choral Union. (Their annual orgy was a mammoth concert at the Crystal Palace.) In one entry, explaining 'Profit on Soirée—4/5d.,' he gets fifteen lines of details into an inch. These are the sort of details:

|  |  | 1891 |  | 18 | 16 | 4 |
|---|---|---|---|---|---|---|
| Jan | 30 | P Cards |  |  | 2 | - |
| Feb | 9 | Fire fire my heart |  |  | 6 | - |
| Ap |  | Triumph of Victoria |  |  | 15 | - |
|  |  | Tempce Choral Union |  |  | 10 | - |
|  |  | B of Hope Meetg Bks |  |  | 6 | - |
| Mch |  | P Cards Peoples Pal |  |  | 2 | 6 |
|  |  | Selectn Song of Miriam | } | 2 | - | - |
| May |  | 4 doz Sol Fa Jubilee | } |  |  |  |
|  |  | O N Song of Miriam |  |  | 1 | - |
| June | 15 | When Allan a Dale |  |  | 8 | 8 |
|  |  |  |  | 23 | 7 | 6 |

('O.N.' would, of course, be Old Notation, for the conductor, as contrasted with the new-fangled Tonic Solfa.)

Irrelevant note: On some otherwise blank pages in the account book are scrawled a few sums in a child's hand, ranging from 1 plus 1 equals 2 —marked R—to 4-figure totals marked X. Then, still in a child's hand: 'If you get this sum R I will kiss you.' The sum is 11 plus 11. The result is R, and I smell romance.

My eldest brother, nicely settled at seventeen by my father in a Trinity House clerkship, left soon after to be a farmer. However, he's kept his clerkly hand, so I suppose 'it runs in the family.' Years before I took to the stage I spent six months at an art school, learning besides lettering how to draw vases, draperies, and chairs put upside down with the legs pointing towards me (for Perspective). Thereafter I did a lot of formal script as a job, including illuminated books, presentation addresses, and single 'pretties,' like this:

# O Mistress Mine

O mistress mine, where are you roaming?
O stay and hear; your true love's coming
  That can sing both high and low.
Trip no further, pretty sweeting;
Journeys end in lovers meeting,
  Every wise man's son doth know.

What is love? 'tis not hereafter;
Present mirth hath present laughter:
  What's to come is still unsure:
In delay there lies no plenty;
Then come kiss me, sweet-and-twenty!
  Youth's a stuff will not endure.

William Shakespeare:
'Twelfth Night'

In the original the staves are red, and the black square notes, though quaint, are not very serviceable. At least they weren't in a book of old English songs I wrote out for reproduction twenty years back. Owing to the necessity of double printing the alignment of notes on staves was often uncertain, giving now and then an effect of quarter-tones or even more Oriental harmonics. The songs were good, and it is a pity that the net result was one of those slim decorative volumes which look nice on a very occasional table.

Naturally for ordinary purposes I use a quicker, more straightforward method of copying music; I think this could be adapted to make a hand-written songbook both pleasant and, like Old Possum's cats, practical. There are many unknown old songs worth singing, such as:

In fact, I have such a book in hand. (Advt.).

The poem 'O Mistress Mine,' reproduced above, was written with a turkey-quill on vellum, a combination which gives great enjoyment to the user, once you've rubbed the greasy surface off the skin and have cut the quill to exactly the right width, angle, and straightness. (May the impatient oaths I've vented while cutting quills be ignored by the Recording Angel! He is after all a fellow-scribe.) But when at last the quill's edge is sharp, clean, perfect, how great is the contrasting content! Writing then is among the sensuous pleasures. As line follows line and builds the balanced mass of lettering on the page, you feel there is no reason ever to stop the easy rhythm. The actual contact of pen and page is at once stimulating and soothing. There is a sort of yielding firmness, a vitality in the meeting of these two ex-animate things, bird's quill and calf's skin, which, as you see, I cannot describe—except that it reminds me of walking on the turf at Vatersay, off Barra. (I remember Professor Ker saying to us—I think of a passage in Spenser—'You may think some of his similes far-fetched'; and, after a pause, 'but they are worth fetching.' I only hope this was.)

The ink is kept flowing gently down the quill by a spring, and I invented mine: an old-fashioned two-pronged paper fastener, with the prongs trimmed, bent up to form a flattened W, and inserted under the pen.

That's not very interesting; but it does lead me on to reveal to the world my other and major invention—my Shoelace Œconomy: You—or shall we say for the present, I—secure half a lace in the left-side toe-nearest shoe-hole by a knot underneath; lace it through straight across instead of diagonally, and tie off at the top right-side hole with a neat loop round itself instead of a floppy bow. (Sinistrals will probably perform this *vice versâ*.) I am probably the only being who does this, and I halve my shoelace bill.

When doing formal writing I used functional lettering, as we'd call it now—something suitable in weight and character for the work in hand. I remember one odd job I had: writing out Kipling's 'If,' translated into German, for some old lady admirer to send to Hitler. I used a whole calf-skin, with ebony rollers top and bottom, and chose a weighty black-letter text. I understand that it had an honoured place in the archives of the Chancellery. And it's futile to accuse me of being pro-fascist; it might have done the man a power of good.

My remarks on the family's handwriting should have included Uncle Henry, who sought gold in South Africa in the '70's. I have his diary of the journey up-country—a tall thin volume with marbled cover, leather corners and blue leaves. Nightly by the camp-fire he recorded in a fluent bank-clerkly hand the day's progress and set-backs, and ended with a few pious words (oddly reminiscent of Defoe), a hope for the morrow's trek, and a thought for those in England. There were no hairbreadth escapes; he found little gold, and returned to Durban, where he was accidentally killed in a shooting-saloon.

Reverting to functionalism in lettering:

It occurs to me that another style might have suited another occasion. One dramatic critic forbore to come to the mime *L'Enfant Prodigue*, in which I was acting, but condemned mime plays in the Press. Perhaps this verse, which I thereupon sent to the paper concerned, would have looked more lapidary, if not quite marmoreal, in spaced capitals:

> # CRITICS WHO CUSS
> # NOT BOTHERING TO COME
> # SHOULD BE LIKE US
> # BEAUTIFUL BUT DUMB

I might indeed have carved the quatrain in marble, had I learned to carve. That I hope to do; for my ambition is to work till I am sixty; play village cricket for the next ten years, and thenceforward do the lettering on local tombs. But the craft would take time to master; maybe I'll just scrape the moss from older, finer headstones.

Perhaps my 'working fist' may be mentioned.

As an example, if I need clear handwritten copy for a typist I use this Upright Nondescript. Being speedy it also serves for makg terse notes in eg. the Readg Rm of the B.M. It is easier to work from than my ordy handwritg, wh= can still be used wj it for titles & other differentiatn. Amid the mass of rounded verticals contrasted names like Tropic of Capricorn or The Jolly Miller, even if they don't shine like good deeds in a naughty world, at least stand out —.

I wrote the following pseudo-Papal couplets for a theatre party, to introduce a mock-seventeenth century mime ballet. The music, a Purcellian pastiche—Overture; Jig; Double; Canaries; Passacaille; Finale

—was written by Herbert Murrill for a broken consort of viols with recorders, hautboys, and bassoons, but for some reason got played on a piano. I think the light formalized hand suits the text. (In case it interests: all the cursive writing for this article was done in ordinary ink with a broadish steel nib, Mudie's 'Squeezer.') The verse needs 'old' pronunciation, please—'tay' for 'tea,' and all that.

## THE
# PROLOGUE

[ Enter AMANDA before the Curtain as if perswaded. ]

OUR Author begs me intercede with you
For what he has eſſay'd and fail'd to do
Poor puny Mortal! who, with beſt intent,
Could scale the height of this great Argument?
T'amuse and warn ye was his pious will;
But on so grand a Theme? Ambitious Quill!
For — now to shake our tim'rous tremors off —
Know, Ladies and Gallants, our Subject's GOLF.

Within a house adjacent to the Links
Dwell worthy FOOZLE and his charming Minx.
A cruel paradox, upon my life,
That Links should separate a Man and Wife!
Yet so it is, for here's the sorry coil:
FOOZLE in phrensy after City toil
Daily will pay an hurried homeward call;
Thence to the Green, to drive the feather'd Ball.
Which miſſing, on the underworld he cries,
The boſky Vale re-ecchoing to his noise.
But, like the Flagellant rev'ling in his Pain,
Good FOOZLE ſtands his ground and swings again.

The lone AMANDA, sighing once or twice,
Looks in her glaß and wonders at his choice;
For gamesome too — within the Boudoir — she,
Whose only Caddy is for Tea, not Tee;
And whom perchance a rescuing Swain w.d find
A little leß than kiß but more than kind.
FOOZLE at length returns and makes report
Of what he's not accomplish'd at the sport.
She liftens to his proweß on the Lawn,
Her ears uneager and her mind a Yawn.

Such is their usual tenour. On this day
Which we, dear gentles, shew you in our play,
FOOZLE retires from his pouting Dame
To don his new apparel for the game.
Next VERDURA and simp'ring LOLL come there,
Another Golf-rent sad-aßorted pair.
She, save for marriage DIANA of the place,
Drags her reluctant Spouse to join the chace.
AMANDA's glance and Tea-pot catch his eye;
How melting-soft were his acceptant Sigh!
Then each to his o'er-careful Stance repairs,
All entertaining Angles unawares.

But I too long detain ye. Sure 'tis time
To see what follows in our antic Mime.
Attend, ye truant Husbands! Learn, I pray,
How Fools who come to Golf remain to Tea.

It may interest the nobility and gentry—as well as impresarios and régisseurs—to know that the little piece was very well received on that its only occasion by the distinguished and crowded assembly, three of whom had to sit on the withdrawing-room floor.

Again reverting to suitability of lettering: I have often thought that it might help readers if, instead of the usual solid block of evenly spaced type, matter were printed according to the sense—a sort of visual onomatopoeia. Slow ponderous sentences would have four heavy words to the line, while a flow of quick, futile chatter would appear as one con-

R

tinuous featherweight word. This could well be combined with the placing of the words high or low on the line according to their vocal inflection, something like this . . . (I beg your pardon, Master Compositor? Oh, very well.) But really I need hardly give an example to readers of SATURDAY BOOK calibre, but can safely

> '. . . let us, cyphers to this great accompt,
> On your imaginary forces work.'

The method I have suggested would be especially useful in the printing of plays. Then the actor would have no excuse for o'erstepping the modesty of nature; the play's sense would no longer depend precariously upon his own; dramatist and printer would together mould his utterance, and Aldus come to Aldous' aid!

(That last, besides being something of a peroration in Ercles' vein, is a rather brilliant *jeu d'esprit*; Aldus being, I believe, a famous mediaeval printer, and Aldous referring of course to the worried Mr Huxley. I am secretly pleased with this, so had better leave the matter quickly, for fear of further ego-inflammation. In any case some of you may have already remembered, as I just have, the mouse-tail piece of printing in *Alice*; and so will realize that this is not a fine, new-minted thought, but merely a case of two great minds.)

I think of offering this final manuscript to Mr Bason for sale in his bookshop as a rare collector's piece. It is a random half-page from a Work in Progress, and my last self-humbling sop to Mr Huxley. For it shows what happens when the Creative Urge, Divine Afflatus, Cacoethes Scribendi seizes this person in its dæmonic grip:

There now. And me brought up to be tidy.

# Men's Tears

## *by C. WILLETT CUNNINGTON*

ENGLISHMEN seem to have abandoned the habit of crying, at least in public. Time was when it was an ordinary accomplishment of the gentleman who prided himself on his sensibilities. He wept publicly more readily than the modern man laughs, and his pocket handkerchiefs were much larger than ours. They had to be.

The present generation has not merely lost this gift but apparently is indifferent to the loss, or regards it as a positive gain. As though an incapacity to cry were a matter for pride! Suppose we lost the faculty for laughter, should we congratulate ourselves as fine fellows on that account? Once we could laugh till we cried, for the two are closely linked; lose one and presently we may lose the other, for if we don't exercise our faculties they wither.

If we bottle up our feelings we shall inevitably in time cease to feel the pleasant as well as the unpleasant things in life. We must practise weeping, then, so that we may still be able to laugh.

Our ancestors appear to have had an immense capacity for feeling and for exposing their feelings. We cannot but envy their ability to weep at a sunset, at the contemplation of their own unworthiness, or over the pages of an affecting novel. Yet those tearful creatures were the men who won Waterloo. Can we picture the younger Pitt, that icicle of a man, facing the House, tears trickling down his cheeks, or Sir Robert Peel sobbing under the lash of Disraeli's tongue? Macaulay, a tough Scot, tells us frankly that a pathetic tale moved him to cry like a child. Stern Victorian papas wept at weddings as well as at funerals, and romantic young men wept as they proposed.

Contemporary novels are a convincing guide to social habits, and in them, at least until the end of the last century, we find a tearful throng of characters each with his own distinctive cry; villains who wept with baffled rage; fathers who poured tears of forgiveness on erring daughters shedding tears of repentance; and mothers weeping tears of joy over prodigal sons discharging tears of remorse. And over them all the reader dropped a tear of sympathy.

Obviously there are—or at least there were—all sorts of tears suitable for various moods, cold tears of despair or warm or even scalding. And when we read of 'blinding tears' we may assume they were the scalding variety. By such means the users were able to emphasize different kinds of emotion. Today the novelist who draws his characters from life has to fall back on expletives, with which the English language is miserably furnished. He does so because as a realist he knows that men have forgotten how to weep. Perhaps this is why novels have become drier reading than formerly.

At any rate, there can be no denying that the old humidity of the male sex has notably diminished and we are faced with the question, what has been the cause? Why have men almost discarded so convenient a method of expressing their feelings and replaced it with parched austerity?

The blame rests on the shoulders of Dr Arnold of Rugby. It was he, a century ago, who founded the tradition among schoolboys that blubbing was 'un-English.' Under his inspiration the old school tight upper lip became a badge of courage, and that generation growing up spread the custom until it became generally recognized that men's tears were bad form. The strong silent Englishman had arrived.

True, the old habit still lingers under exceptional circumstances where silence is apt to be misunderstood. If you are in the dock a few discreet tears may temper justice with mercy, though there is the risk that the judge may call it cowardice and add to the sentence. But such displays are uncommon and to make them needs a degree of moral courage which only cowards possess.

The rest of us regard men's tears in public as a shameful exhibition, and having lost this useful way of expressing our feelings we make a virtue of our loss and call it 'self-control.' As a result, weeping in public now exposes a man to the suspicion of being intoxicated. What! Merely because, like Whitman, he is overcome by the mystical moist night air and sheds camerado tears, is he to be run in? Surely democracy should encourage and not frown on such demonstrations of our common humanity? But no. Men's tears are being limited more and more to strictly private performances. As such they still have a use in those domestic moments when nothing less seems adequate.

Have you never engaged in a discussion with your wife when she suddenly drowns your arguments in a flood of tears? What happens then? The thread of your logic is snapped by this ingenious device, and you meekly surrender. But why not use her weapon, getting in your tears first? She would dry up at once, too startled to continue. . . . Why should women have all the good tunes? As it is, we have abandoned this domestic explosive to her and find ourselves practically unarmed.

There are races, more provident, who have never discarded tears as a masculine accomplishment and so, when they are faced by some personal calamity, such as demands for income tax, it is not only Rebecca whose tears blister the family carpet. But we, more phlegmatic, pride ourselves on keeping our few tears for occasions of greater moment. The family doctor, who sees us without our social masks, is sometimes privileged to witness them. And what kind of feelings are they used most often to express? Not grief: rather to emphasize relief. They mark a sudden end to tension long drawn out. Though the certain knowledge of a dreaded loss may provoke them it is more commonly the certain knowledge of a gain.

To women it seems strange that a man who can face a deathbed dry-eyed may yet welcome a birth with tears. But, as doctors learn, men shed tears of joy more readily than tears of grief—because in the former the sense of relief is inexpressible by other forms, and in the latter discipline forbids. Grief braces a man to silence; joy relaxes. Not facing danger but danger overcome inspires him to weep.

Evidently tears serve the two sexes a very different purpose. In a man the normal control is broken, the situation has suddenly dissolved and every taut nerve is loosened. His tears signalize a relaxation not permissible during suspense. But in women it is not the sense of relief which produces tears, but the tears which produce the sense of relief. They soften suspense by helping to change the appearance of a situation. The load is shifted and becomes a personal appeal for sympathy. Here is no relaxation of effort, far from it, for they are actively engaged in a drama of their own making in which they play 'lead.' And as the drama is more effective in the presence of an audience a woman's tears will flow readily before one. She is employing a technique which, as she knows by instinct, will change the look of things by devastating the spectator—unless, of course, he happens to have seen her perform in that rôle too often.

But no man can be wholly indifferent to such an exhibition, whether he is touched, enraged or entertained by it. The situation is changed even if he walks out on her, leaving her triumphant.

He, on the other hand, is not seeking to dramatize his emotions, and so far from signalizing the rise of the curtain his tears mark its fall. The domestic scene is over. Nor does he seek an audience; indeed, that would be for him like being caught undressed, an embarrassment which only women really enjoy. He, poor fellow, gets no secret satisfaction from exhibiting his private feelings. For the moment his defences are down, and to be caught bending is a shock to man's dignity. No wonder he feels ashamed.

Why, then, if this is how the modern man feels about it, did not our ancestors feel a similar shame when they wept? On the contrary, their tears were positively admired, and poets sang their praises. Though Tennyson was apparently puzzled by them it was only of *idle* tears, not purposive ones, that he confessed: 'I know not what they mean.' But we now know better.

The men of his day used tears as a discharge of their exuberant feelings in harmony with those large appetites, flowing whiskers and flowered waistcoats which signalized the Expansion of England. No nonsense about repression or inferiority complex there. They wept as a luxury, and though it may be only a coincidence it is certainly remarkable that men's emphatic modes of expression went out of fashion with those emphatic styles of dress and appearance.

'The tear that flows down Virtue's manly cheek' marked an exquisite sensibility of which the possessor was justly proud; his feelings bubbled over instead of, as with us, remaining bottled up. And though this form of effervescence is still practised by women, it must be admitted that even they use it with less and less facility.

Heroines in modern plays don't cry as nicely as they did; they have a horrid habit of blowing their noses and muttering 'Hell, gimme a cigarette!' It is these cigarettes which are responsible—they dry up the heroine's tears as well as the man's muffled oaths. You can't smoke a wet cigarette or puff a muffled one.

So, too, in real life the cigarette has become a poor substitute for a refreshing flood of tears, and as we lose this art we are in danger of losing likewise its companion, laughter.

We need to see a revival of men's tears and flowered waistcoats; to hear politicians sob and wireless talkers convincingly 'in floods.' But as it is, a pioneer attempting such a revival is not likely to receive much encouragement. On the contrary, he will be lucky if he is not told to dry up.

# Frenchmen's Fashions

## by HONOR TRACY

A FRENCHMAN, witty of course, once said that dress was a conception of the self carried about on the self. He added that the clothes people wore usually suited them. The afterthought may be accepted with reserve, but the statement admirably sums up a neglected truth.

Sometimes we see a very fat lady in a scarlet dress and we ask ourselves at once: why does such a lady wear a dress as bright as that? Surely she would be more at home in another shade, for instance black, or brown? Surely the sight of herself in a mirror must cause her pain? But the answer is, that the lady does not see herself as fat, nor would the accident of catching sight of her reflection in the mirror ever bring it home to her: she sees herself either as she was once or as she would like to be, or as her favourite actress is: to raise the question of red as a suitable colour, therefore, would only lead to confusion and hostility.

The same is true of others whose costume appears to be slightly off the mark. The bright girls of thirty-five with the pinafore dresses and the fetching little bows in the hair, the adolescent with her holiday dress of satin, her wicked lacy panties and her feather boa, the battle-axe in the sprigged muslin, are not unbecomingly attired at all: merely, the person they are dressing is not apparent to the rest of the world, it is a dream self, a self more real to them perhaps than the other. We should beware, then, of passing hasty judgments on people's clothes: rather, we should pause and consider what it is they have in mind.

In Western Europe, as a rule, it is the female who expresses this romantic urge in her clothes. A learned judge once remarked that all women were childishly fond of dressing up: and the fact that this judge, as Virginia Woolf pointed out, was himself at that moment wearing a kind of scarlet dressing-gown and a wig of glossy white sausage curls in no way lessens the truth of his observations, even if it robs them of their sting. Women want to attract or to irritate by their differences, men to reassure by their sameness. A man who wears brown boots with his evening jacket knows, in England at least, that he is doing something he shouldn't: a woman similarly placed would have only a delightful sensation of stealing a march on other women.

It is pleasant then to find the men of Paris standing out against this tradition and clothing themselves in a manner which not only would appear to express some inner and secret self but which cannot fail to make an ineffaceable impression on all who behold it. And here is a curious paradox: while Parisian women are said to be the best dressed

263

in the world and it is taken for granted in Paris that feminine apparel is a serious affair, it is the male attire in this city which catches and rivets the eye of the stranger as he sits in a café and sees the world hurrying past: and these effects are produced, woman's thunder stolen, with no apparent effort, with even a kind of nonchalance as admirable as it is mysterious.

For men are not, like women, bullied and nagged by great houses of Parisian couture. They have no tradition and no accepted standards to guide them. At the most, the tailor's sheets may let fall a hint or two from time to time; under the sketch of a man in canvas trousers, rope sandals, striped jacket reaching to knee and straw boater draped with contrasting scarf, for example, we may find these words of restrained advice: 'a sailing holiday along the Breton coast calls for the appropriate outfit.' A friendly suggestion, no more: should the holiday-maker prefer to set sail in pleated shorts and jumper with a border-pattern of shrimps or lighthouses, no eyebrows will be raised. And it is precisely this freedom which gives to the male costumes their freshness and excitement: while none can foresee how they will finally appear, few, once they catch sight of them, would allow a single item to be changed.

On the first warm day of this year a man was seen strolling up the Champs Elysées. He was wearing white stockinet plus fours with a green alpaca jacket and butterfly tie. Nothing very remarkable in that, perhaps, but with a little stroke of genius he had crowned the ensemble with a bowler hat. This gift for detail which seems surprising at first but then is seen to be inevitable, is the mark of the true artist, such as it is the glory of France to produce in great numbers.

One characteristic of French male costuming is its great fluidity, its restless changeability, that capriciously and wilfully rejects all that went immediately before. To take one example, the Frenchman of our mothers' day was noted for wide, baggy trousers that nestled about his pumps or elastic-sided boots in concertina folds: if the illustrated papers of the time may be believed, it was almost a national costume: whereas, James Laver says, 'nothing marks the modern Frenchman more than the comparative tightness of his trousers.' And not merely trousers in the limited sense, either, but breeches, shorts and plus-fours, the last being especially restricted in width although, as if in compensation, descending to within six inches of the ground. And it is this restlessness above all which betrays the romantic conception that he has of himself, for while in England striking innovations are made only by cranks or cads, in France a constant search goes on for something new: no, the Frenchman appears to say fretfully to himself as he surveys his reflection in the glass, this is not quite the thing yet, it is not *me*.

In the piping days of 1938, the note was of a controlled exuberance.

Overcoats were cut lavishly and waisted neatly, something along the lines of a *robe de style*, shoes were gay and multi-coloured, jackets were immensely tucked and pleated and flounced: favourite shades for summer and winter alike ranged from lilac to *vert pomme*.

The idea behind it was plain: in spite of the unhappy rivalries and dissensions between the two countries, the Parisian of the 'thirties wished to look as much as possible like an English gentleman. His shoes were spoken of in catalogues as for the *footing* or the *trotting*. Extremists came to London for their clothes, although increasingly they were apt to hand them over to their own tailors for the special finishing touch. They went to their offices in hairy, shapeless tweeds, which smothered them in mild weather or became waterlogged after a five-minute shower, and which they would always describe as 'très pratique.' Their children were dressed in bonnet and kilt of apocryphal tartan, or as simple British sailors in navy blue georgette and white suede boots.

Today the scene has changed completely. The first impression is one of grimness and austerity. The ordinary Frenchman is now dressed in a vile garment known as a *canadienne*, or shapeless reefer jacket with fur collar, knickerbockers, white German socks and hobnailed boots, with or without leather gaiters buttoned to the knee. So dressed he goes to work, to dine or to the cinema, or strolls along the boulevards looking the women critically up and down.

Another deplorable feature of post-war fashion is the peaked cap for civilians: this, however, is so far confined to districts like Strasbourg, St Denis and La Vilette, and goes with a grubby raincoat and a toothbrush moustache. Small boys wear rabbit skins sewn together when it is cold and dungarees or battle-dress when it is warm.

Here, again, the question is, what are they aiming for? Do they enjoy looking like that? Do any group of people on the face of this globe wish to look as they mostly do look at present, or, for that matter, do anything else as they would like? Textiles are short in France and, since —a grave pity in the view of most—the French do not export their male fashions, very few are being made. Further, a great factor in French life this year has been the American war surplus: a *canadienne* may be the only jacket available. A Frenchman may be no more delighted to wear it than he is to go to the Opera in a jeep, but possibly he has no choice.

It would be ungenerous, then, to complain that Frenchmen look like people dressed in American war surplus: and it would be false as well, for their remarkable achievement is to look somehow like people coming straight from the *maquis*. They have the air of men who have buried their weapons in the hills and have come flocking to town to rally at the Vel. d'Hiv. Probably, they know this and are pleased by it, for resistance, at one moment de rigueur, then again rather bad form, now has all the chic of far-off hopeless things, like the cause of Bonny Prince Charlie.

Not that goods are ever displayed in shops as 'très resistant' or 'bien maquisard' or that male fashion papers ever give the man in the street any tips on the subject. *Adam*, which is a sort of male *Vogue*, continues to live in a world of its own, inhabited by enormous blond men with steely blue eyes and the shoulders of a gorilla, bronzed by a lamp, scented with Aroma 3 and dressed in dainty smokings of midnight blue, belonging to Clubs such as Magdalen College or Rules and wearing whatever old school tie happens to tone with their complexion. But the Frenchman is above all a realist: since he knows well he can never be a blond gorilla with eyes of steel he makes no especial effort to look like one; instead, he prefers to give the impression that he has just blown up a railway bridge.

If the style *maquis* is the most common in Paris at the moment, next after it comes the style *marché noir*: and this, as befits an organization as vast and as ramified as the French black market, rings a good many changes. In its simplest form, it merely consists of wearing clothes that are much too tight. Jackets no longer button, trousers creak anxiously as the owner sits down: these are worn by the small fry, by the clerks, petty officials, grocers, concièrges and mechanics who are making enough money to eat as they never ate before, but not enough to buy new clothes. They are to be found smiling over the menu in those comfortable homey little bistros in the centre of Paris, where the price of dishes is not marked and where the best dishes are not even written down. After them, are the people who could buy themselves a dozen new suits if they chose but, feeling that life is uncertain and the future shrouded in darkness, prefer to put their money into things that will not only last but, at a pinch, can be negotiated: gems flash from their fingers and neckties, their ladies are loaded with diamonds in such profusion they can hardly set one foot before the other. And finally come those kings and emperors who, having weathered the occupation, the liberation and the purge, pursue their way with a serene confidence in the future of France and are modestly content with the best of everything.

In general, this cramping influence of economics upon style is to be deprecated and all must look forward to the time when fancy may blossom again as in the palmy days between the wars.

The romantic streak in the Frenchman's character is admirably balanced and offset, as we know, by the classic which reveals itself as far as his clothes are concerned by a mania for the 'correct.' It is as important for the French to feel that their clothes are correct as that their behaviour is gentlemanly. The formidable array of costumes that are seen at shooting-parties, hunts, race meetings and gymkhanas out here is due to the wearer's anxiety not to fall short of what is required : it marks his sense of occasion.

Sometimes, this may be carried to extreme. There was a man living in St Cloud who was fond of giving delicious little dinners tête-à-tête to ladies in his apartment. If he received them *en smoking*, all was well: but if he was wearing a certain jacket of plum-coloured velvet, it meant that the guest was in for a rough passage. There were times when a lady, lulled into a false security by the sight of the smoking, had the disturbing experience of seeing him abruptly leave the room, to return in a few instants arrayed in the velvet: there may have been others, more subtly disconcerting perhaps but unrecorded, where the reverse took place. This character clearly felt that certain moments in life call for plum-coloured velvet and he preferred to throw away the advantages of a surprise attack rather than wear anything else.

This French passion for things to be just so is seen best on shopping expeditions. Nobody who is nervous, or under-nourished, or who has some old, deep-seated trouble that a prolonged strain may revive, should ever accompany a Frenchman when he goes to buy himself an article of clothing. He chooses a collar with twice the care that he puts into choosing his dinner. Box after box is pulled out, collar after collar, all identical to the female eye, is considered and rejected.

'For I must not render myself ridiculous,' he says, gravely.

Everything is tried on, nothing left to chance. Strangers are appealed to, photographs of successful men wearing this or that brand of collar are produced for him to study. Finally the shopman, having talked himself hoarse, mutely folds his arms: he can do no more. Even then, our friend is not to be rushed, for too much is at stake: apart from his reputation as a well-dressed man, a collar costs all of twenty-five francs. He may even go into the country for a while and turn the thing over in his mind: or anyhow request the use of the shop's telephone, to ring up his mother. When at last the purchase is made, his friends may expect to be asked at regular intervals: Say, then, have I done well to take this collar?

But if one should ask him to come into a shop for a moment to buy a reel of cotton, the response is always the same: Ah, the women, the women, one knows what that is, when that gets into a shop.

Briefly, then, French male costume at its best is a nice blend of reason and fantasy, harmonizing the wishes of the individual with what he conceives to be the demands of the community. But what of the future? Will the Frenchman of tomorrow be worthy of his forbears? Or will he allow a horde of Argentinos, Chileans, Hungarians and Unesco conference delegates to snatch away the palms that rightfully should be his? We ask the question in real concern. Already in England a generation is growing up that has never known what a Frenchman can look like as he sets forth, gun in hand, *à la chasse aux renards*.

# Let the English Alone—They Bite

## by *PATRICK CAMPBELL*

THE English have been visiting Ireland on business for more than seven hundred years. Up till 1946 the natives accepted their various appearances with a certain measure of reserve, on occasion even retiring into the hills to avoid the burden of conversation. But in 1946 the sun came out. In that year the English came to Ireland simply and solely in search of pleasure—their conception of pleasure being bordered by beef on one side, and a fresh egg on the other. The Irish provided their new friends with both, and were amazed to find them humbly grateful. But what the English were being humble about was a mystery.

'You know,' I said to my friend Joe, 'these babies are nearly incomprehensible. As a nation they have just won a war, and yet the last thing they want to be when they come over here is English. You might, in fact, divide them into two categories. The first is the Englishman who has no Irish connections, and apologizes for it. The second is the Englishman who had a cousin who was born in Roscommon, and can't forget it. As soon as this second character arrives in Dublin he buys himself an Arran Island bonnet, goes into a pub, and says to the barman : "Be after givin' us, plaze, a drop of Oirish whuskey, shure and bedad." '

'What'd he mean be that?' said Joe.

'He was looking for a ball of malt,' I said, 'but when Englishmen start talking Irish it comes out as a mixture of Sir Harry Lauder, any New York policeman, and the Abbey Theatre on an off night.'

' "Be after givin' us, plaze, a drop of Oirish whuskey, shure and bedad." ' Joe experimented with it carefully. 'Gorra,' he said, 'that's a queer class of talk.'

'It is, Joe,' I said. 'But it's only neck and neck with the stuff that comes out of the other kind of Englishman, the one who has no Irish connections. He says: "Well no, frankly, actually, I'm right off the beam here. Sorry, old boy. Plain sort of Sassenach type, and all that, if you know what I mean." '

'Did you?' said Joe.

'You can sort it out in time,' I told him. 'They usually begin with an overture—"Actually, frankly, as a matter of fact, I mean without any line-shooting or flannel. . . ." You can leave all that out. They're just warming up. Then comes the body of the message. This is very often framed in terms the origin of which is to be found in the science of aerial navigation. But it is a simple matter to decode with the help of an instruction manual. After a while you become familiar with the technical expressions, and can frat like anything. I mean, you can find out their names, and whether they think it is going to rain.'

'You wouldn't back them too heavy,' said Joe, 'at the talking?'

I told him he could go nap on it, and thereby put him on to a loser.

The truth of the matter is that it is a superficial judgment to maintain that the English cannot express themselves with the spoken word. It is merely a matter of goading them beyond endurance to find that they can handle conversation in just as sharp a manner as anybody else.

Twelve months ago I stepped off the Irish Mail at Euston with my luggage full of ham, and a dozen new-laid eggs nesting in the crown of me cap. Dublin was so jam-packed with English visitors that I was losing my Irish accent, and beginning to carry an umbrella. The only thing to do was to get out, before I caught myself saying, 'You've had it.' And, in any case, the wages seemed better in London, too.

Before I left Dublin I had fifty-three farewell parties in the home counties. At one of them I discovered for the first time this latent English talent for suddenly letting go with a rasper, just when you think the silence has shut down for the night.

I heard that some people were having a dinner party, so I said I would be along about eight. Unfortunately, I met a man who was eating live mice in exchange for pints, so that it was closer to nine by the time that I arrived. I drank a bottle of sherry, and we went in to dinner.

Two strangers were seated opposite me, a well-dressed man and his wife. At once I recognized their English accents.

'Well, suffering duck,' I said, 'here's the enemy.' They said nothing. They started picking nervously at bread.

'It's all right,' I told them, 'you can speak if you like.'

They turned down this good-humoured invitation point-blank. They sat there throughout the meal wrapped in rigid silence, not even smiling when I threw a nut at the butler.

After dinner I attacked them directly. I flung myself at the young woman's feet, and said: 'Dear English rose, you are very beautiful, and your tailor-made is clean and neat. Your husband is pretty, too, but how would it be if suddenly one word—something simple like "the" or "but" were to spring from your lips. We Irish, you know, are as friendly as anything, and there is a lively chance that someone might reply.'

The young woman stirred uneasily, but remained silent.

'Beginning with "the" or "but," ' I went on, 'we could work up to the longer words, and then in the course of time achieve a whole sentence. Think, for instance, what a glorious day it would be when, if ever, you were able to express an opinion of what you thought, say, of Ireland. Think of how the audience would hang upon your tiny lips!'

I sat further forward. 'Look,' I said urgently, 'tell us now! Tell us what you think of Eire—this dramatic habitat of saints, mice-eaters, and scholars—this spiritual paradise so carefully tended by Eamonn de Valera and myself.'

The young woman gave a kind of low cry. 'Wrestle with it,' I urged her, suddenly excited, 'fight it out. Let the words come clear. We'll catch them for you. We might even bounce them back.'

Then, for the first time that evening, the young woman spoke. 'Do you mind getting off my foot,' she said, 'I think you've probably broken my ankle.'

I sat back. She rubbed her leg ostentatiously. 'What bores me more than anything else,' she said, 'is clumsiness.'

I was pretty disgruntled. 'Well, anyway,' I said, 'the words are coming out—at last.'

The young woman rose to her feet. 'They are,' she said, 'and while they are you might like to have our views about Eire. We think it's a mess—a silly little mess.'

I was stunned. 'You awful girl!' I said. A thought came to me. 'Listen,' I said, 'if you think the country is a silly little mess what the hell are you doing here at all, wolfing our eggs and steak, and getting cheese and cream all over yourself?'

The young woman looked at me with what appeared to be a fairly deadly smile. 'We are,' she said, 'exacting tribute for your late so-called neutrality.' She turned to her husband. 'Come, poppet,' she said, 'let's bash out of here.' At the door she addressed us again—or me, I thought. 'As for the allegedly humorous part of this evening,' she said, 'I'd rather have Arthur Askey.'

After they had gone we did some imitations of 'poppet' and 'bash out of here,' but we knew what had happened. We had been roped and thrown.


FOR SOME TIME AFTERWARDS I ascribed the outrageous behaviour of this young woman to ill-health. I even started, and began to believe, a story that she had been blitzed in Birmingham, and could not, at times, be held responsible for her actions. But then I left Dublin, and arrived in London, and unfortunately forgot all about it.

Within a week of arriving in London I heard that some people were giving a sherry party, and so I pushed in with a group of invited guests. I became quite gay on several glasses of heady Empire wine, and then looked around for conversation. Everyone seemed to be talking about jobs, or telling anecdotes about rationing—the usual stuff that passes in England for inter-communication of souls. But then I saw a man standing by himself in a corner, cut off from the rest by a grand piano. I closed in on him, told him my name, and said: 'I've just arrived from Dublin, and I was wondering if you could settle something that has been worrying me for a long time.'

He laughed, nervously. 'Glad to help, I'm sure,' he said. He seemed to be sorry that the piano lay between him and the door.

'This theory,' I said, 'is not as yet completely formed. It is, as yet, only in its rough early stages. Isn't it queer how often I'm saying "as yet"?'

I had another go at the nutty Nyasaland, and went on: 'I wish to achieve a certain conclusion about the English. Let us allow, for the sake of argument, that they are one of the very few nations on the face of the earth who appear to have any sense of justice. The Englishman, in general, is honourable, straightforward, and decent, and he does not like to see people who are down getting too powerful a kick in the teeth. Now, is this *conscious* goodness? I mean, is the Englishman born good, and too stupid to become anything else; or is he conscious of the original sin in himself, and fights against it, knowing that *somebody* must save the world from barbarism?'

At this moment a maid came round carrying one of those damn trays of hors d'oeuvres. My new friend carefully chose a varnished sardine. He appeared to be playing for time. He offered me the dish. 'Try one of the sardines,' he said, 'you will find them quite palatable.'

He chewed his sardine for a minute or two in silence. I was wrestling with a piece of string in aspic. Suddenly he looked up. 'Ah, there you are, Muriel,' he said, without the least trace of disappointment, 'I was wondering what had become of you. Let me introduce you to a friend of mine, Mr. Scanlan. He has just arrived from Dublin.'

'Not Scanlan,' I said, 'Campbell—C–A–M–P . . .'

Muriel was dressed in black, with a fox fur and a difficult looking veil. It was my guess that Muriel did not get out to a lot of parties.

'But how nice,' said Muriel. 'I was in Dublin once. We stayed at the Sheringham—Shillington, something like that—Hotel. Mother's leg had been bad, and we thought the change would do her good. I remember one afternoon we went out to Merrion Strand and I bathed, but of course mother just sat on the beach and watched.'

'Mr Campbell has been telling me what he thinks about us here,' said Mr Muriel. 'Tearing off a strip, rather.'

'Tearing off a what?' I said.

'A strip,' said Mr Muriel.

I knew I would never get to the bottom of that, so I transferred my attention to Mrs Muriel. 'Well,' I said, laughing, 'not exactly telling. More asking. I was trying to find out from your husband if the English are consciously decent, or whether they were born like that and cannot throw the incubus off.' After a look at Muriel's face I said: 'And cannot throw it off.'

Muriel giggled. Obviously the water was deeper than she had thought. She looked at Mr Muriel for help, saw no prospect of any, and launched out on her own. 'It all depends on what you mean by decent,' she said, 'like Dr. Joad.'

'Oh, God,' I said, 'is he back?'

Mr Muriel took a hand. He seemed to think his wife was about to be savaged. 'Oh, come now,' he said, 'Dr. Joad is a good chap. At any rate, you ought to feel quite at home in his company—*Commander* Campbell.'

I took another glass of tawny Tanganyika off a passing tray. 'That,' I said, 'is the worst joke I have ever heard. In the name of God, can't we have some *conversation*?'

At that a change came over Mr. Muriel. He seemed to shed his air of indecision. He took his wife firmly by the elbow. 'Wait outside in the hall, dear,' he said, in a steady voice, 'I shall join you in a moment.'

Mrs Muriel nodded. It seemed to me that she came within an ace of saying 'Roger' or 'Wilco,' or whatever those things are. Both of them were clearly being resolute in the face of an emergency.

Mr Muriel watched his wife threading her way through the guests until she reached the door. As she closed it behind her he turned to me and said: 'I don't know who you are, sir, but I do know that you are damned offensive. The only other thing I wish to say is that I have never liked people with red hair and close-set eyes. They remind me of ferrets. Good night.'

At one time I used to hold the theory that Casabianca, silent, with his feet on fire, represented the true picture of the Englishman. Now I have another theory altogether, but I am going to keep it to myself. It seems to me that you can go sauntering along for a certain period, telling the English some interesting things about themselves, and then all at once it feels as if you had stepped on the prongs of a rake.

# Deer Stalker

## by F. FRASER DARLING

SPELT as one word, deerstalker means a kind of hat; spelt as two they mean a kind of man. This article is about the man (who may or may not wear that kind of a hat).[1]

There are about 2,500,000 acres of deer forest in Britain, almost all in the Highlands of Scotland, and if you reckon one stalker to 10,000 acres, on an average, there cannot be more than 250 stalkers. Nowadays there are fewer, considerably fewer; so numerically this must be one of the smallest professions. Stalkers are never found in any great density except at the old peacetime camps of the Lovat Scouts. I say peacetime, because during both wars the members of this famous corps have seemed to be spread about among other troops, supplying expert guides and scouts for rough mountain country.

What is the breed, history, and craft of the stalker, and how does he live? Practically without exception stalkers are Highlanders, though some carry Border blood from ancestors who came north with the sheep from the Southern Uplands after the Jacobite Rebellion of 1745. The failure of that rebellion rendered the Highlands safe for incomers. The vast forests of Scots pine were being felled for iron smelting and were not replanted. The lairds or chiefs found that an acceptance of an increasingly English way of life was more expensive than the self-sufficiency practised earlier, so the offer of high rents by the Border flockmasters brought about an entirely new social order in the Highlands. The people were shifted from the glens to the sea coasts and the little strips of lazy-bed cultivation grassed over to become the wintering ground of the invading hordes of sheep.

These Blackface sheep, hardy and wide-foraging, did amazingly well for many years on the new land where few sheep had ever been kept before. The Border men stayed and became Highlanders, marrying into the Gaels who, though they cursed the sheep and their masters for the clearances they caused, soon became sheep men themselves.

The Gael is inherently a pastoralist rather than a cultivator. But the Gael is also a social being and does not preferably take to a permanent isolation in some remote glen. Crofting townships of the coasts and islands may be sixty miles and more from the railhead, but they are intensely social communities for all that. The stalker is of rather different type, self-sufficient, reserved, able to stand alone without going to pieces.

The craft of stalking in one way or another is as old as mankind. But

[1]The O.E.D. would disagree with me, for it spells both with a hyphen. May I, with the utmost deference, suggest the single use of the hyphen to distinguish the man from the millinery?

S

the Highland stalker is the traditional descendant of the chief's professional hunter whose job it was to keep the pot supplied—no small job
that, in a country where the house of the chief was the headquarters of
the clan and where hospitality awaited all who came, high or low.   The
hunter was called the forester, or in Gaelic *carnach,* the man of the rocks.
The forester lived in his own proud way and was no counterpart of the
servile gamekeeper of southern shires.

The distinction remains today; the stalker would not thank you for
being called a keeper.   His bearing is one of deference to his employer
but with the firm understanding that he is master in his own job.   His
employer knows this—or soon learns it—and the relationship which
grows between an owner of a forest and his stalker is usually one of
mutual respect and deep friendship.   If the stalker says 'No, sir, I think
that beast had better be left another year,' the owner accepts this as a
ruling.

The biggest change between the long past and the present or recent
past is that in the old hunter's day the chief did not go stalking himself.
Now, it is the owner or his guests who do most of the actual shooting,
after being conducted through the stalk by the man who knows the ground
so well.   The change came in the early part of the nineteenth century,
when an increasing leisured class was arising and some of its members
were seeking excitements in wild country, finding pleasure in enduring
physical hardship.   There were the brothers Charles Edward and John
Sobieski Stuart, who had a few wonderful years in the Inverness-shire
glens of Glass, Cannich, and Affric.   Their *Lays of the Deer Forest,*
published in 1848, is still good reading either as natural history or as a
repository of old lore.

Probably the greatest publicist of the new sport of deer stalking was
William Scrope, who had access to the vast Forest of Atholl; his reminiscences appeared in 1830 under the title of *Days of Deerstalking in the
Scottish Highlands.*   Monied Englishmen just lapped it up and began
to offer high rents to the Highland lairds.   The sheep were now cleared
from the roughest areas, where they had skimmed the cream of the good
grazing, and the relatively small population of wild deer was allowed
to increase.   Queen Victoria and the Prince Consort gave the sport that
final touch of *ton.*   Half the aristocracy of England had deer forests by
1880, and in the next fifty years there was constant pressure from
American millionaires, Indian potentates, and the newly rich to buy or
lease.   Rents soared, county councils were able to keep rates low because
of the vast sums they drew from owners and lessees of forests.   Everybody thought it was marvellous.

Indeed, it was fantastic.   The prodigal wealth of an expanding Britain
poured into the Highlands.   Monstrous shooting lodges in the style of

Scots baronial, French chalet, mock Gothic, and so on, appeared in remote places often far from a road. Even if these places had no modern bathrooms they had to have moulded ceilings and other trappings of splendour. Endless chains of maids carried hot water to and from the hip baths in which the Tomnoddys laved their exhausted bodies after a day on the hill. The observer of today who knows the forests and the lodges is amazed at the logistics of the whole thing.

Of course, it was a moment in history, that's all. The crash of 1931 finished the deer-forest era, though it tottered on with some dignity until the second German war delivered the *coup de grâce*.

The stalker himself remained unspoiled through it all, still the simple courteous gentleman, knowledgeable in his craft but never emphasizing it. His job underwent modification from the time of the *carnach*. In those days the stalker carried a heavy weapon called a *culbheir*—plain culver in English—which was loaded *via* the spout and was apt not to go off if the weather was wet. Its killing power was sure enough if the quarry were near and the aim good, but the stalker knew it was a toss-up and took with him a brace of deerhounds to slip after wounded beasts. The old hounds were stronger than the mincing creatures seen in shows today, but not as large as those called Irish Wolfhounds. Chiefs and *carnachs* kept the breed and no one else. There was also a certain amount of driving of deer from a large tract of country towards strategically glaced guns. Queen Victoria describes the scene of one of these drives in her Highland journal. Mary, Queen of Scots, had been present at one not far away more than three centuries earlier.

Then came the invention of Henry's Express rifle, which allowed surer killing at longer distances. There were few drives after that. The straight stalk was the only sporting thing, though hounds were still taken to the hill for tracking wounded animals. Deerhounds were whimpering beasts, nevertheless; they were eager to be running without being intelligent and patient beforehand.

Then someone tried the Border collie cross, which produced exactly the right dog for the job, but almost at the same time the science of ballistics advanced to the stage of the high-powered rifle of small bore. This gave such a degree of certainty that dogs of any kind disappeared from the sport of stalking. It says much for the British temperament that each technical development still further pruned the sport and raised its standard of honour The stalker has played his part in this growing code and no one is its surer guardian.

If one starts arguing about the ethics of blood sports one is apt to get into inextricable positions, whichever way you argue. Deer stalking in the Highlands is not to be compared with the barbarian goings-on in Devon and Somerset. A Highland stalker would walk away in disgust from such a spectacle. As it is, the red deer is truly wild in the Highlands and could be cleared out only with difficulty. No one wishes it to be made extinct. It is a thriving, colonizing species which has to be kept down in numbers if it is not to be a serious pest. Stalking in properly managed country achieves that end of keeping the deer within reasonable numbers, and by means which cause least cruelty and disturbance to the deer themselves.

Indeed, there is no cruelty involved. Stags are stalked in late August, September, and early October, at the time when they are in best condition, when they are on the upper reaches of the hills and most difficult to approach. The females, the hinds, are stalked in late November, December, and early January, when they also are in best condition. Hind stalking on a winter's day can be a good test of endurance, and if there is any snow the animals are very difficult to approach.

Suppose the stalk has taken one, two, three, or four hours; you are within shooting distance—what then? It follows *ipso facto* that the animal does not know you are there, so it cannot be suffering like a bullock in a slaughter-house pen. The stalk is the test of skill, not the shooting. When you have come up to your stag your job is to kill it surely, or leave it. If, therefore, you think you will be surer with a telescopic sight on your rifle, it is not unsporting to have one, *because it is not sport to see if you can hit an animal*. A stag falling stone dead in a herd does not alarm the others. The crack of a rifle is not the roar of a shotgun, and it is remarkable how short a distance the rest of a herd will move from a good, expeditious kill. Owners of forests and stalkers alike are extremely hard on people who wound deer. The code is that, if a beast is hit but not killed, it must be followed and despatched, whatever the weather.

The sportsman, then, has advanced far from the early Victorian period of deer drives. His sport is one for a healthy body, a keen eye, a good knowledge of natural conditions and ability to read the signs of nature. The day without a kill will still be a good one. He stalks when the beast is at its best and the hazards greatest. There is no other method by which the deer could be kept in check with so little suffering to the animals.

Let us leave principles for a while and visit the stalker at home. We find him in a little house of four or five rooms at the head of a glen or in some treeless waste. Forest, after all, is meant in the old sense of a waste place. The house may be seven miles or more from a road, and we have either walked up here or come on Highland ponies. Everything the stalker and his wife needs comes in on the back of a pony, or possibly their little furniture was originally hauled in on a sledge such as is used for carrying hay in steep places.

He himself will look extremely tidy and well dressed in a suit of plus-fours, collar and tie, tweed cap or deerstalker, and excellent shoes, not boots. The tweed of his suit will either be the very best Harris, which the ordinary person finds it hard to get, or a good Sutherland lovat. You will be asked indoors to meet his wife, as if she were in a castle, and welcomed as one who can talk of the outside world.

Tea will be on the table in no time, and home-made fare. The family's two cows provide butter, sometimes cheese, and no stint of cream except in February, when they are dry before calving. There are usually eggs in plenty, and if fresh venison is out of season there will be venison ham, smoked. Sometimes a carcass will be hung in a waterfall near the house, where the meat will keep sweet for several weeks. If the salmon or sea trout are up the river the stalker will have some, no doubt, but you will not ask him if he does, and he will not be so ill-mannered as to lay it on the table before you. It is a matter which laird and stalker, as gentlemen, do not discuss.

Outside, the stalker will have a few acres of inbye land surrounded by a 6-foot deer fence. Here he ploughs an acre or two for potatoes and oats, and sets aside some more for hay. His wife will work as hard on their bit of land as the stalker himself. Well-being depends on it. He may be allowed by the owner to graze a number of cattle in the glen during summer, for this has a beneficial effect on the grazing. So in late April or May we find the stalker going out to the sea coast among the crofters to buy himself half a dozen or ten yearling stirks. These he sells again in October, or if he can harvest enough hay he will keep them on and graze them through another summer, when they will know the ground, make better use of it and go off fat. The grazing for the few beasts is a perquisite to be added to his wage which, before the war, may have been £70–£80 a year.

If the stalking seasons are so short, two months each for stags and hinds, and then not out every day, what does the stalker do with the rest of his time? There is the work of his little farm, the journey out once a week to fetch mails, a newspaper and perhaps a boll of meal. His wife will get out once a year, at the end of October, to visit friends, buy clothes in Inverness and see the dentist. After the spring work there are the peats to be cut, set up and later stacked and brought up to the house; for there is no coal here, and often no wood other than the old pine stumps which may be dug from the bog.

June is a busy month among the foxes. Despite constant effort the grey fox of the Highlands persists in numbers. The stalker may find the cairn of rocks where the young are. His terriers go down into it and finish them off, but there remains the vixen, and that means one or more all-night sittings near the cairn waiting for her to come back. She may be as good a man as he is and elude him. Sitting motionless at 2,000 feet on an exposed hillside through a cold June night is not comfort. Foxes are predators on the deer at this time, taking the newly-born calves by stealth from the watchful hinds. I have myself seen the remains of nine deer calves at a fox den. Wild cats do not affect the deer, but they are attacked by the stalker almost as keenly as the foxes. A few wild cats in a forest are a good thing to have, but they increase fast and spread down country, where they are scourges to hen roosts.

At all times the stalker is watching his deer spread about his beat of 10,000–20,000 acres. He wants to know their habits as a whole, and be able to recognize individual stags by their antlers, and forecast where they may be. He has a habit of wandering about and being little seen, but seeing all. For long periods he may be on his back in the heather, one knee up, with the large end of his telescope held against it, the other end to his eye. Thus if you are yourself ranging about a deer forest in summer, do not make the mistake of assuming that you are with certainty alone with nature. Donald's keen eye may be watching you through his much-prized Ross glass. One stalker's wife said to me of a young couple who passed through the forest, 'Indeed, John was having to lower his glass.' And John, being a gentleman, would lower it.

The stalker's small income is helped a little in the season by hiring his two Highland ponies to his employer for carrying the deer from the hill. He may get a pound or thirty shillings a week for each of them for six weeks. All ponies have to be trained to carry deer—they don't like a dead animal on their back—but some never will carry a stag, and such ponies are no good to the stalker. The pony also needs to be of the native kind that can climb to 3,000 feet if need be and pick its way back without getting frightened of the rough terrain.

Winter is the slackest time for the stalker except for the hind shooting, which he usually does himself. The stags come down about his house in the bad weather and he gets to know them intimately, checking up on their ages in his amazing memory and knowing which part of the forest they are from. A crofter hates deer like poison because they sometimes come down to his crops, but the stalker loves them all the time, without any trace of sentimentality.

While deer remain there will be stalkers, though few men will be able to own forests in the old style. Perhaps many stalkers will become members of the staff of the national parks and nature reserves we hope to see established soon; some will work for big hotels offering stalking, and there is even yet a chance that the forest country may be nationalized and that among its other uses of forestry and cattle grazing it may be possible to take out a one-stag licence. The stalker will be necessary then more than ever, to conduct the amateur and preserve the rigid code of the forest. But he may be a saddened man.

# Lead Belly, Life and Letters

## by IAIN LANG

LEAD BELLY is, among other things, a blues singer. The other things are or have been various—thousand-pound cotton picker, horse-tamer, convicted homicide with a long chain-gang and penitentiary record, performer on the mandolin, accordion, mouth-organ and bass fiddle, and (he claims) King of the Twelve-String Guitar Players of the World. Besides blues he knows other songs from the rich folk treasury of the Southern and Western American States, but his singing and playing of blues has done more for him than any of his accomplishments. It has twice got him out of jail, has secured him a modest but lasting place in the archives of the Library of Congress, and has made his gramophone records prizes diligently collected by people who like and understand such singing.

After I had described, in the first SATURDAY BOOK, some of the obscure and often disreputable Negro musicians who have moulded the blues tradition, the coloured band leader Duke Ellington expressed his amused astonishment that 'serious writers in Europe' should pay such attention to the vagrant musicians of the Black Belts, 'writing monographs and things' about men who had no ambition beyond picking up uncertain dollars and chance drinks, and no dreams of fame outside backrooms in back streets.

Whatever surprise Lead Belly may have felt when he first received serious recognition he has long since outgrown. When he was invited to give a recital at Vassar University, he asked if this was not 'one of the famous women's schools': on being told it was, he commented, 'Well, maybe they don't know it, but they is about to hear the famousest guitar player in the world.'

Yet sixty-three years ago, when he was born, the odds against his becoming famous in any field were considerable. He did not even have the advantage enjoyed by most notable pioneers of blues and jazz of being born or raised in New Orleans and so being awakened by the stir and stimulus of a great cosmopolitan city. Mooringsport, his birthplace, is over towards the western edge of Louisiana, an unmapped spot in the Red River country near the Texas border. Huddie Leadbetter—that is Lead Belly's formal name—is not all Negro; his mother had a strain of Red Indian blood. His boyhood was without any white American influence, for in many of the Red River settlements 'they ain't no white man in twenty miles,' and even the cotton planter for whom his father worked as a sharecropper was a Negro.

In those remote cotton fields and canebrakes the white American was less a present reality than a myth remembered from 'slavery times'—the hereditary enemy referred to evasively as 'the man.' That used to mean the slave-owner or plantation overseer; nowadays any white holder of oppressive authority, a works foreman or chain-gang boss, is 'the man.' As Lead Belly says, 'in slavery times they had so many ways of saying about the man, he didn't know what it was all about.'

He still remembers some of the slave songs he heard then from the old people, but in fact his boyhood in the all-Negro hinterland was freer than it would have been in one of the Mississippi or seaboard cities: and this probably explains the swagger with which he has been able to face his many mischances.

AS WELL AS HELPING in the cotton fields, Huddie learned to ride a horse and play the accordion. These two skills were connected: the horse carried him for miles over the countryside to play the accordion at sukey-jumps, as the Red River Negroes call their parties; so by the time he was fifteen he was in steady demand as a performer, at fifty cents a night, and was ambitious for a wider stage. Out there in the Louisiana-Texas borderland the local metropolis is Shreveport. The first thing Huddie heard about Shreveport was his father's warning, 'Don't go down to Fannin' Street, son.' In Fanning Street there were girls and liquor and music. Huddie soon found out that his father, for all his admonitions, went down to Fanning Street whenever he had the money and the excuse of urgent business in Shreveport. The boy decided to follow the example, and not the advice, when he was old enough. Visitors in short pants were not admitted to the barrel-houses of Fanning Street, but 'soon's my mamma put long pants on me, I flew out the door. When you get long pants you ought to act like a man, if you ain't no man.'

At sixteen Huddie was man enough to be a husband and a father. His wife, Lethe, seems to have been a vigorous young woman, for when two years later they 'banished away' to West Texas to pick cotton, Huddie found she could pick two hundred pounds a day to his hundred. A man named Clarence Ruffing showed him how to go up to four hundred and fifty pounds and then to six hundred, until in the end he was among the few thousand-pickers—a cotton field celebrity.

He became known, too, as a rider who could master outlaw horses. It was, literally, rough-riding: 'you put two spurs on and ride till they fall dead—either they're broke in or dead.' Then he turned to city life, in Dallas, where he met a master of blues-singing, Blind Lemon Jefferson, and went back to music, though now it was not the accordion but the guitar that interested him most.

(The curious thing about Lead Belly's guitar playing is that he formed his style by imitating boogie-woogie piano players he heard in the Fanning Street barrel-houses. 'That's what I wanted to play on guitar, that piano bass,' he has said. But the boogie-woogie men had developed their way of playing by imitating the two-man guitar teams popular before pianos were cheap enough for Negroes to own: the pianist's right hand took the part of the first guitar and 'picked' the melody, while the left supplied the rolling rhythmic accompaniment of the second guitar, or 'frammer.')

Blind Lemon was a noted guitarist, and when he and Lead Belly worked the Texas barrel-house circuit in partnership it was Jefferson who did the singing and playing. Lead Belly danced taps. But he was listening to Blind Lemon and learning fast.

One night he met a man with a twelve-string guitar who challenged him to play it. Huddie tried, without much success; but when he got back to Dallas the first thing he did was to buy a twelve-stringed instrument, and the same night he played it at a dance. 'I put my foot on the door-step,' he recalls, 'and my finger on the strings and said, "Here's Lead Belly."'

Lead Belly presented himself with the same sort of assurance in all situations, in a hard-bitten half-world where assurance needs to be backed up by action. His muscles toughened by horse-breaking and work in the cotton fields, he was as arrogant as he was strong; so arrogant that the coloured courtesans of Dallas plotted to kill him, and, he says, nearly chopped his head off. About that time he was arrested for assaulting a woman and sentenced to a year on a chain gang. Before the year was up he escaped and fled eastwards as far as New Orleans. But not for many years, not until he was fifty did he escape from the cycle of crime and punishment; he kept on rambling through the South-West playing the guitar and singing blues, kept on getting into fights and kept on getting into the penitentiary.

Jail did not break him. He was strong enough for the hardest labour, and he still had his songs and his guitar. In the end his music brought him freedom. Negroes released from the penitentiary spread the legend throughout the Black Belts in many cities of the man back in there who could sing more blues than anybody; and in time the legend reached white students of coloured people's songs. It reached the foremost authority on American folk music, John Lomax, and Lomax and his son Alan worked until Lead Belly was pardoned.

CERTAINLY THE LOMAXES had found a prize. In one man was contained a whole history of Southern folk music, a living link between the primitive rural songs and dances heard at sukey-jumps and plantation hollers and the urban music of blues. Usually there is a gap between the country and the city idiom, a gap to be bridged by patient research and more or less inspired guesswork. Lead Belly has lived through both phases. But he has, as well, a wider significance than the somewhat specialized one that attracted John and Alan Lomax. In his character as a representative blues singer he and his songs throw light on aspects of American life and letters far beyond the scope of blues.

It has been said that in the classic literature of Spain 'almost everything that is not folk lore is pedantry.' Whether this is true or not in the Spanish case, it is fair comment on much imaginative writing by Americans. In nearly every American writer whom circumstance or temperament has insulated from popular values and 'folk' ways of expression—in Henry James and T. S. Eliot equally with James Branch Cabell and Ezra Pound —a seam of *pedantería* can be traced among whatever other ores, of greater or less value, make up that writer's talent. Conversely, it is fairly obvious that the authors of (for example) *Huckleberry Finn, An American Tragedy* and *The Grapes of Wrath* are more deeply rooted in folk culture than their contemporaries among English or French novelists. I am not, of course, arguing that James, aloof from popular values, is a less important writer than Dreiser or Steinbeck, who are saturated in those values, nor that Eliot's *pedantería* makes him inferior to such anti-pedantic poets as Vachell Lindsay or Carl Sandburg; but that the writers who owe nothing to folk culture are less characteristically American than those who owe much. And this is true in a way not applicable in Europe, for nobody would suggest that Flaubert was less characteristically French than Jean Giono, or Matthew Arnold less English than the Dorset dialect poet William Barnes.

There are many folk cultures in the United States. What gives special interest to the form of expression developed in blues is the correspondence between its dominant themes and attitudes and the dominant themes and attitudes of such writers as Ernest Hemingway, William Faulkner, James Cain, Dashiell Hammett—in fact, of the writers whom the general reader would name as the typical American writers of our day.

It is, for present purposes, irrelevant that Mr Hemingway is an artist of great accomplishment and force, while Mr Cain's quality is lightweight. The difference is one of degree rather than of kind. They are all 'tough' writers; but what is a little surprising is that toughness never gets them anywhere; their characters, however violent in action, are always the victims of circumstance, never its masters.

When the hero of *A Farewell to Arms* is not being buffeted around by the vast and incomprehensible currents of war he is being 'biologically trapped.' Jordan, in *For Whom the Bell Tolls*, although a man of lonely and desperate action, a saboteur living precariously on nerve and wits, is equally helpless in the long run, equally at the mercy of uncontrollable, hostile events.  The protagonist of *The Postman Always Rings Twice* is a puppet whose destiny is decided by such impersonal powers as coincidence and the economics of the life insurance business.  A melodramatic fatality hangs over all Mr Faulkner's stock figures.  The view of *la condition humaine* implicit in these representative American novels usually remains implicit because the hero-victims are, as a rule, appropriately inarticulate; but it finds expression occasionally, as in Mr Hemingway's grim conclusion: 'The world breaks every one and afterward many are strong at the broken places.  But those that will not break it kills.  It kills the very good and the very gentle and the very brave impartially.'

BLUES SINGERS SELDOM, if ever, venture on sweeping generalizations about life, but a similar fatalism is implied in almost every blues—a similar stoical acceptance of the fact that the world, the flesh and the devil are hostile powers against which it is not much use to struggle:

> *Talk about trouble, that's all I've ever known*
> *Now if I hadn'ta been a man I woulda stayed at home.*
>
> *If you ever love a woman first you give your soul to the good Lord above*
> *Give your time to the devil and give your love to the girl you love.*
>
> *Sittin' on a kerbstone worryin' my heart an' soul*
> *Just like a 'possum hidin' in a groundhog's hole.*
>
> *Sittin' in the house with everythin' on my mind*
> *Lookin' at the clock an' can't even tell the time*
> *Can't eat, can't sleep, so weak I can't walk my floor*
> *Feel like hollerin' 'Murder!' an' let the police squad get me once more.*
>
> *The blues jumped a rabbit, run him a solid mile*
> *The poor fellow lied down an' cried just like a natural child.*
>
> *What you gonna do when Death comes tippin' in your room?*
> *I'm gonna hang my head, I'm gonna hang my head an' cry.*

These half-dozen fragments give a very imperfect idea of a sentiment, difficult to isolate by quotation, that pervades almost all blues, the feeling that there is nothing to be done in the face of life's unfriendliness but to sit on the kerbstone, to cry just like a natural child, to let the police squad

take over.  The only positive action to combat difficulties that is ever
suggested is to move on somewhere else:

> *Feelin' tomorrow like I feel today*
> *Gonna pack up my grip an' make my gitaway.*

There are endless variations on the getaway theme, the burden of the
innumerable railroad songs: for the blues singer, as for Baudelaire, *cette
vie est un hôpital où chaque malade est possédé du désir de changer de
lit.*  To pick up the parallel, the novels of contemporary America are
uneasy with movement which would be aimless if the aim were not
escape; even the peasants seem to be without roots.  Escape, either by
physical motion or by illusion.  The monotonous alcoholism, which is
pushed to the point of burlesque in Dashiell Hammett's stories, has
nothing to do with the considered enjoyment of drinking, either as a
social or deipnosophic exercise; its statement in blues terms is:

> *I'd rather be sloppy drunk than anythin' else I know*
> *Shoot me the liquor—another half-pint'll see me go.*

And the sequel to that is, of course:

> *I was high last night, but today I'm gully low*
> *Got a dime in my pocket 'n a long, long ways to go.*

Love, for Hemingway and his followers, is either an unreal armistice
in 'the war between men and women' or a ludicrously simple satisfaction
of appetite.  Hemingway has never advanced from the position stated in
his first book *In Our Time* more than twenty years ago, in the
*monologue intérieur* of a demobilized doughboy: 'He would have liked
to have a girl but he did not want to have to spend a long time getting
her.  He did not want to get into the intrigue and the politics.  He did not
want to have to do any courting.'  And, indeed, the Hemingway hero
never does have to do much courting—the absurdly dumb and acquiescent
doll-heroines of *A Farewell to Arms* and *For Whom the Bell Tolls* are
figures of a schoolboy's dream.
   It is not surprising that a similar simplification is found in blues, for
one does not expect a popular song to elaborate Stendhalian subtleties;
but even the least sophisticated European ballads set some value on
qualities of character as well as physical desirability, acknowledging that
loyalty may sometimes be found in men and women and, when found,
is to be prized.  Among hundreds of blues I have come across only one
which suggests that there may be a bond of affection—as distinct from

desire or dependence—between man and woman, and this exception (Lonnie Johnson's *She's My Mary*) is sufficiently unusual in metrical structure to suggest adaptation from an old Scots or Irish song.  A blues equivalent of *My Old Dutch* is almost unthinkable.  'Love that moves the sun and the other stars' comes to this:

> *I got a girl sure do treat me right*
> *What I mean when I say right, man, 's three meals a day an' jelly*
>   *at night.*

The distrust of woman as the born enemy which is expressed in such stories as *Hills Like White Elephants* and *The Snows of Kilimanjaro* and gives whatever force they possess to the novels of Faulkner and Cain becomes monotonous in its recurrence as a blues theme:

> *It's rainin' here, stormin' on the deep blue sea*
> *Ain't no blackheaded woman can make a fatmouth outa me.*

> *These here women sure do make me tired*
> *Got a handful of 'gimme' and a mouthful of 'much obliged.'*

> *I never loved an' I hope I never will*
> *'Cause a lovin' proposition will get somebody killed.*

> *Lord, I don't think no man's love can last*
> *They love you to death then treat you like a thing of the past.*

> *It's ashes to ashes, I mean dust to dust*
> *Now show me a man any woman can trust.*

It would need much fuller quotation from both sides than space here allows fully to exhibit the similarities in the determining attitudes of contemporary American fiction and blues.  One comment, however, may be made.  It is not, perhaps, surprising that blues—the utterance of poor and under-privileged people, mostly Southern Negroes—should regard society as, on the whole, a hostile conspiracy against which it is hopeless to struggle; but that writers speaking for more fortunate groups in the world's most prosperous country should be saturated with a similar defeatism is not at all encouraging.  Lead Belly, the strong and arrogant, thousand-picker and horse-tamer, acquires symbolic stature as he shuffles along in the chain gang.  The chain clanks—as the bell tolls—for more than one victim.

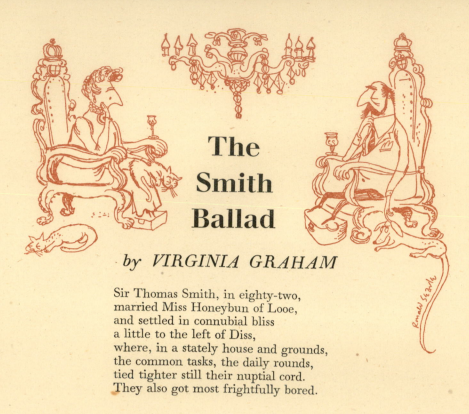

# The
# Smith
# Ballad

## by *VIRGINIA GRAHAM*

Sir Thomas Smith, in eighty-two,
married Miss Honeybun of Looe,
and settled in connubial bliss
a little to the left of Diss,
where, in a stately house and grounds,
the common tasks, the daily rounds,
tied tighter still their nuptial cord.
They also got most frightfully bored.

By Gad! Sir Thomas said one day,
Lettice, m'dear, let's go away,
the spirit of adventure, lud!
is surging madly through m'blood.
No feeble timorous heart was hers,
she threw away her seccateurs,
and rushed upstairs at once to trail
a topee and a motoring veil;
while he was not especially slow
to telegraph the P. and O.

After tremendous preparations,
complete with trunks and reservations,
the Smiths set forth in happy heart
for Africa, (the darkest part)
where it was said one could be sure
to find life much less of a Boer.

Let us slide swiftly o'er the trip,
devoted, as on any ship,
to whist and walks and sleep and soup
and talks with bishops in the poop,
and let us hurry off to where
the Smiths, still gay and debonair,
began on what was soon to be
a slice of English history.

We find them sleeping in a tent,
after an arduous day well spent
in shooting shots both wide and true
at small elusive caribou.

Did we say sleeping? No alas,
for Lettice Smith, the silly ass,
remembering she had dropped a belt
(of all things!) somewhere in the veldt,
stole from her downy fleabag and
went out into the hinterland
to probe with ardent eyes the ground.
When lo, there came from all around
a native tribe, whose fearful cries
vied with the clash of assegais.
In vain she screamed; they bound her tight,
and whisked her off into the night.

Sir Thomas woke. Oddsfish! he swore,
Where have I heard that voice before?
Lettice! He leapt from out his tent,
astounded with astonishment.
Was that her cry? Ye gods above!
Where have you gone, my ancient love?
Lettice, come back, my joy, my pride!
No answer came, and so beside
himself he ran pursued by fear,
far faster than the native deer,
far swifter than giraffe or gnu,
than buffalo or kangaroo,
far fleeter than orangutan . . .
well anyhow, the poor man ran
with speed beyond comparison,
to rouse the local garrison.

The trumpets sounded in the square,
the soldiers combed their horses' hair,
they took their lances from the wall:
We come, they said, we hear your call,

but though you doubtless fear the worst,
let's polish up our buttons first,
and press, they said, our pantaloons
as fits the 7th Cameroons.

At last, at last they were prepared;
the horses' blankets had been aired,
each had a shining bridled face
and oat-cakes in a sandwich case,
each hoof was painted black as ink;
the Colonel said, I really think
we might be off. You will, of course,
ride on Lieutenant Chidwell's horse?
Thus, with a cheer, they went forthwith
to the Relief of Lady Smith.

They journeyed far, they journeyed long,
from Matins unto Evensong,
they circled round, they looped the loop,
retraced their footsteps stoep by stoep.
No sign! the Colonel cried: I grieve
to say, Sir Thomas, we must leave,
for even as it is you see
we shall be *frightfully* late for tea.
Sir Thomas was about to say
something he would regret one day,
when hark! Be still! Who sings a song?
Is it the mating binturong?
The amorous snipe? Oh heart, I die!
It sounds like Madam Butterfly!

They found her sitting quite intact
upon a tom-tom, where in fact
she had been lecturing for hours
to everyone, on English flowers,
and with the voice that breathed o'er Eden
had damned the monocotyledon.
The tribesmen, spellbound, gathered round
in painful posture on the ground
treated in mode avuncular
her love of things ranuncular,
greeted with happy shrieks of glee
the lesser umbelliferae.

Alas, though Lettice thought that this
was nicer than her life at Diss,
Sir Thomas had sufficient, he,
of making English history;
and thus in future years they spent
their holidays in Ashford, Kent.